Tactics of Modern Warfare

Rapid Deployment in the 20th Century

Tactics of Modern Warfare

Rapid Deployment in the 20th Century

Mark Lloyd

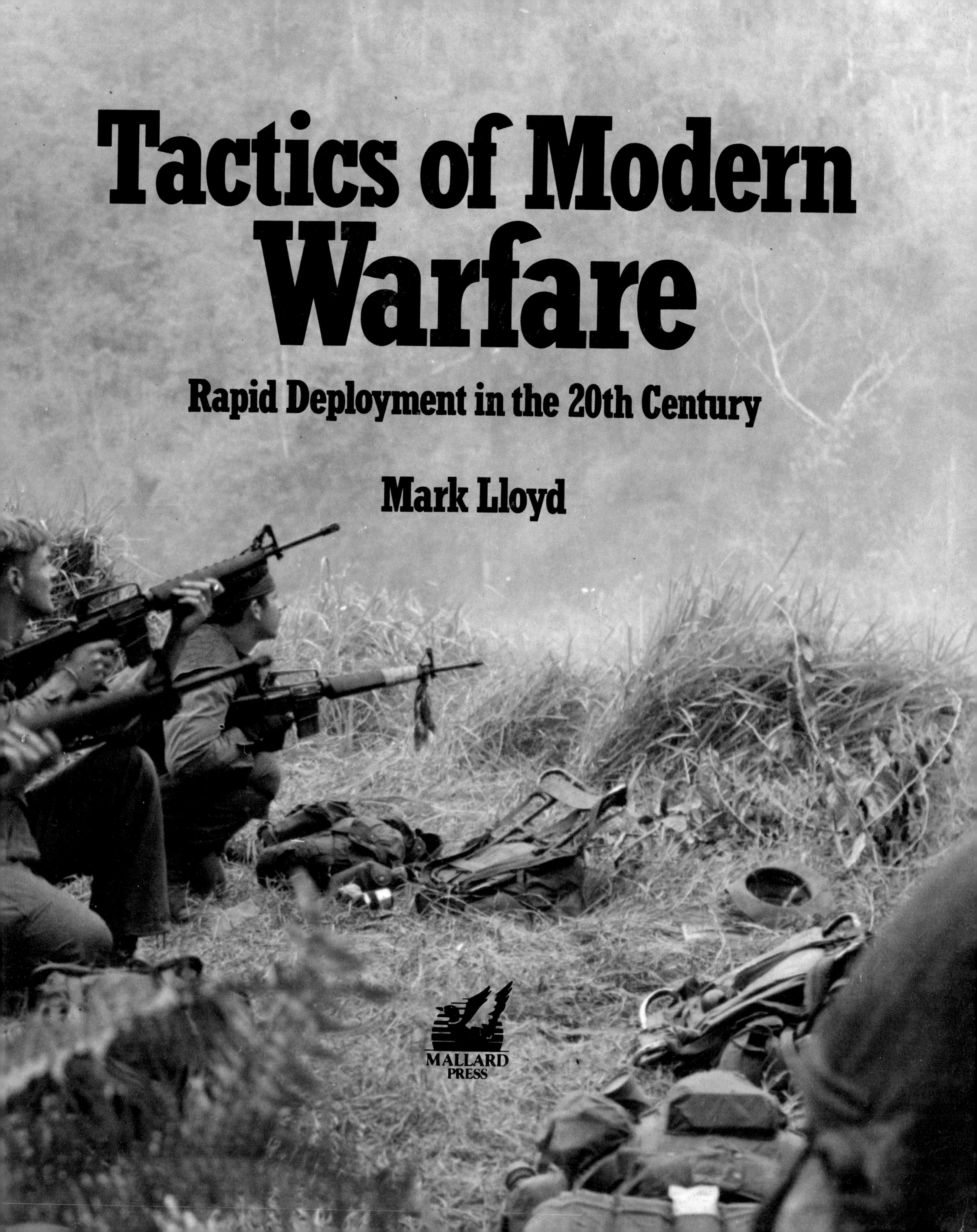

MALLARD PRESS

Above: *A member of 173rd Airborne fires his jeep-mounted M2 machine gun into an enemy position in Vietnam.*

Project Editor: Leone Edwards

First Published in the United States of America in 1991
by the Mallard Press
An Imprint of BDD Promotional Book Company, Inc.
666 Fifth Avenue
New York, N.Y. 10103
"Mallard Press and its accompanying design and logo are trademarks of BDD Promotional Book Company, Inc."

ISBN 0-7924-5467-7

Printed in Portugal

Previous page: A search-and-secure mission, north of the Ai Lao River, returns sniper fire.

CONTENTS

The Mexican-American Wars, 1911–1918

The Mexican wars began in the autumn of 1910 with revolution against the 30-year dictatorship of General Porfirio Diaz. The revolution was headed by Francisco Madero, an idealist son of the all-powerful landowning class whose interests Diaz had guarded. The actual fighting was done by Pascual Orozco, named as commander of the revolutionary forces by Madero, and Doroteo Arango, otherwise known as Pancho Villa. After several early defeats, the revolutionaries managed to capture the important border city of Ciudad Juarez and sweep on to topple Diaz in May 1911. On 6 November Madero was elected President and began to grapple with the immense problems of the country, blocked at every turn by the hostility of the landowners and the ambitions of power-hungry generals.

Madero lead the revolutionaries until February 1913, when he was arrested and shot in a *coup d'état* headed by General Victoriano Huerta, who named himself as Mexico's new president. When Woodrow Wilson was inaugurated as President of the United States in the following month, he refused to acknowledge Huerta. This gave great encouragement to the welter of anti-Huerta leaders who emerged in Mexico tenuously headed by the governor of Coahila State, Venustiano Carranza. Villa, now named as a general of Carranza's 'Constitutionalist' forces, raised a force of over 10,000 men armed with weapons smuggled across the Rio Grande. Washington favoured the anti-munitions - an alignment favoured by the pro-American Villa. Carranza, however, shared the deep-rooted Mexican hatred and distrust of the United States, an early divergence which led to his eventual breach with Villa.

Direct American intervention in Mexico came with two incidents in April 1914. The first was the temporary arrest on 19 April by an aggressive band of Huertista soldiers of a party of American sailors from U.S.S. *Dolphin*, who landed at Tampico to pick up some supplies which had been purchased for the ship. This affront to the American flag was followed on 21 April by American landings at Veracruz intended to prevent the landing of a cargo of weapons and munitions shipped to Huerta from Germany. Although denounced as high-handed aggression by the Mexican anti-American faction – the ensuing ten-week American occupation of Veracruz cut off Huerta from his last source of overseas aid. On 15 July 1914 Huerta resigned from the presidency and left Mexico for exile in Europe.

Huerta's departure from the scene removed the only tenuous bond between Carranza and Villa, although an open breach between them was delayed until November 1914. When it came, most of the initial advantages lay with Villa, who controlled most of the area along the American border and hence had access to American supplies. In alliance with the equally famous revolutionary leader Emiliano Zapata, champion of the peasants of Morelos, Villa marched south to occupy Mexico City and force Carranza to set up his capital at Veracruz.

Villa's run of victories ended abruptly in April 1915 with two heavy defeats by the one-armed Carranzista General Alvaro Obregon. With the European war now in its ninth month, President Wilson was anxious to do anything he could to bring about a peaceful settlement in Mexico. Villa's defeats therefore prompted Wilson to issue a formal recognition of Carranza as the likeliest guarantor of stability and as *de facto* president of Mexico on 9 October 1915. On hearing that Villa was planning to capture the Carranzista border town of Agua Prieta, Wilson sent arms and supplies to help the Carranzistas defend it.

By the time Villa's army arrived at Agua Prieta on 30 October 1915, American aid had rendered the town impregnable, surrounding it with trenchworks, belts of barbed wire, machine-guns, and abundant artillery. The result was a bloody repulse for Villa's men when they attacked on 1 November 1915. Villa headed south-west in the hope of recouping this defeat by taking Hermosillo, capital of Sonora. the result was an even greater loss of men. With his surviving followers Villa now fell back on Nogales in the north with a fiercely burning hatred of the United States.

President Wilson was now obliged to take steps to safeguard the border. On 9 March 1916, Villa's band struck across the border and attacked the U.S. 13th Cavalry Regiment at its headquarters in Columbus, New Mexico. Albeit surprised by the assault of the Villistas, Colonel Herbert Slocum's cavalrymen fought back energetically and drove them off after a savage three hour fight. Major Frank Tompkins then led a small column in pursuit, chasing the fleeing Villistas until the Americans ran out of ammunition and withdrew north across the border.

Villa's raid led Wilson to order a 'Punitive Expedition' into Mexico to disperse and destroy Villa's band. It was intended as a goodwill gesture towards the Carranzista regime, but it backfired badly by the fact that the Carranzistas angrily resented what they regarded as an affront to Mexican sovereignty. The Punitive Expedition was commanded by Brigadier-General John J. Pershing. It was an all-arms force of cavalry, infantry, light artillery, and air reconnaissance provided by the 1st Aero Squadron. Pershing's objective was not, as was popularly reported, to capture Villa dead or alive, but to destroy the menace which Villa's motley army represented.

The Punitive Expedition crossed into Mexico on 15 March 1916 and made rapid progress. Within a few weeks, fast moving American cavalry columns had surprised and scattered every major Villista band in the field. The main opposition came not from the Villistas but from the Carranzistas as had occurred at Parral where, in April 1916, an American cavalry force was attacked first by a mob and then by the local Carranzista garrison. Although he had prevented his men from firing on the mob, the American officer had no scruples about ordering his men to shoot back at the Carranzista troops, who were driven off.

Worsening relations with the Carranzistas were marked by an insolent note sent to Pershing on 16 June 1916 by General Jacinto Trevino, commanding in Chihuahua. Trevino tersely informed Pershing that from that date the American

Above: U.S. battle fleet steaming towards Mexican waters in 1914. The U.S. Navy was then the second most powerful in the world. Her Army, however, was minute by European standards – less than 20,000 strong!

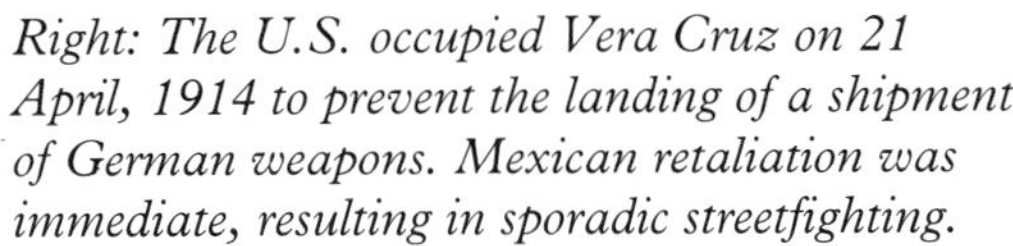

Right: The U.S. occupied Vera Cruz on 21 April, 1914 to prevent the landing of a shipment of German weapons. Mexican retaliation was immediate, resulting in sporadic streetfighting.

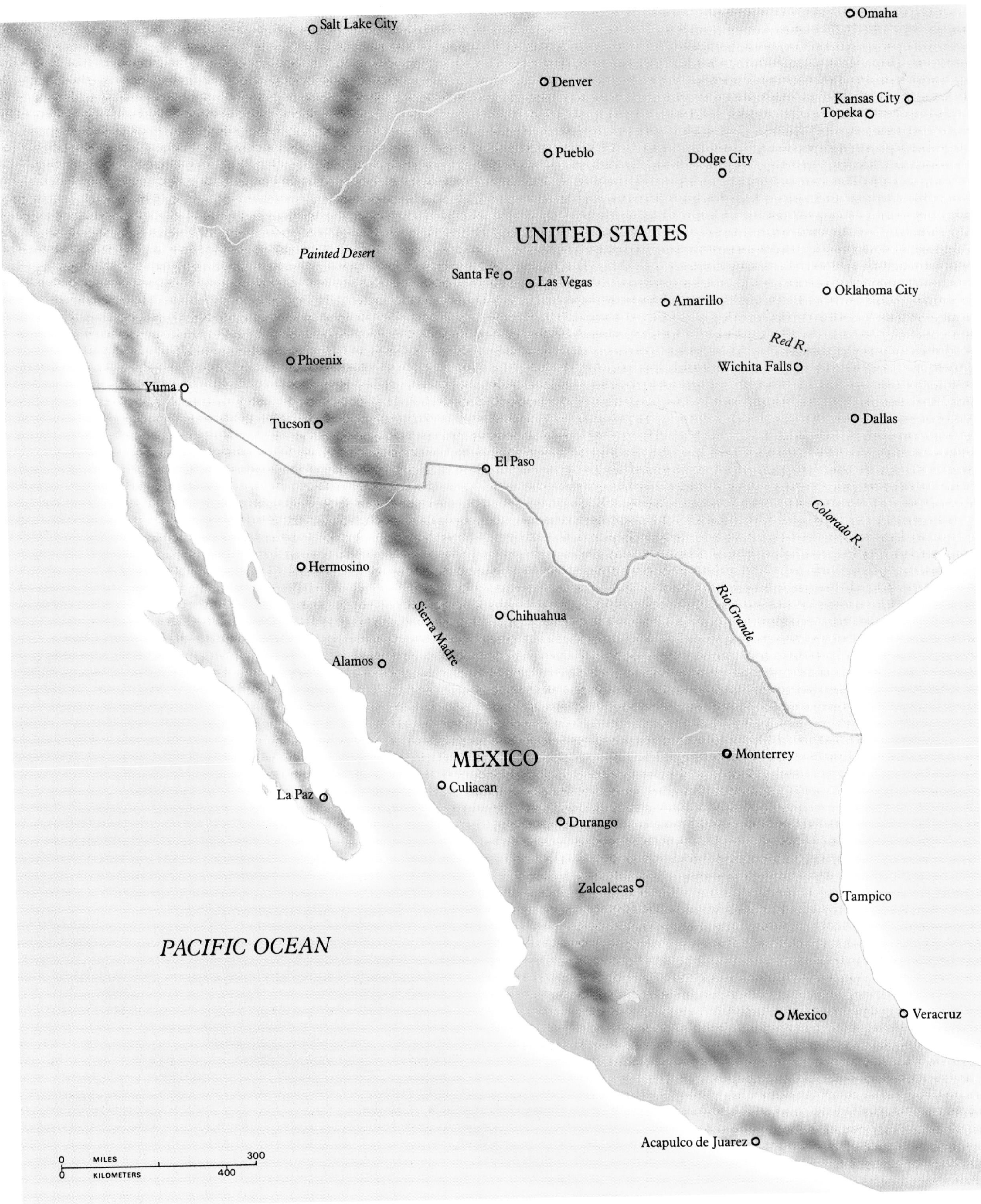
Salt Lake City
Omaha
Denver
Kansas City
Topeka
Pueblo
Dodge City
UNITED STATES
Painted Desert
Santa Fe
Las Vegas
Amarillo
Oklahoma City
Red R.
Phoenix
Wichita Falls
Yuma
Tucson
Dallas
El Paso
Colorado R.
Hermosino
Rio Grande
Sierra Madre
Chihuahua
Alamos
Monterrey
MEXICO
Culiacan
La Paz
Durango
Zalcalecas
Tampico
PACIFIC OCEAN
Mexico
Veracruz
Acapulco de Juarez
0 MILES 300
0 KILOMETERS 400

The Mexican War, which led to American intervention, began in the autumn of 1910 when Francisco Madero rose in revolution, overthrowing the dictatorship of General Porfirio Diaz. Three years later Madero himself was toppled by General Victoriano Huerta. When the newly elected United States President Woodrow Wilson refused to recognize the Huerta regime a series of American-inspired uprisings followed, the most successful of which was led by the famous outlaw Pancho Villa. Direct American intervention followed in April 1914 when the crew of the USS Dolphin was manhandled and the United States flag desecrated. Huerta was forced to resign and flee to Europe for protection, leaving behind him a political void which Villa determined to fill. Relations between Villa and the United States deteriorated rapidly reaching an all-time low in March 1916 when Villa's forces struck across the border into New Mexico. Wilson ordered Pershing to lead a punitive expedition into Mexico to disperse and destroy Villa's band.

force would only be permitted to move north, and that movement in any other direction would be resisted by the Carranzistas. Pershing's reply to Trevino, equally blunt, was that he only took orders from his own government. Trevino's action made open conflict with the Americans inevitable, and it came in less than a week. On 21 June 1916, a small American cavalry force was approaching the town of Carrizal. It consisted of two troops of the 10th Cavalry – a black regiment – and numbered three officers, a couple of civilian guides, and 79 troopers. Emboldened by the small size of the American force, the Carrizal garrison attacked.

For what was little more than a skirmish, the action at Carrizal was extremely hard fought and costly for both sides. The Mexican commander, General Felix Gomez, was killed in the first exchange of fire. Two of the American officers were killed, the third was wounded, and most of the non-commissioned officers were also killed or wounded. For all that, virtually leaderless and heavily outnumbered, most of the black troopers managed to shoot their way clear, with only a handful being taken prisoner. The losses later admitted by the Carranzistas were greater than the American total strength at Carrizal.

The news of Carrizal had momentous effects on both sides of the Atlantic. In Washington, President Wilson was assailed with angry demands for full-scale military intervention in Mexico. Congress voted for the National Guard, the national militia at the disposal of the individual states in time of peace, to be taken into Federal service. Wilson was still determined to preserve American neutrality for as long as possible, but he had come to believe that war with Germany was unavoidable and that when it came, the United States 'would need every ounce of reserve we have to lick Germany'. He therefore refused to escalate the Mexican conflict into all-out war, while ordering Pershing to continue his mission with the Punitive Expedition. Wilson did, however, accept the recommendation his Chief-of-Staff, Major-General Hugh L. Scott, to mobilize the National Guard as authorized by Congress.

Given the lack of time and precedent for an operation on such a scale, a measure of disorder in the National Guard mobilization was only to be expected. It was admittedly humiliating for the Americans, but the delight with which the confusion was derided by the Carranzistas was out of all proportion. On the other hand, the Mexican reaction seemed comparatively statesmanlike against the wild optimism and ignorance displayed in Berlin. At the very moment when the Verdun bloodbath was reaching its dreadful climax with the first phosgene gas bombardments, German newspapers proclaimed, with banner headlines, *'DER AMERIKANISCHE-MEXIKANISCHE KONFLIKT!'*. German journalists and military chiefs alike appeared to gloat over the fact that Americans were failing to volunteer for the war against Mexico, heedless of the fact that no such war had been declared, and therefore no volunteers called for by the American government. Details of the National Guard mobilization were taken as proof positive that the United States was, as a modern military power, a joke. The time had surely come to call Washington's bluff and, ignoring all future American protests, unleash the German U-boats on a campaign of unrestricted submarine warfare in the Atlantic.

A week after the decision for unrestricted U-boat warfare was taken in Berlin (9 January 1917), German Foreign Minister Arthur von Zimmermann dispatched his famous telegram to Carranza proposing a German-Mexican military alliance. President Wilson had already severed diplomatic relations with Germany (3 February 1917) and recalled Pershing's expedition from Mexico. The Zimmermann Telegram, 'leaked' to Washington after being intercepted and decoded by the British, gave the final impetus to Wilson's declaration of war against Germany on 6 April. Not the least of Wilson's achievements was his appointment of Pershing, whose performance in Mexico had been admirable in the face of the problems encountered, to command the American Expeditionary Force in France.

Mystery still shrouds the details of German attempts to ferment open war between Mexico and the United States, which never occurred despite continuing tension along the border in 1917 and 1918. The last serious incident was a fierce cross-border fire fight at Nogales in August 1918 which ended with a temporary American occupation of the town, after which American Intelligence reported that several 'Mexican' corpses interred by the burial parties had blond hair and blue eyes. The true effect of the Mexican civil conflict had been to mislead the German High Command as to American readiness for a modern war. In 1941, the same disastrously fatal miscalculation would be made by Japan.

A Marine officer urges his band of Leathernecks on as they overrun the San Cosmo Gate at Mexico City.

The Tunnellers, The War Beneath the Trenches, 1915–1918

Mining, the science of piercing enemy fixed defences by driving tunnels beneath them, is as old as war itself. Israelite mines crammed with firewood, set ablaze when the signal was given by the blowing of horns, were most probably the secret weapon which brought down the walls of Jericho as recorded in the Old Testament (*Joshua 6*). Apart from the certitude of long-term hunger imposed by siege, mines remained the deadliest weapon against castles and fortified towns throughout the Middle Ages. As early as the 16th century however, it was well known that mining was a game at which both besieger and besieged could play. In Shakespeare's *Henry V,* the touchy Fluellen explodes 'Look you, the mines is not according to the disciplines of the war; the concavities of it is not sufficient; for, look you, th'athversary is digged himself four yard under the countermines; by Cheshu, I think a' will blow up all, if there is not better directions.' Over three hundred years later with World War I, this was as neat a summing up of the 'tunnel war' beneath the trenches of the Western Front as could be found on either side.

When the war in the West began in August 1914, none of the combatant armies was equipped with 'directions' for tunnelling and mining, let alone the trained specialists and equipment required for such operations. These were only developed towards the close of 1914, after trench deadlock had ended the war of movement. First successes in the field went to the army whose engineer units had been given the most training in tunnelling, as opposed to the driving of traditional surface approach trenches or 'saps'. These were not the Field Companies of the British Army's Royal Engineers, or the French *sapeurs-mineurs,* but the Pioneer Companies of the German Army.

The tunnel war erupted on 20 December 1914 when ten German mines, planted inside tunnels on an 800m (half-mile) front under the British line near Festubert, were simultaneously blown. The unit on the receiving end of the blast was the hapless Indian Sirhind Brigade, already demoralized by the intensity of a Flanders winter's cold and German artillery fire. When the very earth beneath their feet blew up, the Indians broke. The Allies were lucky that the Germans had no full-blown assault force poised to flood through the breach which this created. As with the premature British commitment of a handful of tanks on the Somme in 1916, this first successful German mining operation was no more than a live-firing experiment. Even so, it opened a new dimension of the war on the Western Front.

By and large, the Germans retained the initiative in the tunnel war throughout 1915, forcing the British and French into the defensive ploy of counter-mining: listening for sounds of underground activity, then tunnelling forward to neutralize the enemy mine before it could be pushed under the Allied line. Each side tried to entomb the other's tunnelling parties by placing small explosive charges known as *camouflets,* and there were frequent vicious underground combats when rival tunnellers met.

The speed of the British response to the threat of German mining owed much to Major John Norton Griffith, M.P., a politician and tunnelling contractor who persuaded Lord Kitchener to approve the formation of a special mining unit recruited from civilian tunnel workers. The nucleus of this unit consisted of men employed by Griffith's peacetime company to dig sewer tunnels under the city of Manchester. They used the 'clay-kicking' technique, that is, lying at an angle of 45 degrees on wooden frames, and using both feet to drive a spade into the clay at the tunnel face. As the loosened clay was removed, the 'clay-kicker' moved forward on his frame to extend the tunnel. It was appallingly exhausting work, usually carried out in foul air which crude ventilating bellows could do little to freshen. Added to this was the ever-present risk of being killed by underground enemy tunnellers.

Sappers spent hours silent and alone listening for the tell-tale sounds of enemy counter-sapping. Cave-ins were common, often resulting in fatilities.

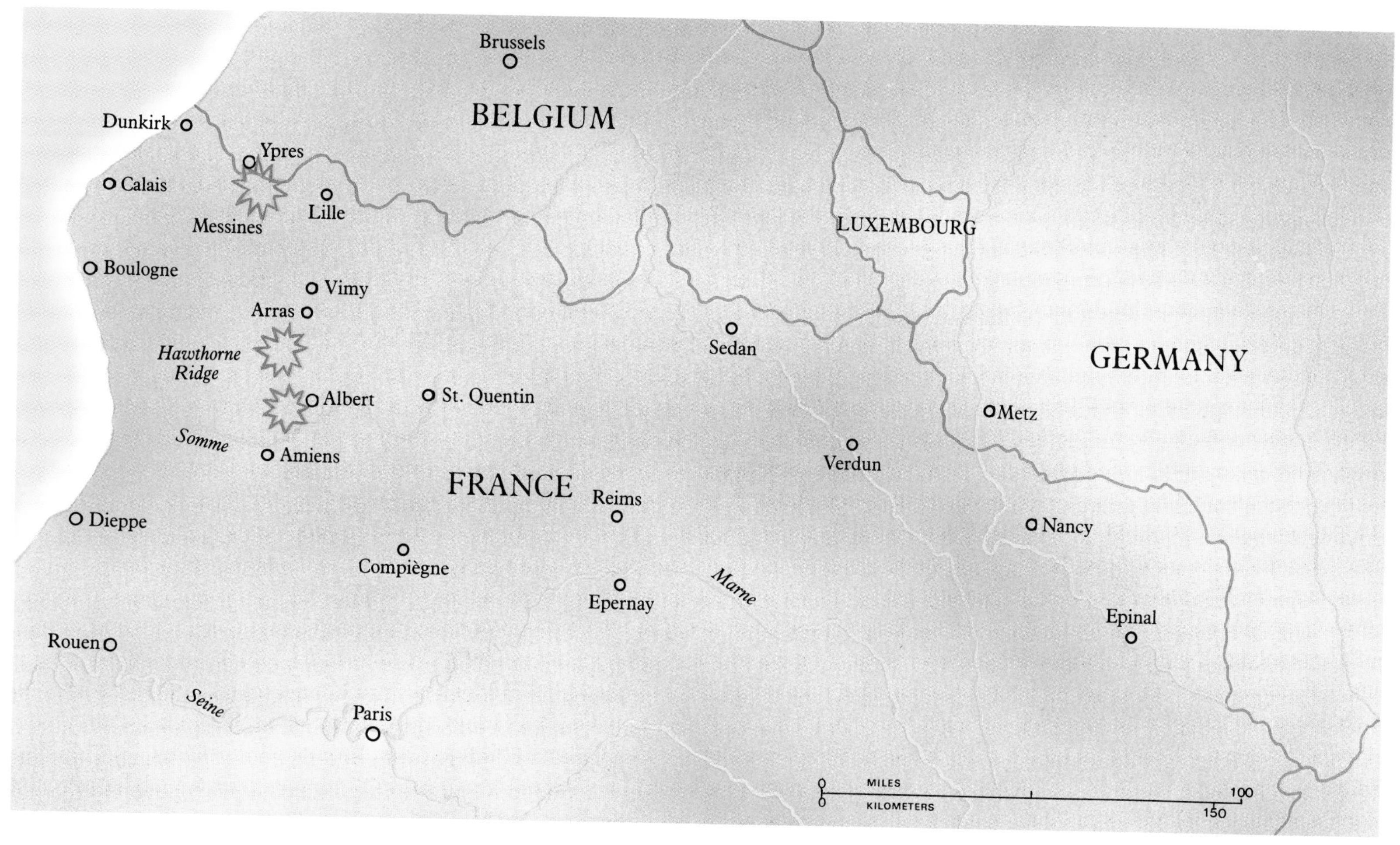

Considering that Griffith only began recruiting his tunnelling specialists in January 1915, the first British success in the tunnel war came gratifyingly early in the form of the storming of Hill 60, on the southern face of the Ypres Salient, in April 1915. Work on three tunnels began on 8 March in appalling tunnelling conditions of almost liquid mud, but was pushed steadily ahead. By the 16th, the tunnellers had detected sounds of German counter-mining, and one British tunnel subsequently pierced a German gallery which was successfully blown in with a *camouflet*. After a month of exhausting labour the tunnels had been driven under the German positions and the explosive charges, the largest of 1,225kg (2,700 pounds) had been tamped in place. The three mines were detonated on 17 April with shattering effect, blasting deep craters in the German line which infantry of the British 13th Brigade had no difficulty in seizing.

The decisive role played by the tunnellers in the capture of Hill 60 ensured the use of mining on an increasing scale in the Allied offensives which battered unavailingly at the German line in 1915, 1916, and 1917. The devastation caused by a well-placed mine was unquestionably better at cutting the enemy's barbed-wire defences than the heaviest artillery bombardment, but there were drawbacks. One was the danger to the attacker's own forward infantry, which was packed into the front-line trench awaiting the moment to attack. When the British blew their first really big mine of 2,270kg (5,000 pounds), at Hooge on the Ypres Salient on 15 July 1915, tragically, at least ten British infantrymen of the assault force were killed by the blast. It was also found that mine craters, though comparatively easy to occupy in the aftermath of the blast, were notoriously difficult to hold against the inevitable enemy counter-attack.

In the build-up to the British 'big push' on the Somme which began on 1 July 1916, British mining and German counter-mining was intensive. On the front of the British 18th Division, this activity created a maze of craters in No-Man's-Land which the Germans occupied, considerably slowing the British assault on 1 July. Along the central 24km (15 mile) front of the British 4th Army, 19 mines had been dug. Two of these contained 24 tons of explosive each. These were recorded as some of the most spectacular photographs of the entire war when blown at 7.28 a.m. on 1 July. What mattered that day, however, was not the size of the mine craters but the intact German dugouts on either side of them,

The tunnel war erupted on 20 December, 1914 when ten German mines were exploded along an 800m (864 ft) front under the Indian Sirhind Brigade positions. The Germans kept the initiative throughout 1915 but, a year later were overtaken by the British. During the build-up to the Somme offensive of July 1916 mining and counter-mining became intensive. On 1 July a series of 19 mines were blown under the German lines creating an explosion clearly audible in London. The effects were mixed. The enemy trenches on either side of the craters were not damaged, while the craters themselves formed obstacles to the advancing infantry, more impenetrable than the trenches which were intended for destruction. Nonetheless the British persevered and a year later exploded an even larger series of mines under the German positions at Messines with equally limited success. The surrounding area was virtually turned into primeval swamp, making further mining impossible. As the war became more fluid in 1918 mining was abandoned as an impractical exercise.

from which the German defenders emerged with their machine-guns to savage the oncoming British infantry.

On the Somme in 1916, the triple alliance of mining, intense artillery bombardment, and methodical infantry advance failed to achieve the hoped-for major breakthrough. This failure on the Somme, however, did not mean that mining had lost its effectiveness against suitable local objectives. This was proved in June 1917 by the most spectacular and horrifying event of the tunnel war – the mining and capture of the Messines Ridge, curtain-raiser to the dreadful Passchendaele offensive of August-November 1917.

Like Hill 60 and Hooge, the Messines Ridge was an essential objective for any British attempt to break eastwards out of the Ypres Salient. Plans to mine the Messines Ridge had dated back to the end of 1915. The longest of the 21 tunnels at Messines, of which 19 were eventually detonated, were more than 914m (1,000 yds) long, and their completion was attended by intense fighting underground. General Sir Herbert Plumer, commanding the British 2nd Army charged with the capture of Messines, ordered that the 19 mines were to be blown simultaneously at Zero Hour - 3.10 a.m. on 7 June. The assault, by nine British, Irish, Australian, and New Zealand divisions, would be prefaced by the detonation of nearly 430,920kg (950,000 pounds, or 424 tons) of high explosive. The biggest mine, to the south of St Eloi, consisted of 43,364kg (43 tons) of ammonal.

What was to prove on the part of the Germans to be the climax of the tunnel war took place on 7 June 1917. It remained the greatest localized military explosion in history until the first atomic bomb was dropped on Hiroshima 38 years later. The bang was not only clearly heard in London, it was reported in Dublin, about 804km (500 miles) away. It made the clay boil like porridge and vaporized thousands of German troops. German 'missing' casualty figures for the day, excluding listed dead and wounded, came to 10,000. Hardly less shaken than the German survivors, Plumer's men swept forward to occupy the Messines Ridge in little more than five hours.

If Messines was the greatest vindication of selective mining to capture a localized objective, it also exemplified the essential futility of the tactic when placed in context of Western Front grand strategy as a whole. The victory of 7 June 1917 was eclipsed by the horror of Passchendaele over the ensuing three months, which resulted in 244,897 British casualties. The mindless artillery bombardments, in causing the terrain east of the Ypres Salient to revert to primeval swamp, also made it impossible for any future mining operations to be undertaken in the only sector of the Western Front where mining had achieved any solid gains.

There was another reason why Messines was the postscript to the tunnel war. In March 1917 the German Army on the Western Front had conducted a masterly withdrawal to the prepared positions of the *Siegfriedstellung* – the Hindenburg Line. This dense belt of reinforced, buried defences-in-depth had been designed to reduce front line manpower to the minimum, not only with regard to reducing the number of casualties from Allied artillery fire, but also from Allied mining operations. The wheel had come full circle and the motive power was still German ingenuity and flexibility, which had opened the tunnel war at the end of 1914.

If Germany had stood on the defensive throughout 1918, it is likely that the Allies would have attempted to mine selected sectors of the Hindenburg Line. It is noteworthy however, that in the final great German offensive of March 1918, which at last restored movement to the Western Front, mining played no part at all. The German breakthrough was achieved by surgical artillery preparation, effectively severing the British front line from its rear areas. This was followed by rapid infantry penetration into those rear areas. After the German 1918 offensive had been fought to a vitual standstill, the Allied counter-offensive moved at far too great a pace for the tunnel war to be resumed. Trench mining had become a part of history along with trench warfare, in which the tunnellers had played a dramatic yet sadly, in the end, a futile role.

Above: Mining before the Battle of Albert, July 1916. Note the officer's geophone used to listen for counter-sapping.

Left: Explosion under the Hawthorn Ridge, 1 July, 1916.

Below: The mine crater at La Boisselle.

The Khyber Pass, The Battle for Control, 1919–1922

Throughout the latter half of the nineteenth century, Afghanistan remained the thorn in the side of the British Empire. Coveted by Britain and Russia alike, it acted as a magnet to the warring and fiercely independent tribes of the North-West Frontier.

Attempts to subjugate Afghanistan by force of arms were abandoned as impractical after repeated military defeats. Instead, Britain embarked upon a policy of diplomacy, hoping to win the hearts and minds of the Afghan leaders if not the loyalty of the tribesmen.

In 1901 Habibullah succeeded his father Abdur Rahman to the throne of Afghanistan and immediately began to show a certain susceptibility to British influence. Even so, he was fiercely resentful of her presence on the North-West Frontier, which he regarded historically as Afghan soil. Habibullah was a man of great bravery and considerable intellect, who accepted British largesse, at the same time continuing in his attempts to rid his country of her influence. On a wholly different score, he was apparently a man of vast sexual appetite, having one of the largest harems in recorded history and being reputed to have sired 200 children.

Although Habibullah accepted an Indian Imperial delegation to Kabul in 1904, reciprocating by visiting the Viceroy in Simla three years later, his precise aspirations remained unclear until 1914. On 4 August the same year, Britain declared war on Germany. Habibullah might have chosen to side with the Central Powers, tying up on sentry duty along the North-West Frontier much of the Indian Army then desperately needed in Europe. Instead, he unreservedly threw in his lot with the British, earning for himself the undying hatred of the majority of his people. When Turkey joined the Central Alliance the war took on the air of a jihad in the eyes of many Afghan Muslim fundamentalists, driving an even greater wedge between themselves and their king.

Habibullah's position became untenable. His younger brother, Nasrullah, inspired by his friend, the ideologue and satirist Mahmud Tarzi, openly conspired against him while his son and presumed heir, Amanullah, disowned him. In 1919 matters came to a head. Habibullah's demand for 'a written agreement recognizing the absolute liberty, freedom of action and perpetual independence of the Sublime Government of Afghanistan', a not unreasonable reward for four years' wartime support, was ignored by Britain as was his less realistic request for a seat at the Versailles Peace Conference.

Arrival at the Afghan peace delegation at a forward British outpost.

On 19 February 1919, Habibullah was assassinated by person or persons unknown. After a brief power struggle between Amanullah and Nasrullah the younger man ascended the throne, having first imprisoned his uncle for life, charging him with complicity in the murder of the hapless Habibullah.

Amanullah, although initially popular with the tribesmen, enjoyed few of the social or academic graces of his late father and soon found his throne in jeopardy. Desperate for a unifying factor around which to rally his people, the young king turned to India for a solution.

India was then embroiled in a state of sectarian and political unrest compounded by the heavy-handed and insensitive activities of the post-war government. On 13 April 1919 thousands of townspeople gathered in the Punjabi city of Amritsar to observe a Hindu holy day in defiance of a Government order banning public assemblies. Brigadier Dyer, at the head of a Gurkha force, was sent to maintain order and decided without further recourse to teach the 'natives' a lesson. Without giving the demonstrators prior warning, Dyer ordered his men to fire volley after volley into the heart of the crowd. Within ten minutes, 379 men, women and children had been killed and a further 1,200 wounded. The survivors were forced to crawl from the scene on their hands and knees as a final act of humiliation. The world was outraged. Dyer was forced to resign, Gandhi began his rise to power and Amanullah seized his opportunity.

Ignoring the fact that the vast majority of the dead were Hindu, Amanullah called for a Muslim holy jihad against the British infidels. Matters quickly got out of hand. Troops had to be called in to protect the British Agent in Kabul, proclamations declaring 'Holy War' were posted in mosques across the country and Mullahs began to infiltrate the Frontier hills to arouse the already volatile Pathan tribes. On their heels marched the Afghan Army, on Amanullah's orders.

Amanullah now began to grow uneasy. It had been his intention to prise a few concessions from a war-weary Britain, not to goad her into open warfare. His army was small, ramshackle and badly trained. More disconcertingly, it had not received a promised pay rise and elements were nearing open revolt. Amanullah could do no more than hold his men on their own side of the Durand Line, the highly artificial border then prevailing, and wait for some chance to withdraw gracefully.

He was to be presented with his opportunity and duly squander it. On 1 May Afghan scouts reported the presence of a British officer and four sepoys in Bagh, a shabby patch of near worthless cultivation in the Khyber Pass. Bagh was occupied by neither adversary, but claimed by both, due to its proximity to the strategically important town of Landi Kotal. Although the British patrol was almost certainly routine, Amanullah over-reacted. General Saleh Muhammed, the Commander-in-Chief of the Afghan Army, was ordered to build a fort in the area. When Britain complained, Bagh was occupied by a force of 150 Afghan soldiers. That night a band of Shinwari Pathans led by Zar Shah attacked a nearby Indian work gang, killing five men. Keen to ferment war, Zar Shah then sent word to the British that he had acted on General Saleh Mohammed's orders. Unprepared for war, the British ignored this obvious provocation and gave the Afghans an opportunity to withdraw. When this was not acted upon, the Indian Government announced a formal declaration of war against Afghanistan.

Above: A jirga, or group of tribesmen, gather to discuss their future with a senior, and well-guarded, British official.

Left: An Indian Army mountain battery deploying into action.

Britain's motive in declaring war was not so much the destruction of the Afghan Army as the prevention of a new and serious Frontier tribal uprising. Saleh had five infantry battalions supported by six field guns in the region of Landi Kotal, which had been garrisoned by Britain with a force of less than 500 sepoys of the Khyber Rifles. If he were to consolidate his position at Bagh and march on Landi Kotal the authorities feared that many of the local Pathan laskars would swell the ranks of the jihad. The 20,000 Afridis, Orakzais and Mohmands under arms in the Khyber Pass would then combine to turn the area into a bloodbath. On 7 May, two days after the declaration of war, mass desertions broke out among the sepoys of the Khyber Rifles forcing the Chief Commissioner to pre-empt a mutiny by disbanding the force and replacing it with regular troops.

The Indian Army of the day was far from being battle-ready, post-war demobilization having left it dangerously below strength. Many of its new recruits had not fired a shot in training, let alone anger, and its British officers were largely unacclimatized to the privations of Frontier service. The British regiments in the area were little better. Manned largely by 'hostilities only' conscripts called up for the war, the majority of officers and men were actively seeking demobilization and had absolutely no desire to become caught up in a frontier war against some of the most vicious tribesmen in the world. When asked to volunteer for action most initially refused, complaining

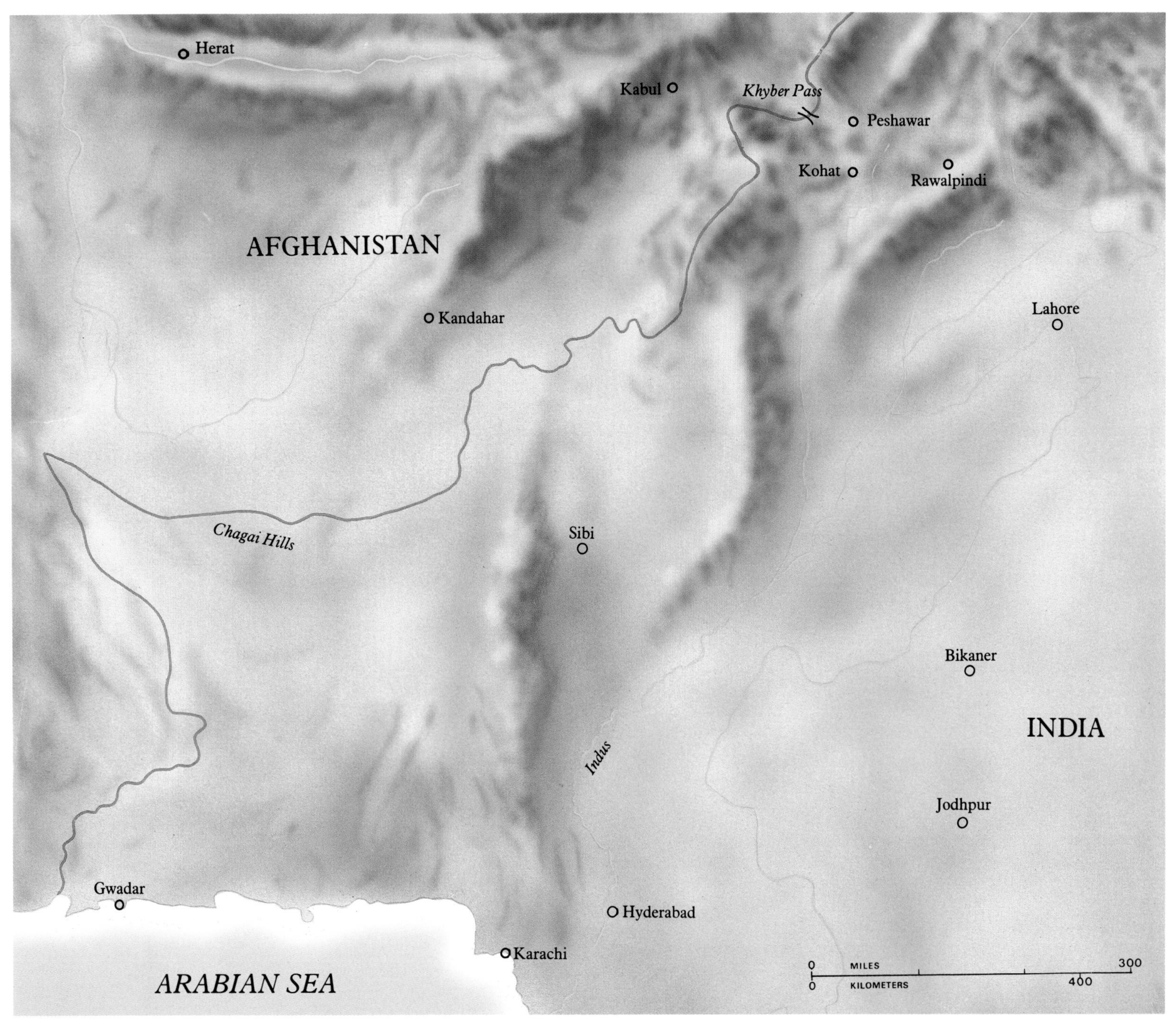

Afghanistan has always proved a grave yard for foreign armies, yet throughout the nineteenth and early twentieth centuries it became too important to ignore. Pivoted between the British and Russian Empires it was fated to become a pawn in a political game in which the interests of its indigenous peoples mattered for nothing. Ruled from Kabul by a king whose power over his disparate people was never more than tenuous, Afghanistan comprised a number of warlike and fiercely independent tribes with little more than religion in common. Usually these tribes were content to fight among themselves, but occasionally their squabbles permeated south across the Khyber Pass into India. When this happened British intervention invariably followed, although rarely with the outcome anticipated by Delhi. The so-called Third Afghan War of 1919-22 was such an intervention.

that their employers in England would not keep their jobs open for them if it were discovered that they had stayed on in India of their own volition. For a while it looked as if insubordination would degenerate into mutiny. Eventually, however, a composite unit commanded by Brigadier O'Dowda, nicknamed 'O'Dowda's Bolshie Brigade' after a second near mutiny en route, was sent north to the Frontier.

With surprising resourcefulness, the British managed to conceal their presence as they moved up the Khyber Pass and were thus left unharmed by the otherwise suspicious tribesmen. On 7 May, only two days after the declaration of war, the 'Bolshies' reached Landi Kotal where they combined with a somewhat more reliable force of Gurkhas and Sikhs under the command of the gallant if impetuous Brigadier Crocker.

Shortly after sunrise on 9 May the force began fanning out west of the fort towards Bagh. Initial Afghan resistance was fierce despite the accurate application of British artillery which speedily silenced the enemy guns. As the troops advanced they became aware of the fact that thousands of Afridi warriors had drawn up in battle formation between themselves and the comparative protection of Landi Kotal. The Afridis had come to watch events. They did not join the battle, though every soldier present knew that they would, with devastating effect, should the allied force fail to take Bagh. Spurred on by the horrific consequences of failure, Bagh was stormed after two days of heavy fighting.

So ended the first stage of the so-called 'Third Afghan War' . The enemy had been forced out of the disputed territory and the Pathans had not risen in their support. Britain knew however, that it would take a far more comprehensive victory than that at Bagh to cement a lasting peace in the area.

Dakka, a village about 8km (5 miles) to the north-west, became the next objective. A squadron of Royal Flying Corps bombers were called in to soften up the target, with little success. It was left to the infantry yet again to bear the brunt of the fighting. The Afghan defensive positions at Dakka were excellent, so much so that Crocker made no initial attempt to storm the village. Instead, he encamped his men in a defensive position outside and awaited events. The conditions in and around the camp were atrocious. Few of the men had been inoculated before the campaign and cholera quickly became the principal killer. To add to the force's discomfort, they were constantly sniped at by Mohmand tribesmen firing clay-filled expanding bullets from the surrounding hills.

The position was eventually taken but with 22 British and Indians killed and 157 wounded, it was a terrible price for so insignificant a prize.

On 28 May the troops received a much needed boost to their morale when a Handley-Page bomber flew low overhead on its way to bomb Kabul. The aircraft's two 45kg (100 pound) bombs killed no one and caused little damage to the capital, although they reputedly created chaos in the harem. They did however herald the next stage in the British advance. On 28 May the British troops were ordered to quit their hated camp at Dakka and resume their westward march to occupy Jalalabad.

General Nadir Khan, Amanullah's third cousin and the only Afghan military leader with a true grasp of strategy, now began to influence events. Discredited since his implied complicity in Habibullah's murder, Nadir was rehabilitated and given overall command of Afghan strategy. He immediately saw that the British forces were dangerously stretched and determined to attack them where least expected. Gathering together a force of 3,000 Afghan infantry regulars and two cavalry regiments supported by ten 100mm Krupp guns and seven 75mm Krupp howitzers, he sought a target of opportunity. Thal, to the south of the Kurram Valley, offered an excellent target. Defended by no more than 800 militiamen with two artillery pieces, it occupied a strategically important position at the northern end of a railway line. If it were to fall, Nadir reasoned that the consequences would be enormous. The British would no longer appear invincible in the eyes of the hill tribesmen who would certainly rise against them, expelling their hated presence from the frontier.

On 25 May, to British consternation, Nadir marched his force across the border and headed north-east towards Thal. Local military posts in his path were evacuated in panic or mutinied, allowing him to continue virtually unhindered to his objective. Soon he was joined by a force of 12,000 Pathan laskars goaded into rebellion by the seeming impotency of their former British masters. Within days 20,000 Wazir and Mahsuds, many of them former allies of the British on the Western Front, swelled the ranks of the rebels.

In the meantime the British position at Thal was becoming critical. The defender's guns were soon silenced by the far superior Krupps and the garrison cut off from its water supply. A relief column had set off but had become bogged down somewhere to the east. Ammunition supplies were running low and defeat seemed inevitable. Had the infamous General Dyer not reached the fort on 1 June at the head of a force of 3,000 British-Indian regulars supported by a dozen large calibre field guns, Thal would have fallen. The attendant massacre of the British defenders at the hands of the Pathans would have electrified the frontier causing those tribesmen still at peace to take up arms in what would have become the largest insurrection in the history of the North-West Frontier.

Instead, Dyer's artillery destroyed the now out-gunned Krupps while his infantry routed the Pathans. The Afghans sued for peace and began to pull back, pursued by the British, until ordered to stop.

The war ended 29 days after it had started, in stalemate. Both sides claimed victory with a certain degree of justification. Although small-scale guerrilla activity continued for the next two years, the British had largely restored order in and around the Khyber Pass. For their part the Afghans had gained the right to implement their own foreign policy independent of Delhi. In this way began an uneasy Afghan-Soviet flirtation which would be destined to end in tragedy some fifty years later.

Despite the primitive state of their weapons, many Afridi tribesmen were excellent shots.

The Taking of Eben-Emael, German Paratroops, 1940

The capture of Fort Eben-Emael by German paratroopers on the night of 10 May 1940 was perhaps the most daring and brilliantly executed commando action of the war. It combined planning with improvisation, and training with resourcefulness to bring about a victory which most would have regarded as impossible. In so doing it helped to change the course of history and bring about the defeat first of Belgium then of France.

By 10 May 1940 Hitler was the master of Central Europe. He had destroyed the Polish Army and occupied Czechoslovakia and Denmark. His troops were fighting a successful campaign in Norway and stood poised ready to launch a lightning strike against the remaining democracies in the West. The forces at his disposal, though fewer in number, were far superior in training and morale to the bulk of his potential adversaries, the French Army in particular being of dubious quality. Poorly trained, ill-disciplined and still mentally exhausted from the blood-letting of the Great War, its members could no longer be guaranteed to fight with their customary panache. The British were of a high standard but few in number, and the Belgians and Dutch ill-prepared for war.

More importantly, Belgium and Holland were still neutral. When Britain and France had declared war on Nazi Germany on 3 September 1939, Belgium had refused to join the old alliance, preferring to join the Netherlands in a policy of strict neutrality. Both non-combatants had mobilized their forces, placing the majority on the German border. At the same time they had strictly forbidden the Franco-British Army to enter their country to make effective preparations for their defence.

Britain had been forced to construct a series of wholly inadequate anti-tank ditches along the Franco-Belgian border during 1939. It was accepted that this created a dangerous gap of some 80km (49.7 miles) between the southern flank of the British temporary defences and the beginning of the massive French *Maginot line*, but this was discounted. The French felt that the densely wooded Ardennes,

Top: On 10 May, the German Army smashed its way across the Belgian border, taking the defenders competely by surprise.

Above: French and Belgian infantrymen relied on Great War tactics and equipment. They were no match for the German Panzers.

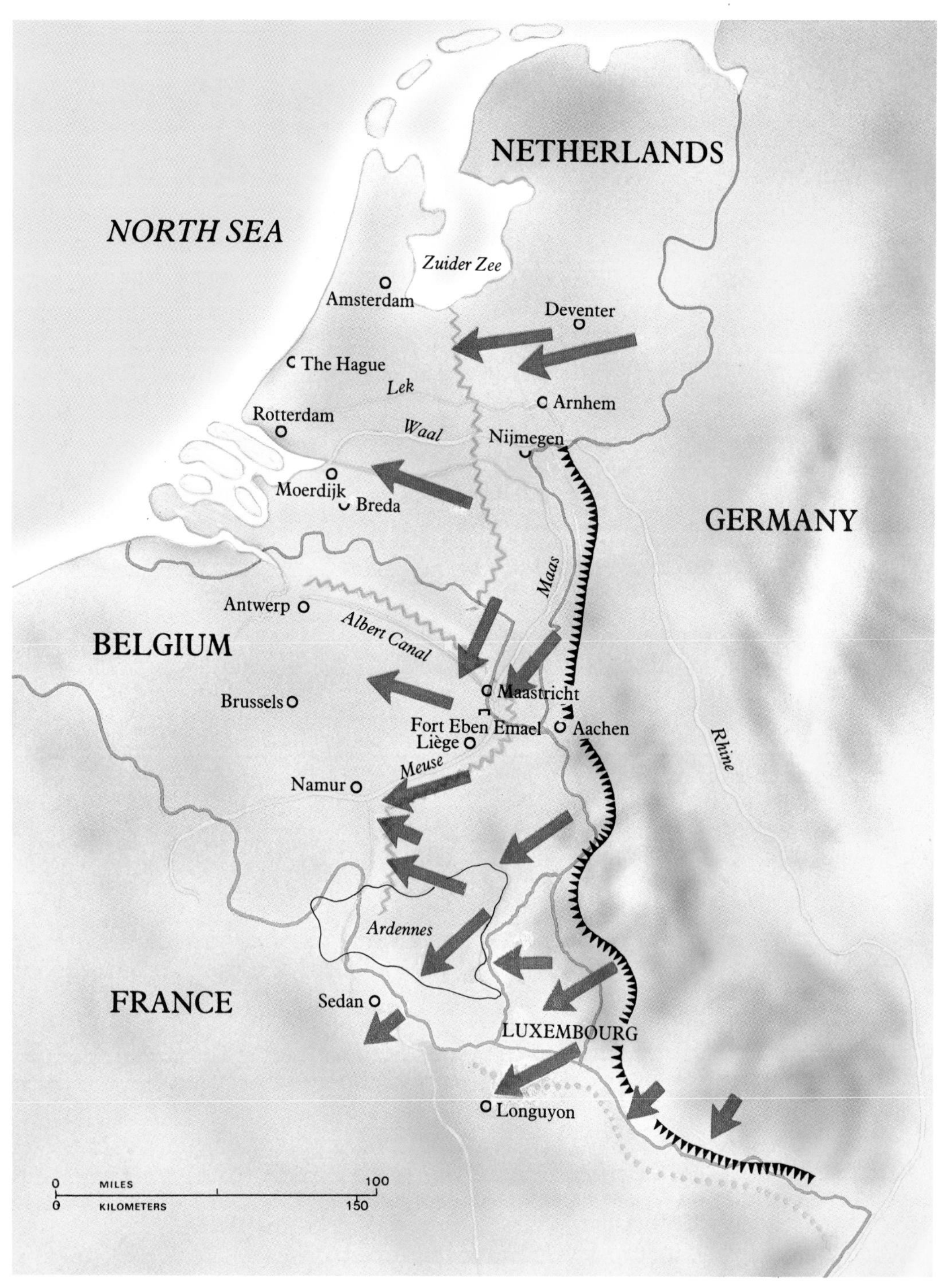

Eben-Emael was considered impregnable to conventional attack. It was in essence a tight complex of inter-related infantry and artillery strong points, 900m (972 ft) long and 700m (756 ft) wide, co-ordinated to provide mutual defence and linked by kilometres of deep subterranean passages. Numerous barrack blocks, messes, cook houses, sick bays, store rooms and magazines were integrated into a single entity capable of sustaining 1,200 servicemen for weeks, if not months. Eben- Emael was eventually assaulted from the air. Nine gliders were landed on the complex roof, taking the Belgian defenders completely by surprise. Within ten minutes the engineer commandos were in virtual control of the upper surfaces of the fortress with the garrison below at their mercy. Within hours Eben-Emael was in German hands and the road into Belgium was wide open.

which occupied the bulk of this lightly defended front, were impassable for large modern armies and declined to place more than nine divisions, only two of which were up to strength, in the sector. Britain, which would later argue that she had concurred only so as not to upset her more powerful ally, did not argue.

Only Hitler and the German High Command fully realized the recklessness of this complacency. Top secret plans were implemented for a lightning strike through Belgium and the Ardennes deep into the heartland of France. The key to German success lay in speed. It would be essential therefore to capture the bridges across the Meuse and Albert Canal intact and to neutralize the massive defences at Eben-Emael in the first hours of the invasion.

Eben-Emael was considered impregnable. Constructed between 1932 and 1935 as the northernmost fortification guarding the strategically important city of Liege, it dominated the network of roads leading from Maastricht to the west and protected the Vroenhaven and Veltwezert high-bridges which cross the Albert Canal.

Eben-Emael, 900m (984 yds) long and 700m (766 yds) wide, was in essence a tight complex of interrelated infantry and artillery strong points coordinated to provide mutual defences and linked by kilometres of deep subterranean passages. Barrack blocks, officers' and NCOs' messes, sick bays, machine rooms and magazines were all integrated into a single self-contained entity capable of sustaining 1,200 servicemen for weeks, if not months.

The fortress was protected on its north-east side by a sheer drop to the Albert Canal some 40m (132.1 ft) below. To the north-west the flood plain of the River Jeker had been raised by the fortifications to frustrate armoured attack fromthat direction. Anti-tank ditches and 4m (13.12 ft) walls had been dug to the south and west. With its own generators, telecommunications and over-pressure

filtered ventilation system, Eben-Emael was designed to withstand any form of attack experienced in the previous war. As history would prove, however, it was not geared for the next.

Responsibility for neutralizing Eben-Emael and capturing the bridges was delegated to the Koch Storm Detachment formed amid great secrecy in Hildesheim in November 1939. Commanded by Captain Koch, it constituted the 1st Company of the 1st Parachute Regiment, the Parachute Sapper Detachment of the VIIth Flying Division (at that time the only parachute division), the Freight Glider Unit, a beacon and searchlight detachment and airfield ground staff. The parachute company was ordered to take the three bridges at Vroenhaven, Veltwezelt and Canne, the sapper detachment to overcome the fortress.

This detachment was unique. Consisting entirely of engineers who had volunteered for hazardous duties, it incorporated within its ranks some of the finest glider pilots of pre-war Germany. Under the command of Lieutenant Rudolf Witzig it had grown into a close-knit, confident and above all self-reliant unit. Its training, order of battle, where possible its very existence, were unknown to the rest of the army.

During the six months before the operation its members were given no leave nor were they allowed to mix socially beyond their own numbers. Their mail was censored, they were not allowed to wear airborne badges and insignia and they were frequently moved around the countryside so as not to establish a pattern. Very few of the men had any real concept of the mission ahead of them and only Witzig knew the exact details.

Top left: German artillery and cycle troops cross the Albert Canal, 11 May 1940.

Above: An optical range-finder transmits its calculations direct to the anti-aircraft batteries.

Top right: Eben-Emael's water defences were formidable. However, they offered no defence against a paratroop drop.

Above: The Eben- Emael gun emplacements were perfectly designed to withstand ground attack, not a parachute assault.

The plan of attack was as daring as it was simple. The group would make no attempt to breach Eben-Emael's impregnable outer defences. Instead it would land silently by glider on the roof of the undefended fortress from where its members would deploy to the various key points, destroying them before the enemy knew that he was even under attack.

The initial assault would be limited to the central installations with priority given to the destruction of infantry support weapons and anti-aircraft guns. Massive 50kg (110.2 pound) hemisphere shaped cavity charges, transportable in two parts, would then be used to penetrate the armoured domes above the artillery positions.

As May approached so the training became more specific. The detachment moved first to the Sudetenland to practise attacking strongly fortified installations then to the Polish town of Gleiwitz to hone its demolition skills. Finally its members attended the Engineer School at Karlshorst to receive an introduction to the theory of fortress construction.

On the afternoon of 9 May Witzig at last received notification that the operation for which he and his men had planned and trained for so long was about to take place. The Koch Storm Detachment met according to plan at the Koln-Ostheim and Koln-Butzweilerhof airfields to receive its final briefings and at 4.30 a.m. precisely took off for its various destinations. The detachment was divided into eleven sections of seven or eight men each with its own glider. The take-off went well but almost at once complications set in. Two of the gliders, including Witzig's veered off course and were forced to land short of their objectives. The remaining nine, however, proceeded according to plan, dropped their tow lines some 30km (18.6 miles) from the border and continued silently and effortlessly towards their objective.

At precisely 5.25 a.m., five minutes before the main German Army crossed the frontier, the gliders landed in a tight configuration, precisely on target. Sergeant-Major Wenzel at once assumed command in the absence of the luckless Witzig and began to coordinate the operation. The nine teams left their aircraft within seconds of landing and moved effortlessly, two to the north of the complex, seven to the south, to locate their targets. The long and unremitting period of training was now paying dividends. A crucial anti-aircraft post in the south-east of the complex (A) fell before its crew members realized that they were even under attack. Seconds later the small barrack block to its north also succumbed to the relentless barrage of German machine gun fire, grenades and bombs. Within ten minutes the engineers were in virtual control of the upper surfaces of the fortress and the garrison below was at their mercy.

Allowing the Belgians no time to recover, explosive charges were now placed on seven of the reinforced artillery domes. Five emplacements were completely destroyed and with them nine of the fortress' massive 7.5cm (3 inch) guns. When it was found that the cavity charges would not penetrate the massive 6m (6.5 yd) diameter flat armoured dome protecting the 12cm (4.8 in) revolving twin cannon situated towards the centre of the emplacement (B) two 1kg (2.2 pound) satchel charges were hurled into the barrels, destroying the breeches as they exploded.

Above: Assault troops from the German 51st Sapper Battalion crossing the Albert Canal under fire.

To their chagrin, the two teams attacking targets in the north of the fortress discovered too late that their objectives (C) were in fact dummy installations uncharacteristically well protected by barbed wire. By a cruel irony the Belgians had intended to cover the entire upper surfaces with barbed wire and anti-vehicle obstacles some weeks earlier but had failed to receive the necessary materials. Had these arrived the fate of Witzig's men might have been very different.

By 8.30 a.m. the commandos had every reason to feel satisfied. Eben-Emael had been rendered ineffective. With the exception of the machine gun positions (D) overlooking the canal from the eastern perimeter and a lone emplacement on the west, the entire upper surface of the fortress was in German hands.

Then the impossible happened. A Luftwaffe glider suddenly appeared from the east and landed with a jolt close to the wrecks of the other craft. To everyone's surprise and relief Witzig descended unharmed and immediately demanded a full briefing before resuming command. It later transpired that the glider's tow-rope had parted soon after leaving Köln, forcing it to crash-land in a field. Fortunately the landing had been comparatively soft and it had been possible to relaunch the glider with the aid of a Ju 52 towing aircraft. Once airborne Witzig had followed his original flightpath, joining the battle some three hours late.

The counter-attack which Witzig's men had anticipated from the outset took some hours to materialize and when it did was initially ineffective. A number of Belgian artillery batteries to the north brought down fire on the German positions but failed to cause casualties. As the day progressed however, the Belgians began to appreciate the full immensity of their problems and brought up larger forces. By nightfall the Germans had been driven out of all but the north-west sector but not until they had managed to drop 100kg (220 pound) charges into the central ascent shafts, burying many of the hapless defenders alive.

Throughout the afternoon, elements of the 51st Sapper Battalion due to relieve Witzig's group attempted to cross the canal in rubber dinghies but were constantly frustrated by accurate gunfire from the remaining operational Belgian machine gun emplacement (D). Although Witzig was able to neutralize the effect of the gunfire to a degree by exploding hanging charges close to the observation slits in an effort to block them with debris, he could not do so completely, leaving the canal temporarily in Belgian control.

At approximately 7.00 a.m., elements of the Sapper Battalion skirted the remaining Belgian defences and approached the fortress from the west. Led by Sergeant Portsteffen they silenced the remaining ditch emplacement (E) and scrambled on to the emplacement roof. By midday, the remaining gun positions had ceased firing and what was left of Eben-Emael was firmly in German hands. The Belgians had lost 23 dead and 59 wounded in the day-long engagement, the Germans six dead and 15 injured.

Considerable speculation followed, particularly in the neutral press, as to why Eben-Emael had fallen so easily. Treachery and subterfuge were blamed but in reality neither was present. Witzig had, in fact, relied on a brilliant plan, comprehensive training and excellent soldiering to win. His few men had never allowed the Belgians, who had outnumbered them by more than ten to one, to gain the initiative, instead causing them to become captives in their own fortress and as such stifling their will to fight. Had the garrison counter-attacked during the night it might well have driven the Germans off, but such was not the case.

The storming of Eben-Emael was the first engineers' attack ever made from the air. There have been few like it since.

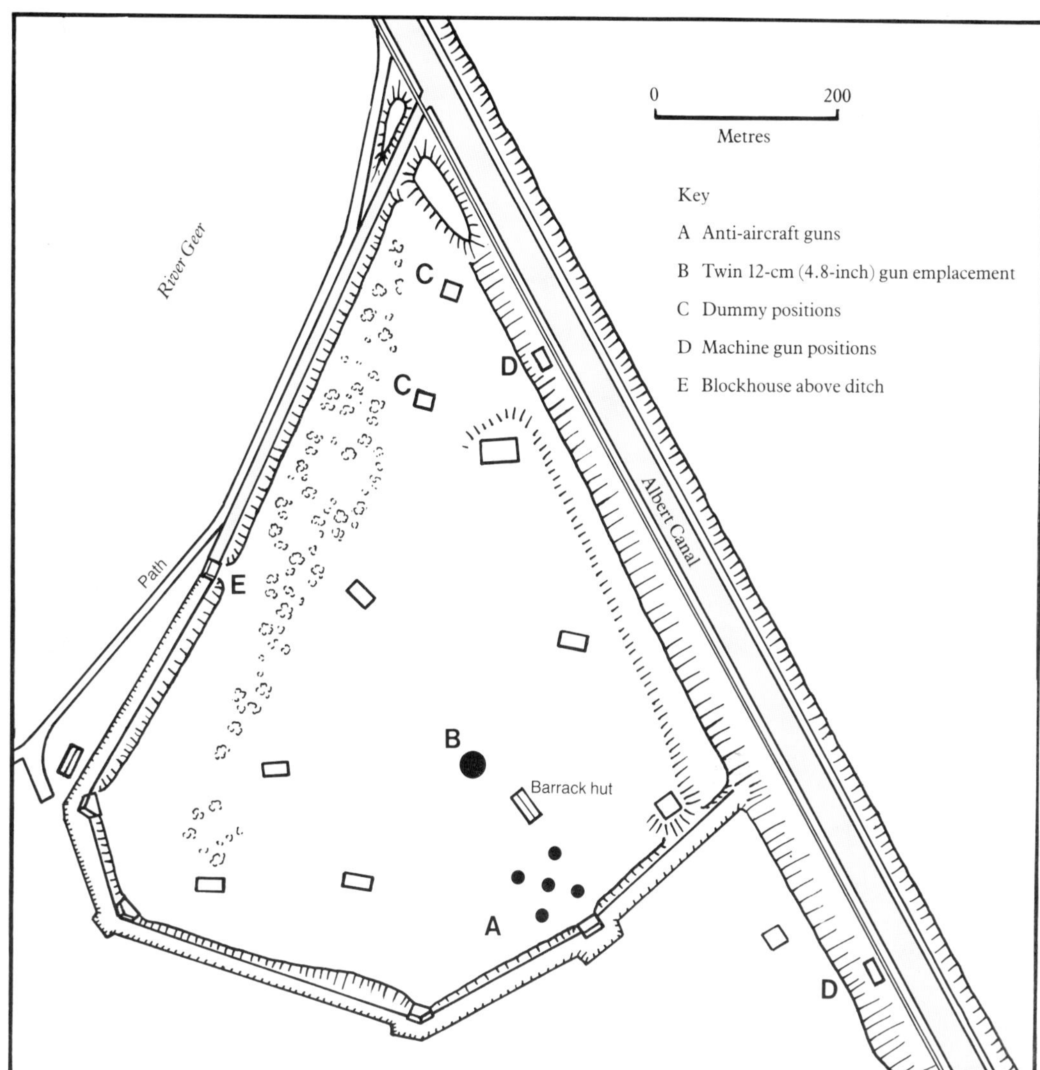

Below: A German machine gun crew during the assault into the Low Countries, May 1940.

The early neutralization of the Belgian fortress of Eban-Emael was crucial to the timing of the German plan for the invasion of France. The fortress itself and its surrounding bridges were attacked on the morning of 10 May, 1940. Almost simultaneously von Rundstedt's Army Group A began its thrust west and south-west through Belgium into the soft French underbelly. Meanwhile to the north, von Bock's Army Group B punched its way through the flimsy Belgian and Dutch defences westward towards Bruxelles, Antwerp and the Channel ports. Within days the Allied defensive plan was in tatters as her shocked and demoralized troops were forced to fall back.

The First Chindit Campaign, Burma, 1943

By the summer of 1942 the British position in the Far East was critical. Her ill-equipped and poorly trained Army had been hurled out of Burma by the much maligned Imperial Japanese Army. *Repulse* and *Prince of Wales,* both the epitome of Royal Naval impregnability, lay at the bottom of the sea. Singapore and Hong Kong were in enemy hands and the Indian National Congress Party were threatening Britain's sovereignty in the sub-continent.

The British command in Delhi nurtured a passion for the recapture of Burma but had neither troops of sufficient calibre nor the equipment and organization to fulfil its dream. The same border terrain which prevented a full-scale Japanese incursion into India frustrated attempts by General Irwin's *Eastern Army* to mount even the occasional localized counter-attack. The border between India and Burma consisted of a long chain of jungle-covered mountains, some 320km (200 miles) across. There were few permanent roads and such tracks as existed meandered grotesquely through the wilderness rising and falling precipitously with every mile.

Above: Wingate poses with his senior officers prior to leading the Chindits into battle.

Below: Chindits crossing one of the smaller rivers in enemy-occupied Burma.

The numerous swift flowing and often deep rivers were seldom bridged and invariably ran north to south making them impossible to avoid.

As if in anticipation of the British plight Lieutenant-General Shorjiro Iada, in command of the Japanese XV Army, pulled the bulk of his troops back from the border area to less hostile bases east of the Chindwin River, leaving a few patrols to monitor the crossroads and river crossings. Responsibility for the border was divided between XXXIII and XLV Divisions, XVIII turned north to face the massing Chinese while XLVI Division was held in reserve. When command passed to Lieutenant-General Renya Mutaguchi, the veteran commander of XVIII Division, in March 1943, Japanese headquarters were transferred to Maymyo but in all other respects the policy of wait, watch and consolidate was re-emphasized.

Lethargy within the region would almost certainly have continued had it not been

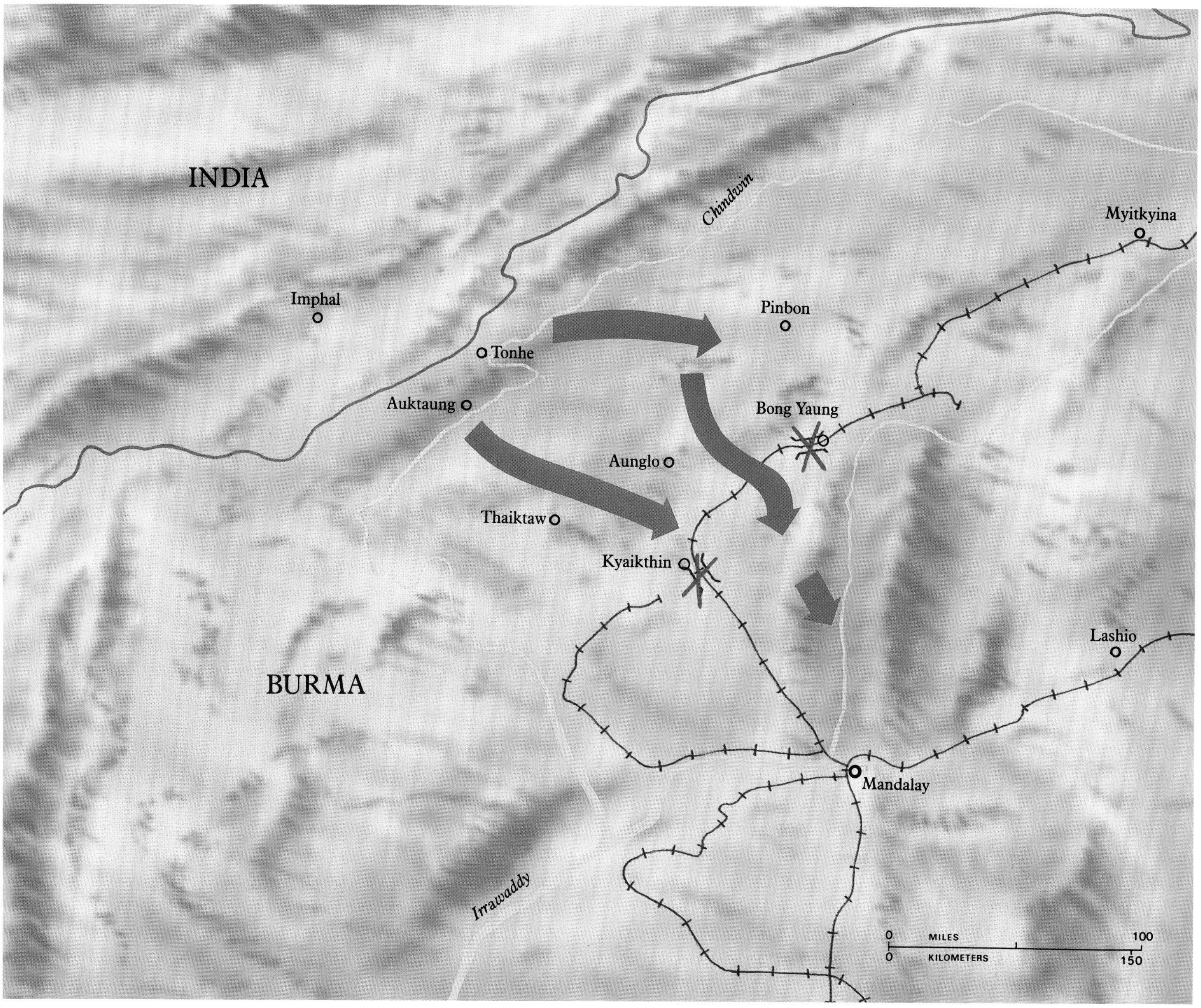

INDIA
Chindwin
Myitkyina
Imphal
Pinbon
Tonhe
Auktaung
Bong Yaung
Aunglo
Thaiktaw
Kyaikthin
Lashio
BURMA
Mandalay
Irrawaddy
0 MILES 100
0 KILOMETERS 150

The first Chindit expedition advanced deep into Japanese held territory along two fronts. A small party moved north from Tonhe across the Chindwin towards Pinbon and then south towards Bong Yaung, the larger southern party from Auktaung and on to Kyaikthin. Initially all went well. The Japanese, taken completely by surprise, assumed erroneously that the British were being supplied along conventional lines and wasted a considerable amount of their resources hunting for the non-existent supply lines. However when they realized that the Chindits were being resupplied from the air they changed their tactics with devastating effect. Two of the Chindit units were ambushed and forced to withdraw in disorder. The others continued ever eastward across the Irriwaddy until, confronted by overwhelming enemy numbers, they too were forced to retire. Although the operation was deemed a success, and repeated later on a far larger scale, it was very costly in human terms. Of the 3,000 men who entered the jungle with Wingate only 2,182 returned of whom no more than 600 were ever considered fit for service again.

General Wingate inside a Dakota aircraft, fitted for the transportation of mules.

for the creation of South East Asia Command (SEAC) under Lord Louis Mountbatten and the arrival in the theatre of Orde Wingate. A man of formidable physical and intellectual energy, Wingate had, by the age of 38, already established himself as one of the most extraordinary officers then serving in the British Army. Before the outbreak of the war his career had been somewhat hindered by his total lack of social niceties, his inability to make small talk even when politically necessary, and by his absolute intolerance of those whom he regarded as fools even when they held superior rank. He was a committed Christian whose unshakeable conviction in the power of God influenced his every major decision. Despite his beliefs he was also a fervent Zionist, a factor in itself guaranteed to upset the pre-war military hierarchy. To many Wingate was a dangerous eccentric, refusing to bathe in the conventional way, instead keeping himself scrupulously clean by scrubbing his body vigorously with a tooth-brush. To the more enlightened however, his was an outstanding military potential simply waiting to be exploited.

Wingate joined General Wavell's staff in March 1942, the two men having met a year earlier. Then, as G.O.C. Middle East, Wavell had come close to court-martialling his junior but instead had learned to tolerate his insubordination. He had listened attentively to Wingate's tales of successful guerrilla raids behind the lines in Palestine and Abyssinia and now wished to investigate the possibility of translating these to the jungles of Burma.

Wingate was immediately promoted from major to colonel and sent to Maymyo, which was then still in British hands, with orders to take command of all guerrilla operations in Burma. With the able assistance of Major Michael Calvert, commandant of the Bush Warfare School, Wingate carried out a series of deep reconnaissances from which emerged a series of radical theories which were later to manifest themselves into the First Chindit Campaign.

Wingate argued that highly trained columns, large enough for independent combat yet small enough for manoeuvrability, could operate in the deep jungle almost indefinitely if resupplied regularly from the air. Once in position they would be perfectly positioned to harry the enemy's supply lines forcing him to divert large numbers of combat troops from the front line.

A sympathetic Wavell concurred and agreed to the formation of a long range penetration (L.R.P.) brigade to be designated 77th Indian Infantry Brigade. Mindful of future needs he also agreed to the promulgation of the 50th Indian Parachute Brigade to consist of the 151st (British), 152nd (Indian), and 153rd (Gurkha) Battalions.

Above: British, West Africans and Gurkhas wait at the ramps to file into transports.

Left: Preparing a ration drop. Chocolate was not only a luxury, it provided much needed energy.

In July 1942, 77th Brigade began a period of long and intensive training. The eight columns which comprised the brigade each consisted of a platoon of jungle veterans drawn in the main from the 13th King's Liverpool Regiment, the 3/2nd Gurkha Rifles and the 142nd Commando Company supported by a small R.A.F section equipped with powerful radios. That many of the Liverpudlians were old for infantrymen did not worry Wingate who argued that age brought with it a maturity invaluable in the severe conditions which lay ahead. Intelligence gathering, sabotage, escape and evasion and jungle survival were all taught while more conventional disciplines such as marksmanship and fitness were honed.

Wingate saw his mission as sixfold: to test the theory of long-range penetration, to obtain detailed intelligence on the potential of future Burmese co-operation, to prevent Japanese infiltration across the Chindwin, to prevent an offensive towards Fort Herz, to frustrate the build-up for an attack on Assam, and to keep the motivation and fighting edge of his troops at a peak. When the Americans aborted a proposed sweep south from China which the 77th Brigade had originally been destined to join, Wingate was not deterred but instead convinced the somewhat incredulous Wavell to let him go it alone. The brigade was ordered to be ready to leave Imphal, the site of Slim's forward base on the Burmese border, on 8 February.

Wingate divided his small brigade into two groups, a larger northern group comprising his brigade headquarters, the Burma Rifles HQ and Columns 3, 4, 5 and 7 with 2,200 men and 850 mules and a smaller southern group comprising a headquarters supporting Columns 1 and 2 with 1,000 men and 250 mules. Wingate took personal command of the northern group, delegating control of the columns to Majors Calvert, Bromhead, Fergusson, Gilkes and Scott. Command of the subsidiary group passed to Lieutenant-Colonel Alexander, supported by Majors Dunlop and Emmett.

Both groups were ordered to advance from Imphal to the Chindwin and to effect a silent crossing on the night of the 14/15 February. The northern group was to cross at Tonhe. Thereafter it was to advance undetected through the hills to the Pinbon-Naungkan area, cut east and sever the railway between Bongyaung and Nankan. Alexander's group was to ford the River Chindwin 56km (35 miles) downstream at Auktaung, cross the hills to Thaiktaw, destroy the railway at Kyaikthin, then cross the Irrawaddy near Tagaung and make for Mongmit.

The epic marches began without incident. Both groups successfully crossed the Chindwin, headed east and received their first air drops. Wingate's audacious plan depended upon discipline, excellent timing and above all, luck. After only three days the southern group suffered its first set-back when it encountered an enemy position near Mainyaung and had to take a time-consuming detour. Wingate was more fortunate, succeeding in reaching his intended bivouac site five miles to the west of Pinbon on schedule.

Once established, he dispatched Calvert with Column 3 and Fergusson with Column 5 to the railway with orders that they should carry out extensive demolitions. Column 4, under Major Bromhead, was ordered to carry out a feint to the north of Pinbon to confuse the enemy but, in the process, they encountered a large Japanese concentration near Pinlebu. Bromhead's troops were dispersed and, in fact, played no further part in the action although, true to their orders and training, a number did succeed in making their way back to the safety of the Chindwin. As though in retaliation, Fergusson reached his objective on the following morning and after a bloody encounter with a Japanese patrol destroyed a bridge near Bongyaung. Later that day he dynamited a gorge to the south causing hundreds of tons of debris to block the line while Calvert demolished two railway bridges.

Careless of the hornets' nest which he had stirred up and obsessed with the need to prove that the concept of long-range pentration was viable, Wingate refused to consolidate after his initial successes, but instead ordered his by now disparate groups east across the Irrawaddy. Suddenly things began to go terribly wrong. The southern

Above: Chindits preparing a demolition behind Japanese lines.

Below: Mules were the lifeline of the Chindit columns. When superflous or injured they could always be eaten.

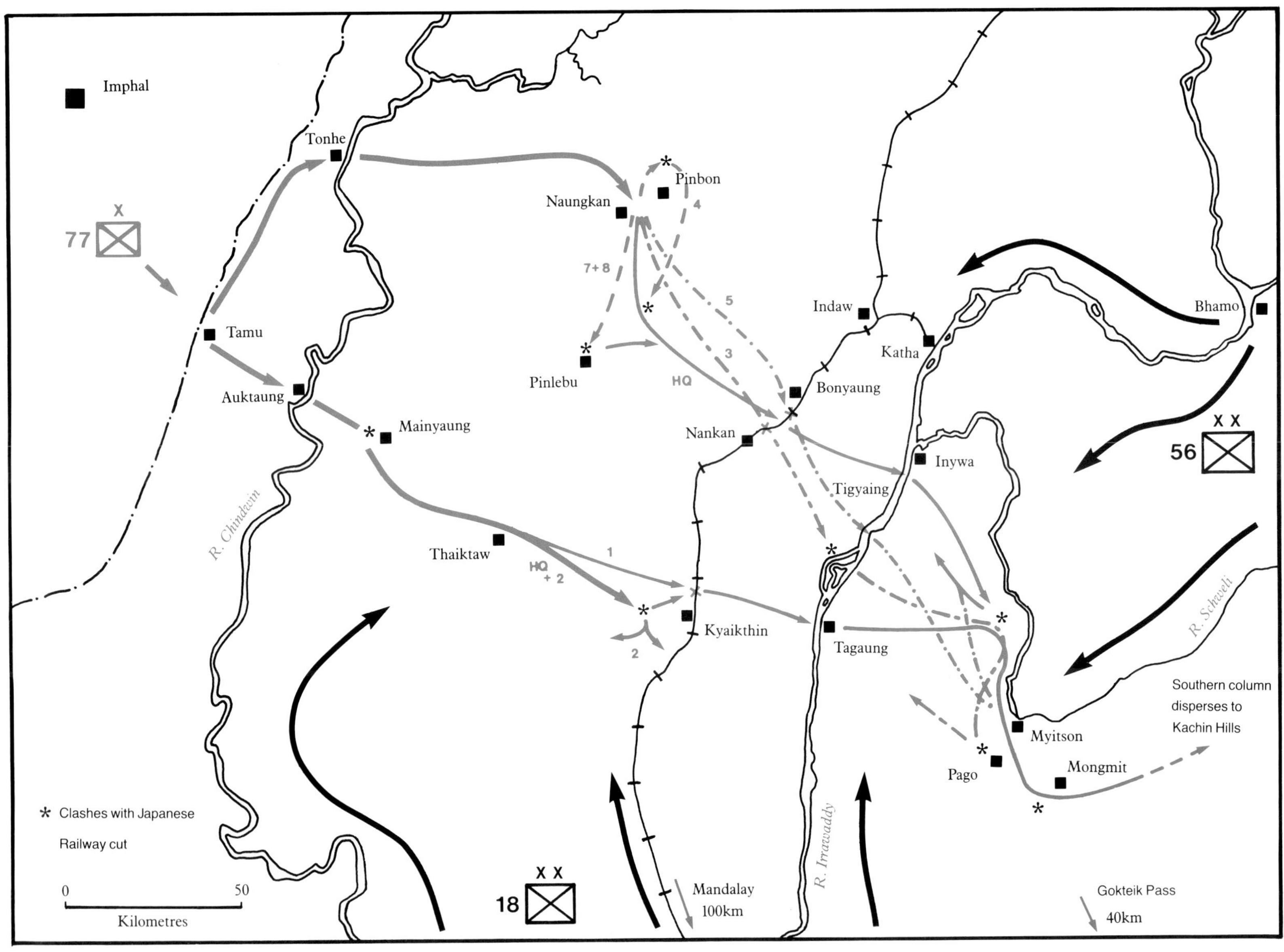

Wingate's volunteers were designated the 77th Indian Infantry Brigade and divided into eight self-sufficient columns. The brigade was split into two groups, a larger northern group comprising brigade headquarters and Columns 3, 4, 5 and 7 with 2,200 men and 850 mules, and a smaller southern group comprising Columns 1 and 2 with 1,000 men and 250 mules. Both groups advanced without mishap from Imphal to the Chindwin, crossing the river without incident on the night of 14/15 February. Thereafter they successfully completed their initial objectives and continued east across the Irriwaddy. Luck deserted the Chindits when the southern group headquarters and Column 2 were ambushed and an air drop to Columns 7 and 8 were spotted by the Japanese. Wingate was ordered to retire but not until the enemy bridge had been blown at Bong Yaung. Of the 3,000 officers and men who entered the jungle with Wingate only 2,182 returned of whom no more than 600 were ever again deemed fit for service.

group headquarters and Column 2 were ambushed and the latter dispersed, the northern column lost most of its mules during the river crossing, and the Japanese unfortunately discovered the secret of Wingate's resupply.

The Japanese XV Army had responded immediately to the first explosions but had assumed, as Wingate had hoped and intended, that the raiding parties were being resupplied by land. Accordingly they had begun to patrol the area to the Chindwin, in depth looking in vain for signs of a line of communication which did not, of course, exist. Suggestions of aerial resupply were dismissed as fanciful until a drop to Columns 7 and 8 was actually witnessed by a rear area patrol. Realizing the truth, Mataguchi at once changed his tactics, recalled his patrols and concentrated his forces. Orders were given for 3/56th Regiment to proceed to Tagaung and the 2/146th Regiment to the triangle between the Irrawaddy and Schweli Rivers. This was precisely the area designated by Wingate for his next operation.

To compound his problem Wingate discovered too late that the area between the Irrawaddy and Schweli consisted of dense virgin jungle, impenetrable save for the established roads and tracks by which it was intersected. It was a completely impossible area for attempting hit-and-run warfare.

Undaunted and still unaware of the converging Japanese regiments, Wingate ordered Calvert and Fergusson south, tasking them with the destruction of the viaduct at Gokteik Gorge. The plan was frustrated when Fergusson's column encountered large-scale Japanese troop movements in the area of Myitson. Scorning a suggestion by Lieutenant-General Scoons commanding IV Corps that he should retire, Wingate now determined to move eastwards into the

Kachin hills with a view to operating towards Lashio and Bhamo. Fearful that aerial resupply would be difficult if not impossible over so great a distance, the realistic and by now thoroughly alarmed Scoons ordered Wingate to abort his plans and instead to consider an attack on Shwebo. When Wingate reported that such an attack would prove impossible due to the lack of available boats on the Irrawaddy he was ordered to withdraw.

Wary of the enemy now massing to his rear, Wingate planned a staged return. Calvert, whose Column was somewhat to the west of the others, was ordered to close the Gokteik Pass if practical and thereafter to proceed to safety independently. Realizing the difficulty of keeping so large a force secret from the enemy, Calvert split his column into ten dispersal groups, jettisoned all but his essential equipment, released his spare mules and set off on his epic journey.

The remnants of the southern group were given the unenviable task of decoying the Japanese by continuing eastward while the rump of the northern group moved on Inywa, near the junction of the Irrawaddy and Schweli, where it was hoped that boats would be available.

Above: A wounded Gurkha being 'casevact' to an L5 Sentinel aircraft.

Fergusson's Column 5, ordered to act as rearguard, suffered catastrophically during the withdrawal. Tricked by an unsympathetic boatman, his party was marooned on a sandbank in midstream while negotiating a crossing of the Schweli. With daylight rapidly approaching, Fergusson was forced to order his men to wade the fast-flowing river in the certain knowledge that any who lost their footing would undoubtedly be swept away. Some were too weakened by disease to attempt the crossing and were left behind to be taken prisoner. In all, Fergusson lost 46 men, who were either dead or marooned, in this single incident.

Above: Air Commando bombers attack Japanese stores and supply depots in the path of the Chindit advance.

Right: Sergeant Len McElroy and Corporal Jimmy Walter; exhausted but safe.

Of the 3,000 officers and men who entered the jungle with Wingate only 2,182 returned, of whom no more than 600 were ever adjudged fit for service again. Yet the expedition had not been a failure even though the railway was soon repaired and the Japanese divisions were as secure as ever. The legend of Japanese invincibility in the jungle had taken a savage blow and to the forgotten men of SEAC it became clear that with fitness, the right sort of training and above all motivation, the enemy could be beaten in his own environment.

The Fall of Cassino, The Poles Take the Fortress, 1943–1944

After the first Battle for Cassino the rains began to fall steadily in Southern Italy, turning the valleys into swamps and grounding the Allied Air Force. A break in the weather had therefore to be awaited before Allied attacks could be resumed.

The exhausted Germans used the period to regroup. On 20 February, General Heidrich's I Paratroop Division relieved the 90th Panzer Grenadiers. The 71st Infantry Division was moved to the quieter Monte Arunci sector to the north of the 94th Division while the 44th had its sector reduced to a narrow strip either side of the Terelle. Only the veteran V Mountain Division, under General Schrank, was left in its original position. The paratroopers were critically under strength after the weeks of hard fighting around Ortona to the south with few of their battalions mustering more than 200 fit men. None of the units was up to strength, supplies were critical and air support totally lacking.

General Alexander, on the other hand, was able to prepare for a powerful assault on the enemy positions in the knowledge that his forces were growing steadily. The U.S. 5th Army alone had 600,000 shells designated for the operation while General Eaker, in command of the Allied air forces in the Mediterranean, had promised to make available every bomber in the theatre.

The Allied plan was simple. The German lines in front of Monte Cassino would be subjected to the largest artillery barrage in the history of the Italian campaign. The 2nd New Zealand and 4th Indian Divisions would then assault a small area, the New Zealanders taking Cassino and Hill 193 (Rocca Janula). This accomplished, the Indians would then storm the steep sides

Top: German troops rest in a lull in the battle. Note the grenades stacked ready for immediate use.

Right: The ruins of Cassino lie under a pall of smoke.

of Monte Cassino, driving the Germans from the monastery. Finally, the British 78th Division would cross the Rapido and push ahead into the Liri Valley.

General Freyberg, in overall Allied command, launched his attack on 15 March 1944. Having withdrawn his forward units under cover of darkness, he ordered the air attack to begin at 8.00 a.m. Wave after wave of aircraft crossed the front line in a four hour orgy of destruction. Bombers numbering 550, supported by 200 fighters and fighter-bombers, pounded an area some 1,300m (1,421 yds) by 400m (437 yds) surrounding the Abbey with 1,250 tons of high explosive. On the withdrawal

Left: Sherman tanks manned by New Zealanders roll into action in support of the attack.

Below: Nestling beneath the monastery, the town of Cassino was totally destroyed in the months of fighting.

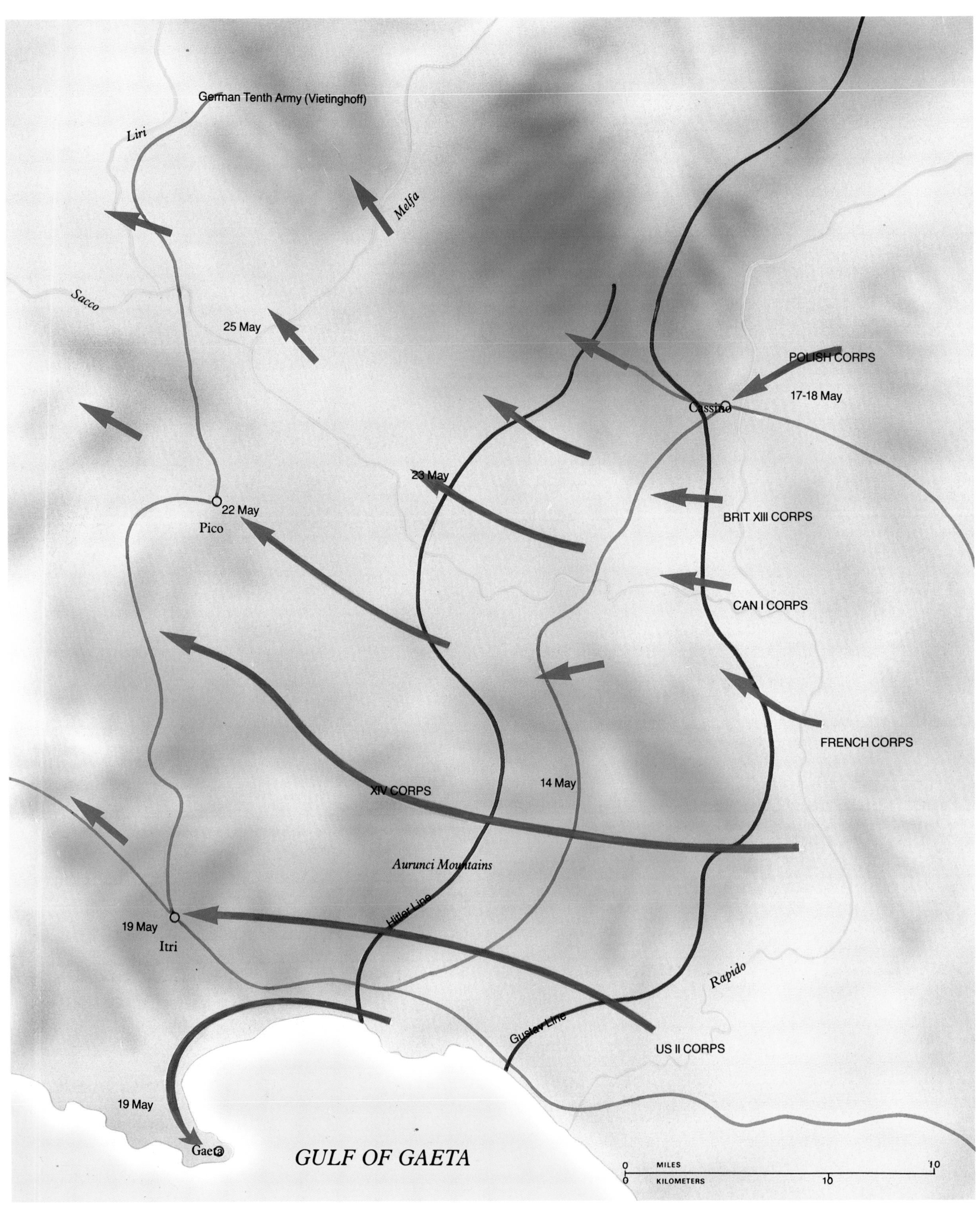
German Tenth Army (Vietinghoff)
Liri
Melfa
Sacco
25 May
POLISH CORPS
17-18 May
Cassino
23 May
22 May
Pico
BRIT XIII CORPS
CAN I CORPS
FRENCH CORPS
XIV CORPS
14 May
Aurunci Mountains
Hitler Line
19 May
Itri
Rapido
Gustav Line
US II CORPS
19 May
Gaeta
GULF OF GAETA
MILES
KILOMETERS
0
10
0
10

Left: The monastery at Cassino; a pre-war view taken in 1927.

Below: One of the great cultural tragedies of the war. The monastery lies in ruins.

The 15th Army began its offensive against the Gustav Line on 11 May when 21 Allied divisions and 11 brigades joined battle with 14 depleted, battle-weary German divisions and no more than three brigades in reserve. The assault began with a barrage of 2,000 guns along a front stretching from the upper Rapido to the Tyrrhenian Sea. An hour later the armour and infantry of the 5th and 8th Armies began their advance. The first major attack was launched by the French Expeditionary Corps now brought up to four divisions. During the night they stormed the German 71st Infantry Division's position on the upper Garigliano securing the tactically important Monte Faito and opening the path to Monte Maio in the process. The U.S. 2nd Corps advancing along the coast made slower progress, failing to make their first objective until 13 May. To the north, the British XIII Corps, supported by the Canadian 1st Corps, succeeded in crossing the Rapido into the Liri Valley. Thereafter they pushed forward unabated, reaching the Cassino-Pignataro Road on 15 May. Simultaneously, the French entered San Giorgio turning the German flank , thereby allowing the Canadian 1st Corps to take Pontecorvo. By 16 May the Allies had reached the Adolf Hitler Line, Germany's last line of defence.

of the last bomber, 748 artillery pieces of various calibres opened up a bombardment against the town and hill, firing 195,969 shells in the space of ten hours.

The defending Germans were taken completely by surprise by the timing and ferocity of the attack. The worst casualties were suffered by II Battalion, III Parachute Regiment actually stationed in the otherwise deserted town. They lost 160 killed and wounded out of a complement of less than 300. Only the Battalion's reserve company, the VIth under command of Captain Foltin, managed to avoid the carnage by seeking the protection of a nearby cave when the bombing started.

The infantry assault began at 3.30 p.m. led by the 5th Brigade of the 2nd New Zealand Division. Almost immediately it came under fire from Foltin's paratroopers who had resumed their defensive positions as soon as the barrage had lifted. Progress was slow. By nightfall the 25th Battalion had fought its way 200m (216 yds) into the north of the town and had captured Peak 153 but the brigade had then stalled. Ironically the New Zealanders' tanks had been delayed by the sheer quantity of debris produced by the earlier shelling and had been unable to follow the infantry into the town, leaving the latter almost totally devoid of support. To compound the New Zealanders' problems, German artillery and mortars around Cassino began firing into their positions, adding to their mounting casualties.

During the course of the next day the 2nd Division continued its painful progress into Cassino, capturing all but the centre and an area around the railway station. That night the Germans brought in strong reinforcements to create a stable defensive line along the Via Casilina.

Meanwhile, the 4th Indian Division had begun its assault on Monte Cassino itself. Under cover of an eight hour barrage the Essex Battalion, 5th Indian Brigade had advanced through the ranks of the New Zealanders on Peak 193 to take Peak 165, badly mauling 1/3rd German Parachute Regiment in the process. A subsequent attempt by the Rajputanans to take Peak 236 was repelled with heavy losses but an attack by 1/9th Gurkhas against Peak 435 succeeded bringing the Indians to within 400m (433 yd) of the rear of the monastery.

When the 26th New Zealand Battalion still fighting in the town below succeeded in capturing the railway station a few hours later, the German defenders found themselves almost completely encircled with a corridor of no more than 1,000m (1,095 yd) between the station and Peak 435 remaining open. Unperturbed, Heidrich set about closing the gap to his front. During the night of 18/19 March the survivors of the 1/4th Parachute Regiment formed up amid the ruins of the monastery. Under cover of darkness they crept down the mountain and at dawn attacked the Essex Battalion who were dug in on Peak 193. Although the assault was eventually repulsed with heavy losses it unnerved the Essex to the extent that they withdrew to their defensive positions, allowing the Germans to retake the ground between themselves and the Gurkhas on Peak 435.

Unknown to the Germans the timing of their counter-offensive was particularly

Above: A wrecked Allied Sherman tank offers testimony to the ferocity of the fighting for the town.

Below: A German StuG III 75mm assault gun deploys in the town.

fortuitous. The 5th Indian Brigade was about to mount its own assault on the monastery from Peak 435 and was awaiting the arrival of a company of New Zealand tanks when the Germans attacked. Unaware that the Indians had become bogged down the tanks duly arrived at their start line and, receiving no orders to the contrary, commenced their attack. Every vehicle was destroyed by German gunfire before the New Zealanders could even reach Monte Cassino.

On 21 March, Alexander held a conference to consider the immediate suspension of the operation in the face of the unexpectedly fierce opposition. However, Freyburg argued that he could still achieve a breakthrough on the Cassino front and was given leave to launch one further attack on 22 March. When this failed miserably Alexander resolved to halt the battle.

It had now become obvious to Alexander that the troops facing Cassino were too weak to prise open the coveted 'Gates of Rome'. More comprehensive measures would be needed to achieve this aim. The British 1st and U.S. 12th Tactical Air Forces stepped up their raids against the German lines of communication in northern Italy destroying railways, roads and bridges in an attempt to starve Kesselring's army group of supplies. The German High Command had, however, anticipated the Allied move and had already brought forward sufficient food and ammunition for a lengthy campaign.

Kesselring now began to speculate when and where Alexander would start his new thrust. He felt it probable that the Allies would mount a large-scale amphibious landing north of Rome, possibly in the Civita Vecchia region. An operation of this kind, if successful, would have allowed the Allies to close the passes through the Etruscan Apennines, blocking off the German line of retreat north from the Gustav Line.

He reasoned that if they did not mount a landing then, they would almost certainly attack in depth along the southern and central sectors of the Cassino front. He assumed that the crux of the attack would be in the region of Monte Cassino itself. He regrouped and awaited events. Group Bode, a formation consisting mainly of the survivors of the old 305th Infantry Division replaced XV Panzer Grenadier Division which was pulled back from the front as a reserve. Overall command for the region that extended from the Tyrrhenian coast to the Liri River passed to XIV Panzer Corps. The divisions between the Liri and Alfedena came under control of General Feuerstein's 51st Mountain Corps while Cassino itself remained firmly in the hands of Heidrich's paratroopers.

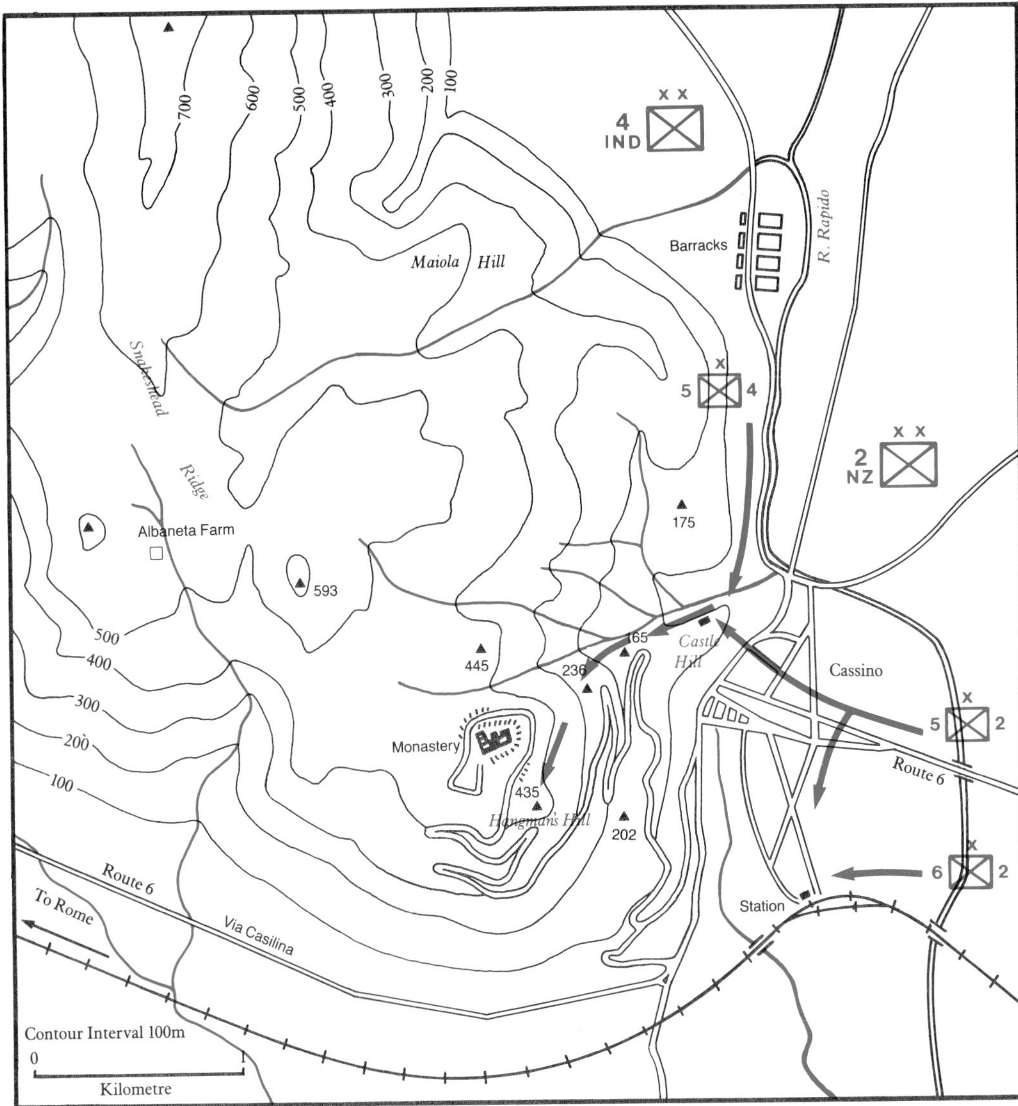

The Allied plan for taking Cassino was simple. The German lines to the front would be subjected to the largest artillery barrage of the Italian campaign. Thereafter the 4th Indian and 2nd New Zealand Divisions would assault the area, the New Zealanders taking Cassino and Hill 193, and the Indians storming the steep sides of Monte Cassino itself. However, General Freyberg's plan reckoned without the tenacious defence of the German paratroopers dug into the rubble of the ruined town. The New Zealanders succeeded in taking Hill 193 and the Indians Hill 165 but the latter were badly mauled in their subsequent attempts to take Hills 236 and 435. Only when the attack was suspended on the direct orders of General Alexander and relaunched by massively superior numbers did it succeed. Eventually the ruins of Monte Cassino fell to the Poles, but not until the German Fallschirmjager had successfully evacuated all but the most severely wounded of their troops.

The Allied 15th Army Group likewise girded itself for the coming battle. The French Expeditionary Force, the unit most feared by Kesselring, moved forward to the upper reaches of the Garigliano to take over British 10th Corps' bridgehead. Its previous sector in the hills north of Cassino was given to General Anders' Polish 2nd Corps while the U.S. 2nd Corps, comprising the 85th and 88th Divisions, made ready on the lower Garigliano. The New Zealanders were relieved by the British 13th Corps with the Canadian 1st Corps behind it. Finally Britain's 10th Corps was shifted to the upper Rapido, bringing into play all but two divisions of the entire British 8th Army.

The Allied 15th Army began its massive offensive late in the evening of 11 May. Twenty-one full strength divisions, together with 11 brigade-size formations, now joined battle with 14 depleted, battle-weary German divisions which had no more than three brigades in reserve. At precisely 11.00 p.m., 2,000 guns began to lay a barrage along a front stretching from the upper Rapido to the Tyrrhenian Sea. An hour later the armour and infantry of the 5th and 8th Armies began their advance. As dawn broke Allied aircraft attacked the German positions in depth destroying X Army's headquarters in Avezzano.

As Kesselring had anticipated, the first major attack was launched by the French Expeditionary Corps, now brought up to four divisions. During the night of 11/12 May they stormed the German 71st Infantry Division's positions on the upper Garigliano, securing the tactically important Monte Faito and opening the path to Monte Maio in the process. General Brosset's French 1st Division took Sant' Andrea, Sant' Ambrogio and Sant' Apollinaire, reaching the Liri in the north. To the south the Moroccan 4th Mountain Division, supported by the Algerian 3rd Division, ejected the remnants of the German 71st Divisions from their defensive positions and scaled Castleforte with its commanding view of the Ausente Valley.

The U.S. 2nd Corps advancing along the coast made slower progress. The 85th and 88th Divisions, both fresh from the United States, had little battle experience and were soon stalled by the German 94th Infantry Division. Indeed, it was not until 13 May when the Germans were obliged to withdraw because of the speedy advance of the French on their flank, that they succeeded in securing their first objectives.

The spirited French advance also assisted General Kirkman's British 13th Corps in its progress across the Rapido and into the Liri Valley. After savage fighting sappers succeeded in bridging the Rapido, allowing a Canadian armoured regiment to follow through and establish a firm bridgehead.

The now desperate Germans had no choice but to bring in to play their meagre reserves. This last ditch attempt had little effect however. The British 13th Corps was able to continue its attacks unabated, reaching the Cassino-Pignataro Road on 15 May. Simultaneously, the French entered San Giorgio turning the right flank

Right: German prisoners taken by the Poles in the Monte Cassino area, 1944.

Below: An 8th Army Bren gunner takes up a defensive position amid the ruins of Monte Cassino.

of the German 51st Mountain Corps. The British 8th Army immediately exploited its success by bringing forward the Canadian 1st Corps with instructions to take Pontecorvo. On 16 May the Canadians attacked and two days later were able to report that their forward elements had reached the Adolf Hitler Line, Germany's last line of defence.

Throughout the early stages of the battle the position in the immediate area of Monte Cassino remained static. The Polish 5th Division attacked Colle Sant' Angelo on the night of 11/12 May but was driven back by the ferocious resistance of the remaining paratroopers.

The Polish 3rd Division succeeded in taking the strategically important Peak 593 (Mount Calvary) only to lose it the next day to a German counter-attack. Although little ground changed hands, the fighting in this sector was some of the most vicious of the campaign. In the fighting for Mount Calvary only one officer and seven men of an entire Polish battalion survived the German counter-attack. The Poles made four further spirited attempts to take the monastery on 13 and 14 May but without success. Not only did they have to contend with the toughness of the paratroopers' resistance, but with the accuracy of the Germany artillery which was ranged down

Right: 194mm guns of the Italian 1st Armoured Regiment in action.

upon them from observation posts up on the 1,000m (3,280 ft) Monte Cifalco commanding the entire battlefield. On 17 May the Poles received a tremendous boost when the British 13th Corps succeeded in pushing west of Cassino up to the Via Casilina and in so doing cut the German paratroopers off from their supplies and communications.

By then the German right flank had collapsed. The French had fought their way 40km (25 miles) through the front and the Americans had linked up with their 6th Corps comrades at the Anzio beachhead. Anders renewed his attack on Monte Cassino but without success. In a ten hour battle, during which control of Mount Calvary passed first to one side and then the other, the Polish forces sustained fearful losses but still failed to carry their objective.

Above: British ammunition trucks ablaze on the road to Cassino.

Above: 2nd Polish Corps loading a pack mule in the Monte Cassino area.

By now Monte Cassino had lost its tactical significance. To avoid encirclement, Kesselring gave orders for the entire Cassino front to be evacuated and during the following night the 1st Parachute Division began its retreat westward over the mountains. When the Polish 12th Podolski Regiment stormed the ruins of Monte Cassino Abbey on the morning of 18 May they found only wounded troops who were too weak to be carried away by their comrades, remaining to be taken prisoner.

The Allies had taken Cassino and opened the 'Gateway to Rome' but at a terrible cost of human life. The American 5th Army sustained 107,144 casualties between 15 January 1944, when the first battle for Cassino began, and 4 June when Rome fell. The British 8th Army, which included the Polish 2nd Corps, lost 7,835 men killed and injured during the third battle alone. As for the Germans, nobody knows precisely how many were lost. It is enough to say that the bodies of 20,002 dead lie in the German military cemetery at Cassino.

Above left: Monte Cassino under fire as seen from the ruins of the town below.

Above: A German mortar platoon takes post amid the ruins of the town.

Right: The ruined monastery as witness to the ferocity of the fighting.

Merrill's Marauders, U.S. Involvement in Burma, 1944

The speed with which the Japanese conquest of Burma took place in 1942, a campaign which lasted little more than three months, had a profound effect on Allied thinking and planning. Confusion and dithering pervaded the British staffs throughout the region as a dangerous air of unrest began to spread through the Indian sub-continent. In China the loss of the Burma Road caused many loyal Chinese actively to consider the possibility of reaching peace with Japan.

General Sir Archibald Wavell, Commander-in-Chief of British forces in India, was deeply worried about the psychological impact of defeat on his troops. He knew that it would be at least two years before his forces would be strong enough to embark on a full-scale campaign, yet equally realized the necessity of at least a limited offensive.

The United States War Department was of a similar opinion. It realized that the fate of India and China were inseparably entwined and determined to send combat troops to the area to bolster, if not eclipse, the British effort. In July 1942, Lieutenant-General Joseph Stilwell was appointed commander of the new China-Burma-India Theatre of Operations with the Joint tasks of providing logistical support to China and controlling all American combat forces in theatre.

Stilwell attempted to form a Chinese Army in India (C.A.I.) based on the Chinese 38th and 22nd Divisions which had escaped westward from Burma during the earlier fighting. Not for the last time Stilwell's plans fell foul of the British authorities who feared that the Chinese would ferment pro-nationalist unrest among the local Indian population. When Delhi vetoed Stilwell's plans, the latter appealed direct to General Marshall in Washington. He in turn put pressure on the British government, which quietly ordered Delhi to withdraw its objections. Stilwell was allowed to open a new training centre in Ramgarh, in east-central India, but from the outset was given little help from his British hosts.

To compound British embarrassment, Wavell's limited offensive, an attack on the isolated Burmese coastal province of Arakan, failed miserably. Indeed it was only saved from total disaster when Lieutenant-General Slim was ordered to the front to conduct a spirited and typically brilliant withdrawal. By contrast, Wingate's first campaign, conducted further to the north, met with a far greater degree of success, convincing Churchill that the immediate course of the war in the Far East lay in large-scale commando-style sorties behind the enemy lines.

Orde Wingate (centre) was one of the few British commanders whom Merrill trusted.

Wingate was promoted to major-general and given command of an over-strength division. He at once began to create a force capable of defeating the enemy 'at his own game'. Meanwhile Stilwell, who had been unable to convince the Chinese to mount an offensive in the spring of 1943, gained their support for a winter campaign. It was agreed that Britain would advance into southern and central Burma by way of Arakan and Tiddim while Stilwell's C.A.I. invaded northern Burma through the Hukawng Valley. The C.A.I. would then link with the Chinese forces in Yunnan, reopen the land route between India and China and combine with the British for a united attack south towards Mandalay. Stilwell appealed to Washington for the release of one or more American divisions to take part in the repeat conquest but had to accept the promise of a single regiment.

Ironically, as Stilwell warmed to the proposed invasion so the British became more cautious until eventually the frustrated American was forced to concede a reduction in his aims. By now Stilwell's C.A.I. formed one of the four corps under command of Admiral Lord Louis Mountbatten's newly established South-East Asia Command (SEAC). Initial plans for the C.A.I. to operate semi-autonomously within General Giffard's 11th Army Group had to be shelved when Stilwell refused to serve under anyone but his friend and confidant General Slim. Matters were however resolved

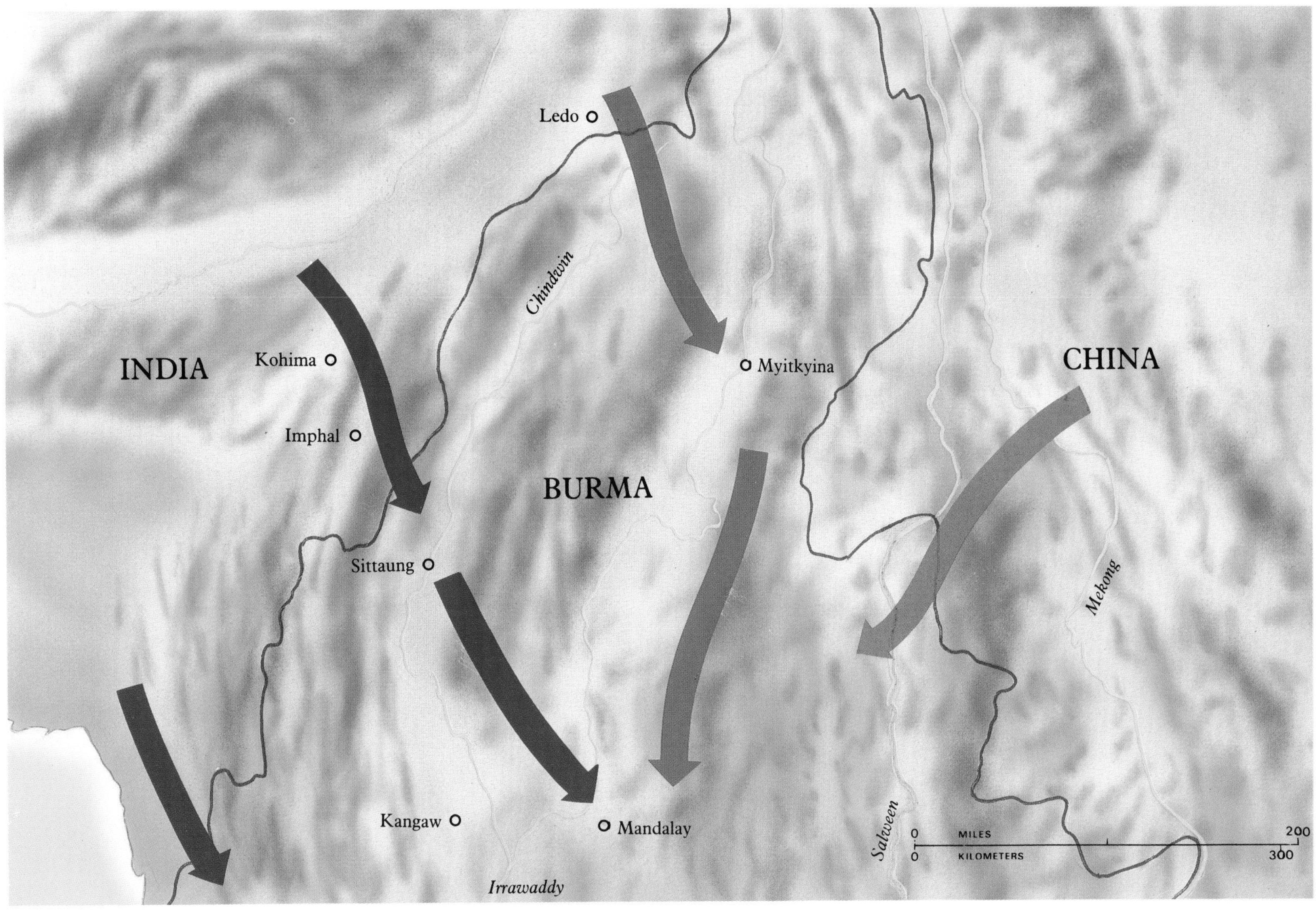

When Lieutenant-General Joseph Stillwell was appointed commander of the new China-Burma Theatre of Operations in July 1942 he immediately put his forces on an offensive footing, determined to take the war to the enemy as quickly as possible. However, his initial plans fell foul of the wary British authorities who felt that the Chinese element would ferment unrest among the local Indian population. When Stillwell was eventually allowed to attack he did so on three fronts, from China in the north-east, from Ledo in the north and from Kohima through Imphal and the mountains of north-west Burma. Although Mandalay was the overall objective none of the three columns came close to reaching it. However the 5307th Composite Unit (Provisional) - the famous Merrill's Marauders - succeeded in reaching Myitkyina, taking the strategically important neighbouring airfield in the process.

successfully, allowing the Chinese to begin their advance in October 1943.

Initially all went well, the leading elements of the Chinese 38th Division encountering little resistance as it moved slowly down the Hukawng Valley towards Shingbwiyang. However, the Japanese had been fully prepared for the advance and suddenly counter-attacked, quickly regaining the lost ground. Stalemate ensued as the campaign died among the encroaching monsoon rains.

Merrill's Marauders now arrived in theatre to provide Stilwell with his only American combat unit. Known locally by its codename *Galahad* but officially designated the 5307th Composite Unit (Provisional), this unique and somewhat macabre unit would only later gain the nickname of 'Merrill's Marauders' in honour of its commanding officer, Brigadier-General Frank Merrill.

Stilwell had requested hardened jungle fighters. Instead, the War Department sent him a peculiar mixture of the bored, the restless and the indifferent. Some were excellently motivated, others suffered from psychiatric disorders. A few yearned for adventure, many others saw the assignment as a stepping stone back to the United States. Fate was to prove them sadly wrong.

Shortly after their arrival in India the Marauders began intensive combat training with the Chindits. They adopted Wingate's organizational concept with each battalion divided into two columns, but refused to accept the British doctrine of avoiding battle with larger or equal enemy forces. Their cockiness and brashness upset the far more experienced Chindits who soon began to discount them. Nonetheless, when Stilwell insisted that his Marauders be used as shock-troops to spearhead his campaign in Burma, Mountbatten reluctantly agreed.

At the end of October 1943 Stilwell ordered elements of the Chinese 38th Division into the Hukawng Valley of Burma where they promptly became bogged down and surrounded by the Japanese. With typical dash he moved at once to the division's headquarters at Yupang Ga, goading the Chinese into action and ultimate victory. Although it was not a big fight and the Chinese casualties were high, it proved to them that, properly led, they could be a match for the Japanese.

Because the Japanese were preparing for a big offensive against the British in Assam, their 18th Division to Stilwell's front was stripped of unnecessary troops and ordered to go on to the defensive. In an attempt to take advantage of the situation Stilwell sent his forces in a series of wide swings against the heavily outnumbered Japanese in an attempt to envelop them. However his forces were far too ponderous and could never quite close the gap. In February 1944 Stilwell determined to use the Marauders as a blocking force across the Japanese line of withdrawal, trapping them between the Americans and the advancing Chinese.

The 18th Division commander, Lieutenant General Shimishi, realizing what was happening, decided to capitalize on the slowness of the Chinese to throw his entire force against the Marauders then deployed near the tiny settlement of Walawbun.

Dug in along the Nampyek Nha River the Marauders repulsed the Japanese attacks. The Japanese now found themselves in serious trouble. A force of tanks from the Chinese First Provisional Tank Group joined the battle from the north forcing its way between two of the 18th Division regiments to attack Shimishi's headquarters. Thoroughly shaken, the Japanese general ordered his men to break off battle and withdraw south. In the confused fighting which followed the Japanese lost heavily, but still made good their escape.

Encouraged by this partial success, Stilwell resolved to send the Marauders on another long, enveloping swing to cut off the Japanese retreat to Kamaing, nestling in the Mogaung Valley, while the Chinese continued their frontal assault. The Japanese counter-attacked so strongly that Merrill, concerned that his command might be annihilated before the slow-moving Chinese came up, ordered them to withdraw and disperse into the hills. Exalted, the Japanese now turned to attack the flank of the advancing Chinese.

Learning of this move, Stilwell ordered Merrill to take his men to the village of Nhpum Ga to cut the Japanese trail. For

Above: The Chinese forces supporting Merrill were armed with a wide variety of British and American weaponry.

Right: Mortars were manhandled through the jungle to provide invaluable support to the advancing infantry.

Below: A C-47 drops ammunition and rations on the Myit Kyina front within 1,500m of the enemy.

the already exhausted Marauders, the move to Nhpum Ga meant another energy sapping trek through the jungles of North Burma. It also meant that they would have to conduct a static defence rather than fight the fast-moving, slashing battle to which they were far better suited.

At Nhpum Ga Merrill placed one battalion on a hilltop near the village with another at Hsamshingyang, three miles away, to protect the airstrip which was his only means of supply and communication with the outside world. The Japanese attacked almost immediately pounding the American positions mercilessly with artillery and mortar fire. However they were unable to take either strongpoint and, after several days of vicious hand-to-hand fighting, withdrew.

By now the Marauders had been through two arduous jungle campaigns. They were underweight through constant marching and poor diet and in their weakened state were rapidly falling victim to disease. To compound their problems they were now informed that their air supplies, which had been faithfully provided by the U.S. 10th Air Force from its bases in Upper Assam, were now to be severely curtailed as the transports were required elsewhere.

Many of the Marauders had understood (quite erroneously) that they would be released from the jungle and sent home after three months. According to the rules of jungle commando operations they should certainly have been relieved. Instead, they were given one more mission; the capture of Myitkyina, the main objective of the campaign in northern Burma.

On 28 April the Marauders, accompanied by elements of the Chinese 30th Division - 7,000 men in all - began an advance eastward over the Kuman Mountains to the Irrawaddy River. Using trails known only to their Katchin guides, they reached Myitkyina, taking the strategically important neighbouring airfield on 17 May.

Things then began to go wrong. Allied intelligence underestimated the number of Japanese in Myitkyina and an early attack on the village was bungled. By now the exhausted allied force had shrunk to less than 3,000 men, no more than the Japanese, and was falling daily at the rate of 75 to 100 a day as disease and exhaustion took its toll. Reinforcements could scarcely keep up with the losses as Stilwell pressed engineers, clerks, cooks, any American who could carry a rifle, into action. After the death of Wingate, the Chindits had come under Stilwell's command. Although in an even worse state than the Marauders after four months in the jungle, Stilwell had not allowed the British to withdraw from the fighting and did not believe that he could now offer his Americans the same option.

Had the Japanese made a determined counter-attack at Myitkyina they might have swept the Chinese-American forces from the airfield. Fortunately they overestimated the strength of the besieging forces and remained behind their own defences.

Myitkyina eventually fell to Stilwell on 3 August 1944 after months of vicious fighting. Its garrison had been cut off since the beginning of the summer but had refused to surrender forcing the Marauders and their Chinese allies to contest every inch of the town. Indeed it is unlikely that Myitkyina would have fallen when it did had General Kimina, the new commander of the Japanese Burma Area Army, not ordered its garrison to attempt a withdrawal. Japanese killed in the siege numbered 3,000, but 600 managed to escape. The Chinese lost 972 killed and 3,184 wounded, the Americans 272 killed and 955 wounded while 188 Chinese and 980 Americans were evacuated sick, of whom 570 were Marauders.

Stilwell's personal triumph in taking Myitkyina was undoubtedly tarnished by the collapse of the Marauders. As the battle had proceeded they had become less brash, far less contemptuous of the British then fighting on a far larger scale in the hills around Imphal and Kohima. They had expected to fight for no more than three months and had literally fallen apart when ordered to do so. The Chindits had suffered a not dissimilar fate although the Chinese 38th and 22nd Divisions had spent seven months in the jungle without complaining. For their part the Japanese had fought for years suffering far greater casualties.

Whatever the cause of the collapse, which is still not certain, it had nothing to do with any apparent inability of the Occidental soldier to withstand hardships if he was properly trained and conditioned. Later the British 36th Division would spend eight months of almost constant action in the jungle without flinching. Of significance was the fact that these soldiers had not been exposed to Wingate's theory, and the seed of doubt as to their ability to carry on without relief from combat after three months' jungle fighting, had not been sown.

The Anzio Bridgehead, U.S. Rangers in Italy, 1944

Operation *Shingle,* as the Anzio landings were called, was the brain-child of Winston Churchill. He saw it as a 'cat's-claw', a single dramatic event destined at one stroke to break the deadlock in Italy. To men like Lieutenant General Mark Clark, commander of the U.S. Fifth Army, however, it was a nightmare. Because *Shingle* was due to be launched on the west coast of Italy, within Fifth Army area, Clark was offered, and accepted, overall command despite his obvious misgivings. Throughout the planning stage he remained unhappy about the number and disposition of the German reserves in the Rome area, refusing to believe British reports that they were slight. Unable to forget the carnage of the earlier U.S. amphibious landing at Salerno he tried to the very end to have the operation cancelled.

Major General John P. Lucas, commander of the Anglo-American forces in VI Corps destined to make the landings, was even less optimistic. At the time Lucas was tired, unhappy and ill – totally unfit to lead so audacious an operation. He had been appointed corps commander at Salerno where dire experience had taught him the necessity for creating a firm base for a beachhead. Since then he had grown pessimistic, constantly underestimating the potential of his own troops while overestimating the power of the enemy.

When advised therefore that he would be given absolute discretion as to how far, if at all, to advance from the beachhead, he resolved to go immediately on to the defensive until adequate reinforcements could be brought up in subsequent waves. Certain in his own mind that his troops would meet heavy resistance, he made few plans for a break out from the beaches and none for an advance on Rome.

Whatever his faults, Lucas was an excellent, if ponderous, administrator. It was no mean feat to gather together a fleet large enough to transport an assault force of 110,000 with all their weapons, vehicles and supplies a distance of 200km (124 miles) when all spare shipping was being recalled to Britain in preparation for D-Day.

Above: U.S. personnel, jeeps and ambulances aboard an LST in Anzio habour await debarkation.

Right: The Anzio convoy was a miracle of logistics, taking into account the total lack of available transports.

Above left: Black South African troops of the 1991 Swazi Smoke Coy await embarkation at Castellammare.

Left: The initial landings were virtually unopposed, the few German defenders being taken completely by surprise.

He did succeed however, and on 21 January a multinational conglomerate of 243 ships, including 19 LCTs and 56 LSTs, set sail from the Bay of Naples.

Those on board were drawn almost equally from the British and American armies. The British included the 1st Infantry Division, commanded by General Penney, the 2nd Special Service Brigade comprising the 9th and 43rd Commando battalions and the 46th Royal Tank Regiment. The American contingent included the 3rd Infantry Division, under General Truscott, the 751st Tank Battalion, the 504th Parachute Infantry Battalion and three battalions of Rangers.

It seemed impossible that so large a force would not be spotted by the enemy but luck remained with the Allies and they slipped through unseen. The first ships dropped anchor outside Anzio at midnight. The assault craft were lowered and at 2.00 a.m., after a five minute barrage, they made for the shore. The sight which greeted

Left: Survivors of the Anzio beachhead enter the open city of Rome.

master of improvisation and manoeuvre, he at once set about mustering all available troops, throwing them into a defensive ring around the Allied beachhead. Troops from Rimini, Genoa, and Leghorn were ordered south immediately, the two divisions were recalled from the front and fresh troops summoned from Germany. By daybreak on 23 January, less than 30 hours after the initial landings, he had seized the psychological initiative. The road to Rome still lay open and Lucas might even at this point have smashed his way through the meagre German lines but instead he remained passive behind his own defences. Only when the second wave of 60,000 troops, comprising the 45th Infantry Division and most of the 1st Armoured Division, was landed did he agree to send out reconnaissance patrols in depth.

During the next day a series of events

Below: LSTs unloading reinforcements at Anzio harbour.

them was macabre. Anzio was a ghost town. Its civilian population had been evacuated some time earlier and the military had abandoned it. The landings had taken the Germans completely by surprise and were allowed to proceed with virtually no opposition. The British, landing some 10km (6.2 miles) north of the port were slowed when the sea was found to be mined and the sand dunes too soft to support vehicles. However the delay was short-lived and the British 1st Division was soon astride the Moletta River. The Americans, experiencing no such delays, advanced without incident to the Mussolini Canal. Everything seemed promising for an immediate advance inland but instead Lucas ordered his men to dig in and await the inevitable counter-attack.

By nightfall some 90 percent of the assault force, with 3,000 vehicles, was ashore but still Lucas refused to send reconnaissance patrols inland. By now he had become obsessed with the need for defensiveness, even refusing Penney permission to land lest he should get caught up in the impending counter-offensive.

Field Marshal Kesselring could not believe his luck. He had committed his last two reserve divisions (III Panzer Grenadier and Hermann Goering) to X Army in the south only days earlier and would have been altogether incapable of withstanding an Allied breakout had one materialized. A

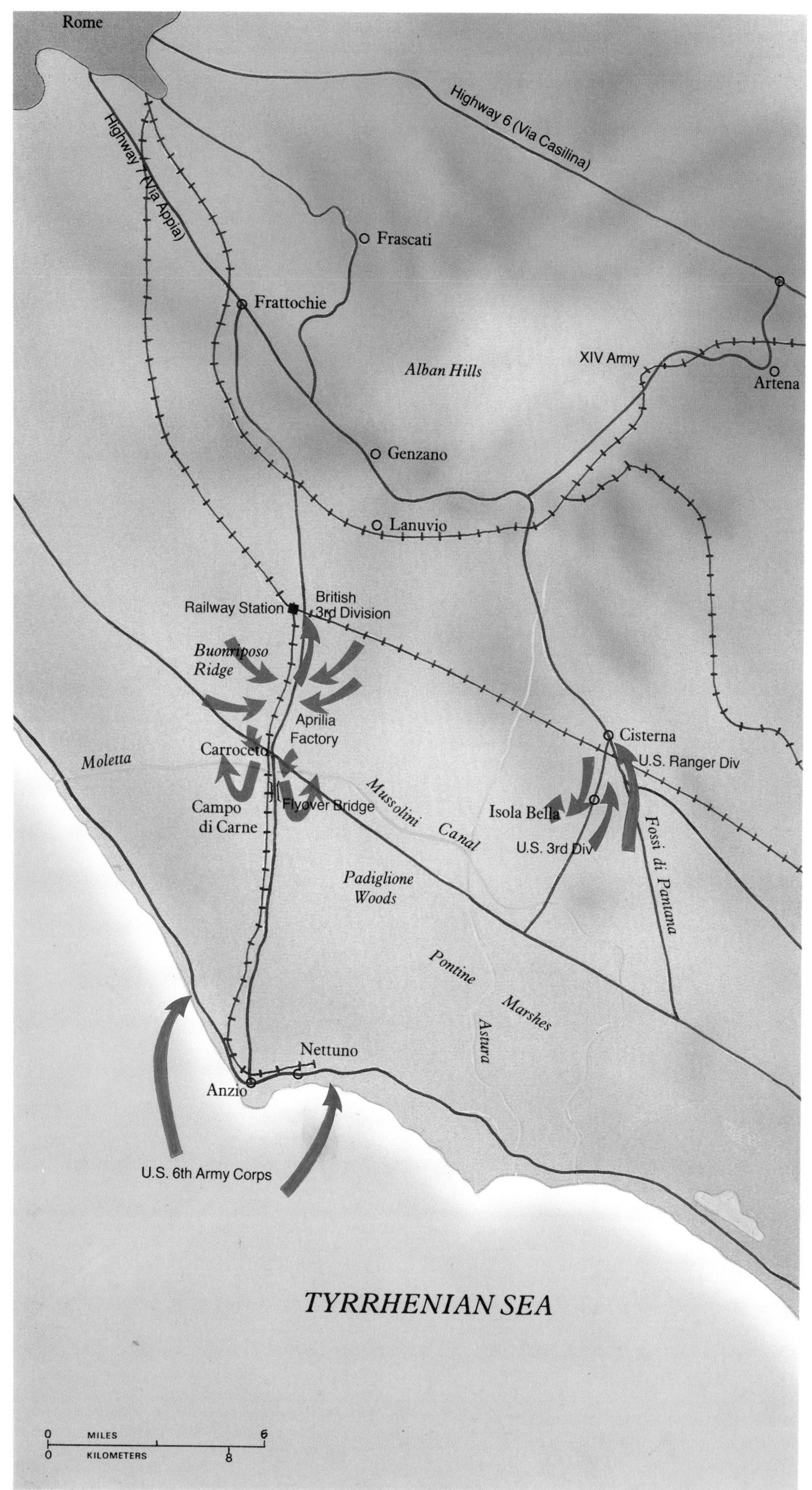

occurred which did nothing to ease Lucas's growing air of pessimism. A number of landing craft were destroyed in a gale and almost simultaneously intelligence, which Lucas had so far heavily discounted, reported the approach of 40,000 Germans under the command of General von Mackensen.

At last he decided to send patrols forward to investigate the enemy's strength along the roads to Campoleone and Cisterna. The 24th Guards Brigade was pulled out of reserve and at last allowed to move gingerly forward along the Anzio-Campoleone-Albano road. Having crossed Flyover Bridge it advanced some 6km (3.72 miles) to the hamlet of Carroceto. Almost immediately it came under fire from elements of XXIX Panzer Grenadier Regiment dug into a nearby farmstead. It cleared the area (later to become known as *the factory*) with difficulty and later withstood a spirited counter-attack. Meanwhile to the British right the Americans advanced along the Cisterna Road until halted by the leading elements of the Herman Goering Division. German heavy artillery in the Alban Hills now began to shell the Allied lines. It now seemed to the experienced Anglo-American troops on the ground, if not to their commander, that a perfect opportunity for victory had been squandered.

Operation Shingle *as the Anzio landings were called, was intended at one stroke to break the deadlock in Italy. Instead, due to indecision and dithering among the leadership, it turned into a bloody stalemate. The initial landings went well with the majority of the 6th Armoured Corps coming ashore virtually unopposed. However, instead of then exploiting the situation, the Allies dug in, anticipating a counter attack. Those patrols which did go forward reported an enemy weak and in a state of confusion yet General Lucas did nothing. When he eventually did decide to move it was too late. The Germans, having rushed reinforcements from every quarter to halt the Allied advance, were now too strong. The fighting which followed was vicious with many proud and famous battalions suffering annihilation at the hands of German armour and artillery. However despite Hitler's personal order that the 6th Army Corps was to be thrown back into the sea at all costs, the bridgehead held, to be relieved later by forward units of the U.S. 5th Army advancing from the south.*

Still Lucas concentrated on building up supplies at the beachhead as though ignorant of its actual purpose. On 28 January Clark visited Lucas to goad him into action. At the time U.S. 6th Corps had 70,000 men ashore, 27,000 tons of supplies, 508 guns and 237 tanks but no definite plan of action. The Allied force was the equivalent of four divisions but now faced elements of eight German divisions. The entire beachhead was under artillery fire and matters were becoming desperate. At last Lucas acted and ordered a general advance. The assault was to be conducted along two fronts, one British, the other American. The Americans were to secure Cisterna, thereby cutting Highway 7, the British to seize Campoleone railway station, five miles beyond the factory, and break out towards Albano. By a cruel twist of fate the XXVI Panzer Grenadier Division, one of the finest units in the German Army, arrived from the Adriatic to reinforce the Hermann Goering Division at Cisterna only hours before the American attack took place.

The day ended catastrophically. A proposed attack by the crack U.S. Ranger Division against Cisterna ended in carnage when the Americans, trying to approach their objective at night along a 6km (3.7 miles) long irrigation canal, were spotted. Subjected to withering small arms and tank fire they were cut to pieces, over 500 being forced to surrender. Of the 767 Rangers who took part in the battle for Cisterna only six returned safely. The 3rd U.S. Division, trying to fight its way along the main road to Cisterna, was fought to a standstill 1,000m short of its objective and forced to retire. To the north, the British fared no better. The terrain west of the Anzio-Albano highway was pitted with gullies and totally impenetrable to the Allied tanks. Denied armoured support, the infantrymen of Penney's 3rd Brigade were annihilated. One of its battalions, The Sherwood Foresters, ceased to exist as a fighting unit after a last desperate assault on Campoleone.

Disheartened, VI Corps made no further attempt to advance but instead went firmly on to the defensive. The British 56th Division was withdrawn from the Cassino front where it was badly needed, and transferred to Anzio. The U.S. and Canadian 1st Special Service Force was also dispatched in a desperate attempt to avert total collapse.

Predictably, the German counter-attack, when it came, was concentrated against the British positions in the area of *the factory* isolated and exposed some 20 km (12 miles) to the fore of the main Allied

Top: German infantry reinforcements seek temporary shelter behind an advancing tank.

Above: A dead German lying among the ruins in Cisterna Di Littoria.

Above: Ruined tanks behind the German tracked mortar testify to the ferocity of the fighting.

defensive line. The North Staffordshire Regiment was dug in with the Guards brigade along the Buonriposo and Vallelata Ridges west of Carroceto, the Gordon Highlanders were to the east in the *Smelly Farm* area and the U.S. 1st Reconnaissance Regiment to the rear by the factory. Furthest forward of all, closest to Campoleone, the remnants of the 3rd Brigade prepared desperately to hold on to its untenable position.

The German counter-attack was launched late on the afternoon of 3 February. After an intensive artillery barrage, massed infantry attacked both sides of the salient, or *Thumb* overrunning *Smelly Farm* and cutting off the 3rd Brigade. Determined to rescue his stalwarts, Penney organized a spectacular break-out by the remnants of the 3rd Brigade. While fresh troops from the London Scottish and U.S. 504th Airborne Regiment drew the bulk of the German fire, the survivors of the three battalions fought their way back through the enemy lines to safety. Over 1,400 men were lost of whom 900 were taken prisoner.

Two nights later *the factory* and neighbouring village of Carroceto were attacked. For 48 hours the fighting raged, during which time famous and proud regiments – the London Irish, the Royal Berks, the Sherwood Foresters to name but three – were pounded into oblivion. Eventually the British 1st Division was forced to pull back. Every battalion had had its share of hand-to-hand fighting and had suffered serious casualties. The 1st British Division was down to 40 percent operational strength and was rapidly ceasing to function as a cohesive entity. When attempts by the U.S. 45th Division to retake the factory failed, the Allies pulled back to their last line of defence along the Albano-Anzio road.

By 15 February it had become apparent that Anzio held no further tactical significance. It was essential, however, for political as much as military reasons to avoid a second Dunkirk. Major Generals Evelegh and Truscott were appointed deputy corps commanders, with a view to the latter replacing Lucas as soon as convenient and fresh units were ordered into the beachhead. The exhausted British 1st Division was pulled out of the line and replaced by the 56th Division under command of the gifted General Templer. The U.S. 45th division dug in astride the Albano-Anzio road in front of *the factory*, Carroceto and Buonriposo Ridge. To its right the U.S. 3rd Division took up its position before Cisterna and as far as the Mussolini Canal.

The Germans attacked with 10 divisions,

Below: Veterans from the 4th Parachute Division move south to reinforce the German lines at Anzio.

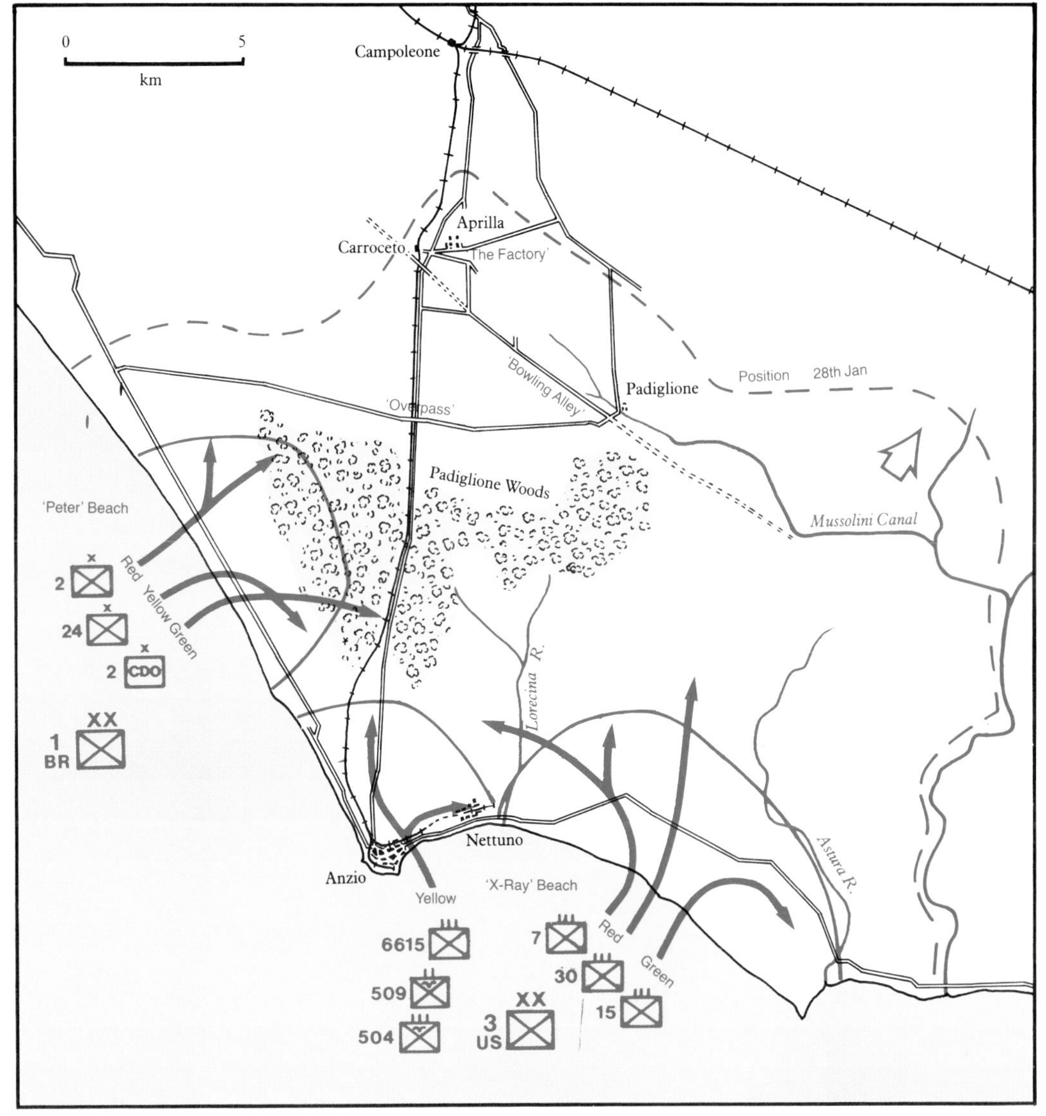

many of them fresh, on 16 February. Forming up behind *the factory*, the Germans attacked along a broad front rolling up the Allied forward positions as they went. Suddenly all 452 German guns available began to bring down concentrated fire on the Flyover as horde upon horde of infantry, supported by tanks, swept down on the American troops who were guarding the position.

Several American outposts fell under the pressure but, almost incredibly, the main front held. During the night, however, the attack was renewed with increased fury and by dawn the German 715th Infantry Division had forced a wedge through the defenders' positions. Despite a massive Allied air counter-offensive the Germans continued on, seemingly regardless of casualties, until the Americans were forced back to the Flyover.

The moment of truth had now come. The U.S. VI Corps had been forced back to a beachhead no bigger than that secured two days after the original landings. Should the Germans manage to carry the flyover, their armour would be able to break out into the Allied rear. All reserves available were brought to play in the area. The warships offshore, the artillery within the beachhead, every fighter that could be spared from the Cassino front was brought into play against the enemy.

The U.S. VI Corps was drawn almost equally from the British and American armies. The British forces, comprising the 1st Infantry Division, the 2nd Service Brigade and the 46th Royal Tank Regiment, attempted to land some 10km (6.2 miles) north of Anzio. However when it was found that the beach was mined and that the sand dunes were too soft to support the weight of the armour the plan was changed to allow the heavier equipment to land in the port itself. The Americans, comprising the 3rd Infantry Division, the 751st Tank battalion, the 504th Parachute Infantry Battalion and three battalions of Rangers, experienced no such problems and succeeded in landing south of the town without incident. Anzio was a ghost town, its civilian population having been evacuated some time earlier. Having landed safely, Lucas had the opportunity to take the initiative but declined to do so, thus allowing the enemy sufficient time to rush in reinforcements.

Below: Troops take shelter from German shelling in an irrigation ditch.

Then suddenly, as if by a miracle, the attacks abated. The German infantry, pounded by artillery and from the air, had had enough. Their casualties had been far greater than the Allies but, unlike VI Corps, they had the option to run. To compound their difficulties the leading elements of General Harmon's tanks advancing from the south now joined the battle as did hundreds of Flying Fortresses, Lightnings and Thunderbolts released from the Cassino campaign.

The fighting continued for the next few days but at a much reduced level. There was patrolling on both sides but little else until the final Allied breakout towards Rome on 23 May.

Anzio had been turned into a charnel house: thousands of troops on both sides had been slaughtered. Some however, Churchill among them, still argued that their sacrifice had been worthwhile. Many useful lessons were learned for the Normandy landings and the advance on Rome was made easier. Whether, however, these advantages were enough to offset so tragic a loss of life can only remain a matter for subsequent debate.

Above: British and American troops get together during a brief lull in the battle.

Left: The O.C. of C Coy 1st bn Green Howards briefs his officers before an attack.

Below: German POWs await shipment from the Anzio beachhead. Forlorn but alive!

Nijmegen,
U.S. Airborne Advance to the Rhine, 1944

By the summer of 1944 the outcome of the war was beyond dispute. Victory was only a matter of time and the Allies were becoming impatient. However, enemy opposition was stiffening as the front moved closer to the Fatherland. Veterans from convalescent battalions, garrison units manned by old men, redundant Luftwaffe pilots with no more planes to fly, even young boys were combining together to take a toll of the advancing troops slowing down their progress to a frustrating standstill.

When Montgomery proposed that his British 21st Army Group and Bradley's 12th United States Army Group should combine into a single 40-division mass (naturally under his command) to thrust its way northwards through the German defensive positions, his plan was vetoed by Eisenhower. The Supreme Commander recognized the value of a push north, particularly if it were to secure a good deep water port which would shorten the Allies' protracted supply routes. He also appreciated that General Patton, the hero of the American public, was advancing with great panache in the south and that any attempt to deny the latter's 3rd Army its fair share of supplies and materiel would be greeted with considerable domestic hostility.

Disappointed but not defeated, Montgomery formulated an alternative, more audacious scheme. By seizing a succession of bridges between the Dutch frontier and the Lower Rhine he argued that the British 2nd Army would be able to smash its way through Holland on to the North German plain. Five major bridges over three rivers, the Maas, the Waal and the Lower Rhine, and two canals, the Wilhelmina Canal some 30km (18.6 miles) beyond the Dutch border and the Zuid Willems Vaart Canal 15km (9.3 miles) further north, would have to be captured intact.

One airborne division would be landed in the 30km (18.6 miles) stretch between Eindhoven and Uden to secure the two canal bridges and the road between them. A second division would be assigned to the Maas bridge at Grave and the Waal bridge at Nijmegen. A third division would have the hardest task of all, to drop at Arnhem to secure the crossing of the Rhine.

Montgomery's bold plan met with almost immediate United States' disapproval. General Bradley felt that it would drive a dangerous wedge between the British 2nd Army and the U.S. 1st Army, while General Dempsey argued that it would be irrelevant to the outcome of the war and would commit lightly armed troops into an area of growing enemy activity.

Eisenhower was in a dilemma. He was under pressure from London to neutralize the V-2 rocket bases in Piemonte and desperately wanted to establish a sea port closer to the front. Yet he had no desire to divert transport aircraft from Patton in the south, particularly as the 3rd Army was about to link up with the U.S. 6th Army Group advancing from the Mediterranean.

Above: U.S. 101st Airborne Division prepare to move out. Note the 'Screaming Eagles' worn on the left shoulder.

Below: Generals Gavin (right) and Dempsey (left) examine a map of Nijmegen.

Below: U.S. paratroopers undertake final checks before emplaning at Cottesmore.

Initially Eisenhower concurred with the plan but only on the basis that available resources be shared equally between Montgomery and Patton. When Montgomery complained however, that any starvation of supplies would cause a delay in the attack and lead to stronger resistance and slower progress, the American begrudgingly conceded. Supplies due to Patton were diverted to 1st Army in the north. True to his nature Patton refused to accept defeat and, interpreting an order to 'carry out a continuous reconnaissance' in the most liberal way, put in an attack. Supplies were rediverted to him, and in some instances actually requisitioned by his men, and Montgomery once again found himself denied the necessary support required for the successful prosecution of his operation.

Notwithstanding detailed planning for the execution of the operation, now code named *Market Garden*, began at the Allied Airborne Army's Headquarters on 10 September 1944. Available were four divisions, two American and two British, together with the Polish Independent Parachute Brigade. The United States 101st Airborne was commanded by General James Gavin, the 82nd Airborne by General Maxwell Taylor. Both were men of high attainments and wide experience. The two British divisions were the 52nd (Lowland) Division and the 1st Airborne Division commanded by the far less experienced but vastly popular Major General Urquhart. The 1st Airborne had not jumped in the Normandy landings but had been held in Britain as a strategic reserve. For the past three months it had trained for a series of objectives all of which had been cancelled. The energetic Urquart, who had never jumped in his life and who suffered from air sickness, insisted that his division be included and that they be given 'the toughest, most advanced assignment'.

Planning for *Market Garden* — *Market* referring to the airborne corps' activities and *Garden* to the follow up by the British 2nd Army — was completed in only six days. The 101st Airborne Division was allotted the task of landing close to Eindhoven, of capturing the town and of securing a series of road and railway bridges crossing the Aa River and Willems Vaart Canal at Veghel, the Dommel River at St Oedenrode and the Wilhelmina Canal at Son. The 82nd Airborne Division was to capture the bridges over the Maas at Grave and the Waal at Nijmegen. The capture of Arnhem, the final and most crucial bridge, fell to the British.

Priority in aircraft was given to the Americans on the premise that it would be pointless for the British to capture Arnhem if the bridges over the Maas and Waal

Above: Fully laden troops of the U.S. 101st Airborne boarding a C-47.

Below: C-47s of the U.S. Air Force mass for a take off en route *to Belgium.*

remained in German hands.

At this stage Allied intelligence began to commit a series of critical blunders. Ignoring the necessity for objectivity at all times they began to see what they wanted to see and submitted a series of reports stating that enemy activity along the intended corridor was light. Dutch Resistance reports of S.S. troop movements and the arrival in the area of at least one armoured division were ignored as fanciful. Instead, it was reported that General Brian Horrock's 30th Corps, which would spearhead the 2nd Army advance, could expect to encounter no more than six weak infantry battalions supported by 25 guns and no more than 20 tanks. The several headquarters complexes spotted by aerial reconnaissance were reported as non-operational while the thousands of troops seen were reported to be broken and on the run back to Germany.

Even if the intelligence summaries had been more accurate it is unlikely that *Market Garden* would have been cancelled. The airborne forces were now raring to go and it was becoming increasingly important to Eisenhower that a Channel port be captured soon.

The operation began on the morning of Sunday 17 September. Visibility was good, winds were light and cloud coverage high as the first of 1,545 aircraft and 478 gliders of 38 Group R.A.F. and 9th United States Troop Carrier Command lifted off from eight British and 14 American airfields. It was agreed that the base airfields for the entire operation would be divided into two distinct groups, the southern group forming over Hatfield in Hertfordshire and the northern group over March in Cambridgeshire.

Above: Private Bernard Nakla of the 101st Airborne stops to hand out gum to a grateful child.

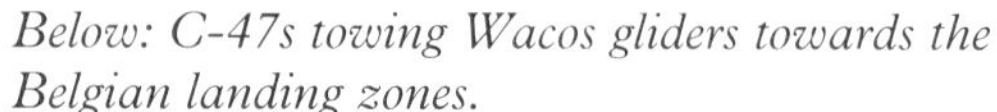

Below: C-47s towing Wacos gliders towards the Belgian landing zones.

The 101st Airborne Division was to fly by the southern route towards the North Foreland and then due east across the Channel to Geel where it would turn north for Eindhoven. The 82nd and 1st Airborne Divisions would fly by the northern route over Aldeburgh and Schouwen Island towards Hertogenbosch where the streams would divide, the Americans making for Grave and Nijmegen and the British for Arnhem.

Nothing was left to chance. The routes were marked by beacons and coded lights aboard ships in mid-Channel and by ground strips, coloured smoke and beacons on the dropping and landing zones. Enemy airfields, barracks and anti-aircraft sites on and near the route were bombed, diversionary bombing raids made well clear of the intended targets and dummy parachutists dropped west of Utrecht, at Emmerich, and east of Arnhem. Finally

1,000 British and American fighter aircraft were allotted to defend the flight and, as far as practical, offer support to the troops once on the ground.

It had been thought that the greatest danger to the slow moving aircraft and virtually unprotected gliders would come from flak with losses of up to 40 percent predicted. In the actual event the earlier fighter attacks did their job and the flak was far less than expected, causing only minimal loss en route. The few Luftwaffe fighters that did attempt to attack the air convoys failed to penetrate the R.A.F. and U.S.A.F. umbrella and were either shot down or forced to abort their missions.

Maxwell Taylor's 101st Division landed without incident having survived relatively heavy fire on the approach to Eindhoven. The bridges across the Zuid Willems Vaart Canal at Veghel were captured intact but unfortunately the bridge across the Wilhelmina canal at Son was partially demolished by retreating enemy sappers before the Americans could reach it. It was repaired that night. While the repairs were taking place an airborne regiment crossed the canal and secured the road into Eindhoven in readiness for the British advance. The 30th Corps did not let its allies down and by nightfall the tanks of the Irish Guards, spearheading the Guards Independent Tank Division, had passed through Valkenswaard and Eindhoven and were on their way north. The first phase of *Market Garden* had been completed to plan and ahead of schedule.

Gavin's 82nd Division landed with equal ease in the area of Grave and Nijmegen. One battalion, by landing astride the bridge over the Maas at Grave, was able to secure it within the hour, registering the first Allied success. Six hours later the bridge across the Maas-Waal Canal fell, allowing the division to continue its advance towards Nijmegen.

Suddenly things began to go wrong and the timetable, always uncompromisingly tight, began to fall apart. Resistance in the Nijmegen area was found to be far tougher than expected, making the capture of the vital bridge over the Waal impossible. Gavin's plans to assault the bridge with fresh troops on the Monday morning were frustrated when a German counter-attack from the Reichwald overran the proposed landing zones intended for the glider-borne artillery and infantry which he had meant to employ in the attack. Although the Americans managed to retake the lost ground and the landings eventually took place, the planned attack was aborted. Throughout that day the Germans brought increasing troop numbers to bear until it seemed that Gavin's forward units would be overwhelmed. Indeed, when he was joined later that day by the leading elements of the Grenadier Guards Armoured Group who had taken over point duty from the Irish, he was only able to spare one of his three regiments to assist in the capture of the bridges across the Waal, his remaining troops being required simply to hold the perimeter.

Above: Gliders landed safely near Wesel. Not all of these flimsy craft were so successful.

Below: Gliders of the 101st Airborne Division landing in open fields near the village of Zon.

By Tuesday morning the approaches to the road and rail bridges, both natural defensive positions in their own right, were heavily defended. Several spirited attacks were launched that day by Gavin's men, supported by the British armour, but all were beaten off with heavy losses. It began to look as though *Market Garden* would end in stalemate with the British isolated and abandoned over 30km (18.6 miles) to the north.

On the morning of Wednesday 20 September, General 'Boy' Browning, in overall command of the operation, landed

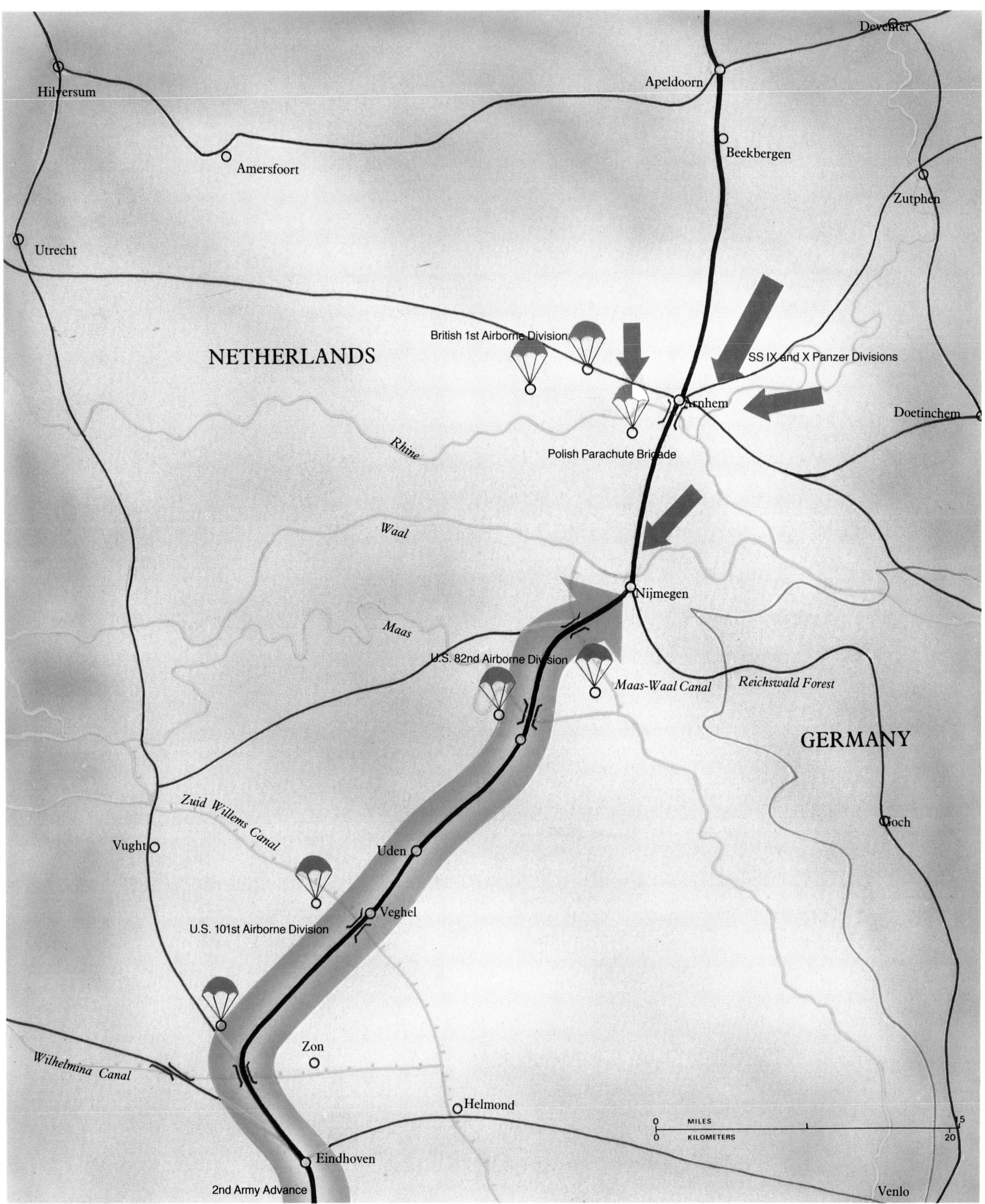

Deventer
Apeldoorn
Hilversum
Beekbergen
Amersfoort
Zutphen
Utrecht
British 1st Airborne Division
NETHERLANDS
SS IX and X Panzer Divisions
Arnhem
Doetinchem
Rhine
Polish Parachute Brigade
Waal
Nijmegen
Maas
U.S. 82nd Airborne Division
Maas-Waal Canal
Reichswald Forest
GERMANY
Zuid Willems Canal
Goch
Vught
Uden
Veghel
U.S. 101st Airborne Division
Zon
Wilhelmina Canal
Helmond
0 MILES 15
0 KILOMETERS 20
Eindhoven
2nd Army Advance
Venlo

It was intended that Operation Market Garden would lay an airborne carpet to the Rhine over which British armour would thrust its way forward into the soft and defenceless underbelly of industrial Germany. It was planned that the 101st Airborne Division would be landed in the 30km (18 mile) stretch between Eindhoven and Uden to secure the two canal bridges and the road between them. A second American airborne division, the 82nd, would secure the Maas Bridge at Grave and the Waal Bridge at Nijmegen. The British 1st Airborne Division, supported by the Polish Independent Airborne Brigade, would have the hardest task of all – to drop at Arnhem and secure the crossing of the Rhine. Montgomery's plan met with almost immediate United States disapproval but was nonetheless proceeded with out of political expediency. Almost from the outset it proved to be over-ambitious. The 82nd Airborne was held up on its objectives for far longer than anticipated by unexpectedly strong opposition. Thereafter the British tanks were forced to proceed almost suicidally along a single raised road ideally suited to defensive warfare. After eight days, virtually destroyed and unable to hold out any longer, the survivors of the 1st British Airborne Division were forced to retire across the Rhine leaving Arnhem Bridge destroyed and the town in enemy hands.

near Nijmegen to take personal control. Despite the losses of the previous day and the growing strength of the German perimeter, the attacks were continued throughout the morning. Gavin's men were by now openly, if unfairly, scornful of the efforts of Horrock's 30th Corps and fearful for the future of their airborne colleagues in Arnhem.

A daring if desperate plan was hatched to enable the bridges to be assaulted from both ends simultaneously. After several hours' delay due to the fact that their use had not been anticipated and they had been stowed towards the rear of the long supply column, British assault boats were brought up, and men of the U.S. 504th Parachute Regiment were ordered to cross the river a mile downstream of the town.

This crossing represents one of the bravest actions in American military history. The boats were launched into a strong current and under heavy fire in broad daylight. Less than half of the first wave reached the bank some 400m (437 yds) away. Those who did, managed to establish a small bridgehead, making it easier for the second and subsequent waves to cross. By late afternoon the Americans had broken out from the bridgehead and were flying the Stars and Stripes from the northern end of the railway bridge.

Inspired by the sight of the flag, the British Guards Armoured Divisions now launched a further, and final assault on the southern approach to the bridge. Under constant and heavy fire from German 88s and supported by Gavin's remaining two regiments the leading tank troop reached the bridge just after 9.00 p.m. Two of the four tanks were destroyed by German anti-tank guns concealed among the girders but the other two succeeded in forcing their way across to the waiting Americans. An hour later the bridge was firmly in Allied hands and the road to Arnhem open. By this time the British had been holding out for three days in all, a day longer than had been anticipated, and against the combined might of two German panzer divisions.

Above: 1/505th Paras return from the front at Nijmegen.

Below: The bridge at Nijmegen still intact after German bombing on 25 September, 1944.

Operation Market Garden, British/Polish Paras at Arnhem, 1944

When Major General Urquhart learned that his paratroopers were to be involved in Operation *Market Garden* in a large-scale advance through Holland followed hopefully by a breakout into Germany, he demanded that they be given a prominent role. His 1st Airborne Division had been kept in reserve during the Normandy landings while their rivals in 6th Airborne Division had gained all the glory. Since then they had trained for mission after mission only to find the missions were cancelled, often at the last minute. They were now, in the words of one of his officers, 'restless, frustrated and ready for anything'. Browning realized that if his men were not committed soon they would lose their fighting edge and quickly disintegrate as an élite unit. He was delighted and relieved therefore to discover that his division had been allotted the task of taking the road bridge at Arnhem. This was the furthest and most crucial objective of the entire operation.

Urquhart was given little time to plan the finer points of the British operation. Despite his strenuous objections he was told that his men would have to be transported to their drop zones in three separate lifts with at least 24 hours between each. This in itself presented tremendous logistical problems and not a few dangers. The first men to land would not only have to take and secure their objectives, but also continue to hold the drop zone until reinforcements arrived. If they failed in their task the enemy would be able either to strengthen his defensive positions around the objectives or make preparations to resist subsequent landings.

Urquhart found himself on the horns of a dilemma. He could either land his men close to the bridge or designate a drop zone some miles away. If he adopted the former course he ran the risk of sustaining heavy initial losses. On the other hand a distant drop, although initially far safer, would allow the enemy time to recover from the shock of the landing and regroup.

Fearful of the heavy flak which he was advised he might encounter over the town centre and mindful of the need to give the R.A.F. towing crews room to manoeuvre without flying too deep into enemy territory, Urquhart elected for landing zones well outside of the town. He rejected the open area around the main bridge just south of the river as too swampy and exposed for the initial landings. Nonetheless he reserved it for the third drop, by which time he reasoned that the bridge would be in British hands and the area cleared of enemy flak batteries.

Five initial landing zones were chosen to the west of the town, three north of the Arnhem to Utrecht railway to Ginkel Heath, two to the south of it on Renkum Heath. The plan in essence was simple. The 21st Independent Parachute Company would drop two hours before H-Hour to mark the ground with strips of coloured nylon tape. The 1st Parachute Brigade together with the men of the Staffordshire Regiment, the Royal Lancashire Regiment, the Border Regiment and the glider Polish Regiment comprising the 1st Airlanding Brigade would land with the divisional troops on day one. Brigadier Hackett's 4th

Above: Major General Urquart places the 1st Airborne Division flag outside his headquarters in defiance of enemy fire.

Below: Air Chief Marshal Tedder discusses final plans with Lieutenant General Browning before the latter's take off.

Left: Support troops bid members of the 1st Airlanding Brigade an emotive farewell as their Hausa glider takes off for Arnhem.

Left: Elements of 4 Para Brigade land on a site already occupied by abandoned Hausa Gliders.

Below: German prisoners taken within minutes of the British landing. Most would later be released.

Parachute Brigade would join them on day two, and General Sosabowski's Polish Independent Brigade on day three. Although Hackett warned his subordinates of heavy losses, it was left to Sosabowski to muse the fate of the British if, 1st Airborne having gone 'a bridge too far', 2nd Army was delayed and unable to drive through quickly enough to relieve it.

Urquhart was not one to allow anything to temper his optimism or the morale of his men once the decision had been made to proceed with the operation. When, therefore, his namesake major Brian Urquhart, the Chief Intelligence Officer at Airborne Army Headquarters, began to issue disturbing reports of growing German strength in the Arnhem area, even hinting at the presence of a panzer division, he had the young major removed, medically examined and diagnosed as suffering from mental exhaustion: suppressing his reports as worthless. It was only later, tragically too late, that Urquhart learned of the young major who had been the only man in the intelligence world to have identified the presence of two panzer divisions within the area.

The British landings took the German High Command completely by surprise. Field Marshal Model had envisaged a thrust by the 2nd Army across the Maas and into the Ruhr, perhaps to be enforced by large-scale airborne landings south of Munster, but he had discounted completely the use of airborne troops west of the Rhine. Ironically, this nearly led to his capture as his headquarters in Oosterbeek lay close to one of the drop zones. Had he and his Chief-of-Staff, General Krebs, not reacted quickly to the sight of falling paratroopers and evacuated in haste to the safety of Arnhem, they might well have become Urquhart's first prisoners.

Unknown to Urquhart, the men under Model's command did not constitute the few dispirited third-rate troops he had been led to anticipate. Instead, they comprised two full battle-hardened S.S. panzer divisions resting and refitting in preparation for a move south and eager to rejoin battle with the Allies.

Commanded by Lieutenant Colonel Walter Harzer, IX S.S. Panzer Division had its main bivouac area around Zutphen. Under S.S. Major General Heinz Harmel,

X S.S. Panzer Division was situated between Zutphen and Ruurlo. Both had units in villages near Arnhem, in the suburbs and in woods, and Dutch Army barracks immediately to the north. Although neither division was up to strength, IX Division had a large number of relatively serviceable tanks and guns, while both had excellent mortar companies. To compound Urquhart's problems, General Willi Bittrich, in command of II S.S. Panzer Corps of which the two divisions formed a part, was also in the area. Brilliant, decisive and, in contrast to most S.S. officers, cultured, Bittrich was destined to make his devastating presence felt almost from the outset.

In addition to the 8,500 men of the two divisions, the area also held three highly experienced infantry battalions; Colonel Lippert's S.S. Officer Training Battalion and two S.S. line battalions under command of Majors Kraft and Eberwein. Of these, Kraft's battalion was actually stationed outside Arnhem, between the town and the advancing British.

Finally, the town held a number of *Fliegerhorst* (Luftwaffe ground staff) battalions, *Schiffstammabteilungen* (naval shore battery) crews and Dutch S.S. originally employed in guarding the concentration camp at Amersfoort.

Bittrich did not await the arrival of Model at his headquarters before acting. Realizing that the British 2nd Army would now be attempting a breakthrough in relief of its own paratroopers, he ordered X Panzer Division south to Nijmegen to halt their advance. In so doing he engineered a clash between the Panzers and Gavin's 82nd Airborne which would slow 30th Corps' advance by three days and cost the British any hope they had of victory.

More importantly, in the short term Bittrich ordered Kraft's battalion to dig into defensive positions along the roads into Arnhem. As Bittrich was subsequently able to comment with a degree of accuracy, 'Almost before the British had touched the ground we were ready to defeat them'.

The size and disposition of the German forces were of course unknown to Urquhart who began to suffer a series of unrelated mishaps almost immediately upon landing. Although the 21st Independent Parachute Company had done an excellent job in marking out the drop zones many of the gliders following had been lost or forced off course when their tow ropes parted. Virtually all the vehicles of the 1st Airborne Reconnaissance Squadron, due to lead the race for the bridge, were lost.

The advance into Arnhem began at 2.45 p.m., led by Lieutenant Colonel Frost's 2nd Battalion of Lathbury's 1st Parachute Brigade. The most southerly route into Arnhem was taken, through Heelsum and south of Oosterbeek. Progress became painfully slow due to a combination of local civilian exuberance, poor radio communications and grossly inadequate maps.

The other battalions met with greater difficulties. Fitch's 3rd Battalion attempting to advance along a more northerly route through Oosterbeek, were delayed by sustained mortar fire from leading elements of Kraft's battalion which had been reinforced by the guns and armoured cars of IX Panzer Division, when still two miles east of the village. With fanatical bravery, and by now suffering severe losses, the paratroopers attempted to continue their advance towards Arnhem but were finally halted on the outskirts of Oosterbeek. As night fell they dug in, still miles from their objective.

Dobie's 1st Battalion met with no greater success. Ordered to make for the high

Above: German troops dig in to oppose the Paratroopers' advance into Arnhem.

Below: 2nd Battalion, Parachute Regiment seen holding the nothern end of the bridge.

Below right: British 1st Airborne Division support troops make good their escape across the Rhine.

Below: The ruins of a Dutch school being searched for snipers by members of the Glider Pilot Regiment.

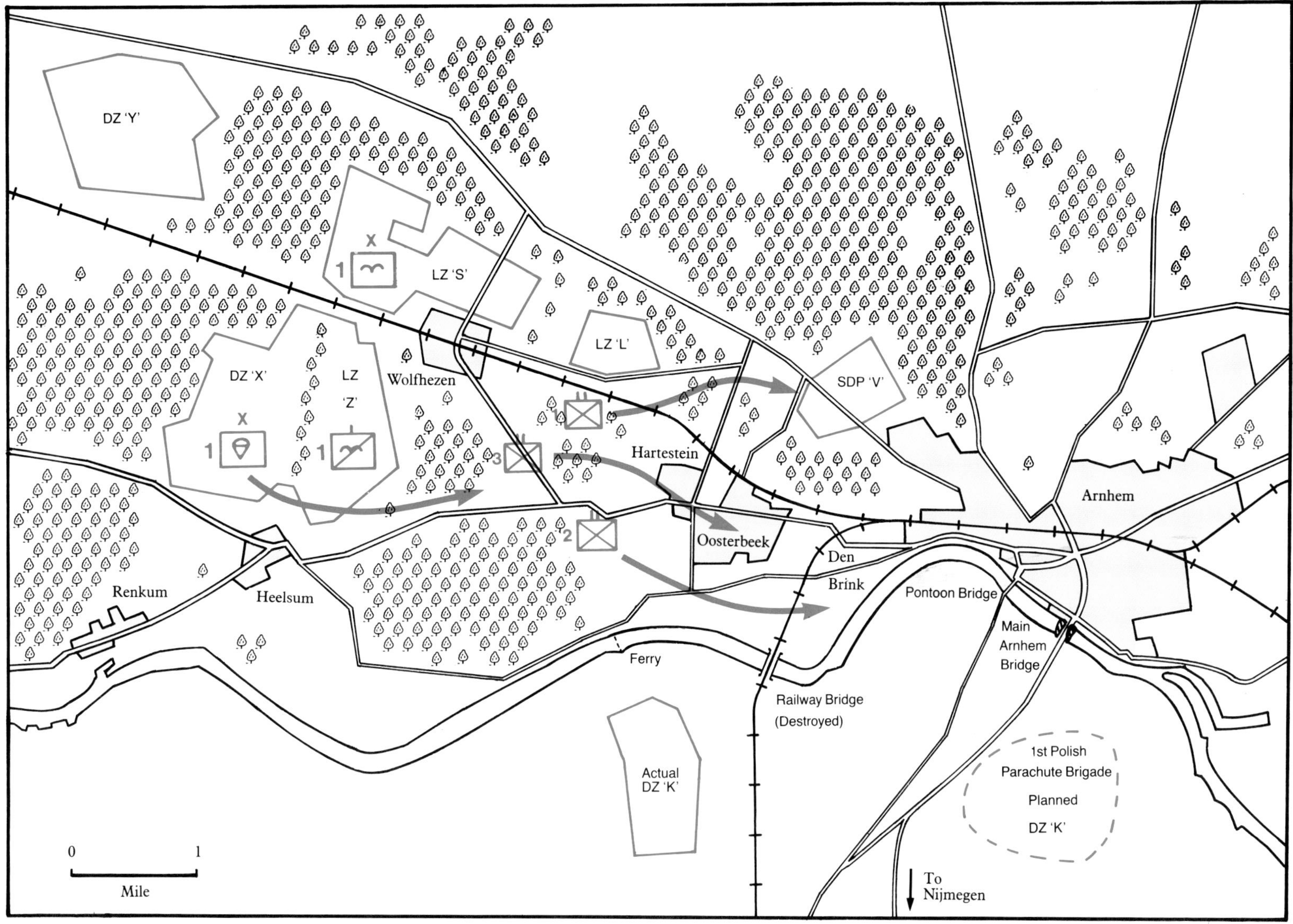

The British plan for the capture of the bridge at Arnhem was in essence quite simple. The 21st Independent Parachute Company would drop two hours before H-Hour to mark the ground with strips of coloured nylon tape. The 1st Parachute Brigade and the 1st Glider Brigade would land on day one, the 4th Parachute Brigade on day two, and the Polish Independent Brigade on day three. However the British were unaware that the town and its environs were held by two Panzer Divisions resting and refitting in anticipation of a move south. Almost immediately the British plan began to fail as the advancing troops met far greater than anticipated resistance. The 3rd Parachute Battalion advancing from the drop zone along the central axis was forced to dig in on the outskirts of Oosterbeek while the 1st Parachute Battalion, advancing to the north, was halted in the Arnhem suburbs. Only Frost's 2nd Parachute Battalion reached its objective. The 4th Parachute Brigade, which dropped next day, was forced to land under fire and the Polish drop had to be postponed for three days when their planned drop zone fell into enemy hands.

ground north of Arnhem and enter the town along the Apeldoorn Road, his men came under withering fire in the woods on the northern outskirts of the town. Decimated and hopelessly outnumbered, the survivors could only dig in and await events.

Colonel Frost succeeded in reaching the northern end of the bridge with about 500 men but, despite two gallant and costly attempts, was unable to dislodge Harzer's Panzers from the southern end. Harzer received reinforcements in the form of infantry, artillery and armour from Army Group B throughout the night and by morning Frost's position appeared to be critical.

Both 1st and 3rd Battalions attempted to continue their advance in the morning but both were soon stalled by murderous artillery and mortar fire from the massive Gothic structure of St. Elizabeth Hospital and the railway station nearby. In the midst of the mayhem, Lathbury was severely injured throwing the command structure into chaos. To compound the problem, Urquhart, who had been advancing with 3rd Battalion, suddenly found himself cut off and in imminent danger of capture. For over twelve hours, throughout the most crucial stage of the battle, he had to hide in an attic listening to the sound of German troops brewing up in the rooms below.

At Divisional Headquarters Brigadier Hicks, in command of the 1st Airlanding Brigade, assumed overall control. Although the stated role of his men was to guard the drop zones, he realized that his priority lay in assisting the remnants of 1st Airborne in its advance to the bridge, but he had little idea how. As ever when clarity is crucial the fog of war prevails. His radios were not strong enough to communicate with the forward airborne elements and neither he nor anyone had any idea what had happened to Urquhart.

Hicks ordered two companies of 2nd South Staffordshire Regiment forward into Arnhem to reconnoitre and report back. He could not release a larger force as the enemy were tightening their cordon around the drop zones. These had to be kept open at least until the arrival of Hackett's 4th Airborne Brigade, which had been delayed by fog over the airfields.

When Hackett did arrive some hours late, he began at once to restore some order to what he regarded as 'a grossly untidy situation'. When Urquhart was able to escape from the attic and return to headquarters, Hackett was able to report that parties from four battalions were making valiant attempts to fight their way through German cordons into the town. Hackett's own three battalions were ordered to join the battle from the north, leaving a single battalion in reserve.

Tuesday 19 September was a day of tragedy for the British forces. Concerted attacks by all the units in the town were repulsed with heavy loss of life, while Hackett's men suffered severe casualties from German mortars and artillery firing from the Johanna Hoeve and Lichtenbeck areas. As a final blow to British morale they were forced to watch the spectacle of R.A.F. aircraft flying through heavy flak to drop supplies onto predetermined targets, all of them in enemy territory.

Above: Two German prisoners. On the right, in his multi-coloured suit, is one of the few snipers taken prisoner.

Left: Major 'Jock' Neill and Lieutenant McCartney of the Border Regiment pass orders to a forward mortar position.

As darkness fell, the battalions within Arnhem continued to press home their attack with undiminished energy, but to no avail. Confusion reigned as all four battalion commanders were wounded and over half their officers killed. Unsure of what to do, the remnants of the leading elements began to fall back.

By now Frost's position on the bridge had become desperate. Denied sleep, food and water and with little ammunition left, the men of the 2nd Battalion could only mole their way into the cellars and hope to survive. The final German assault came at dawn on Thursday 21 September, by which time the exhausted paratroopers had been holding out alone for nearly 90 hours. It met with fanatical resistance and was contested in every room, stairway and yard still in airborne hands. By 9.00 a.m. however, the unequal contest was over. Arnhem bridge was again firmly in German hands, and the British paratroopers prisoners of war.

By then the rest of the 1st Airborne Division had been forced to withdraw into

an irregular horseshoe-shaped perimeter to the west of Oosterbeek and north of the Heveadorp ferry. Urquhart hoped that if he could hold on here there might be an opportunity for 2nd Army to cross the river and reach him, even with the bridge in enemy hands. He reckoned without the fanatical defence of the German X S.S. Panzer Division along the 16km (10 miles) of road separating Nijmegen from Arnhem. Despite their every effort, 43rd Division now spearheading 30th Corps' advance found it impossible to proceed beyond Nijmegen at more than a crawl. The only route open to the lead tanks lay on top of a high dyke, exposing them to the accurate fire of the well-placed German anti-tank guns which had been rushed forward from Army Group headquarters. The advancing column had to halt every few metres in order to bulldoze the wreckage of a destroyed tank from the road. Although recriminations would follow and the Airborne would blame Horrocks for exercising unnecessary caution there was, in truth, nothing more that he or his men could have done.

As the British perimeter shrank into an area known to the Germans as *the cauldron* it came under increasing fire from tanks, snipers and self-propelled artillery discharging phosphorus. Denied sleep, short of food and ammunition and without water, it became clear that the men could not hold out for much longer. On 23 September the Border Regiment was forced

Above: The remains of a column of British jeeps destroyed by enemy shell and mortar fire.

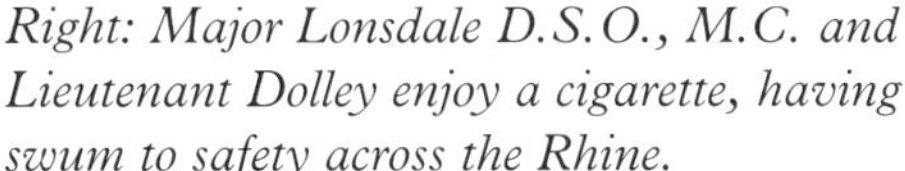

Right: Major Lonsdale D.S.O., M.C. and Lieutenant Dolley enjoy a cigarette, having swum to safety across the Rhine.

off the high ground at Westerbouwing overlooking the Heveadorp ferry with the result that when Sosabowski's Poles dropped south of the river that afternoon, they were unable to cross to the support of their British allies. A number tried to swim across the Rhine under cover of darkness but most were drowned. Only 50 finally made it to the British positions.

During the course of the next day, 4th Battalion, the Dorset Regiment, spearheading 30th Corps advance, reached the Rhine and attempted an abortive crossing. Most were cut to pieces in their assault boats. Those who survived were swept down river to be taken prisoner.

The evacuation began on Monday night, 25 September, eight days after the first landings and six days after Urquhart had been told that he could expect relief. Initially the Germans were taken unawares and did not react. When they discovered what was happening however, they began to bring down concentrated fire on the crossing points adding to the carnage.

Over 1,200 Britons and Poles died at Arnhem. Over 3,000 more were taken prisoner. Several reasons have been advanced for the ultimate failure of the operation. There were too few aircraft available, communications did not work, resupply failed, intelligence was inaccurate, no one expected there to be two full S.S. panzer divisions in the area. Whatever the truth may be, one thing is certain. In those eight days of vicious fighting the officers and men of 1st Airborne Division and the Polish Independent Airborne Brigade, suffering great hardship and deprivation, managed successfully to uphold the time-honoured traditions of excellence for which the airborne soldier is renowned.

Operation Houndsworth, 1 SAS in France, 1944

By 1944 the Special Air Service (SAS) had gained itself an international reputation for living up to its regimental motto *Who Dares Wins.* Spawned from the Long Range Desert Group (L.R.D.G.) in the North African desert, its members had carried out raid after daring raid far behind enemy lines leaving a trail of destruction among the installations, airfields and arms dumps. Blair (Paddy) Maine had even gained the record for the highest number of German aircraft destroyed — on the ground!

In 1943 the Regiment had expanded its area of interest to incorporate Italy and the Balkans, infiltrating singly or in groups from the air and by boat, to arm and organize local partisan groups. Almost single-handed, McGonegal, later to become a Northern Ireland High Court judge, operating in the hostile mountains of Central Yugoslavia, had turned a disparate and highly suspicious rabble into a coherent fighting force.

The Regiment had so angered and frustrated Hitler that he had issued his infamous Commando Order in which he had directed that all special forces, including SAS personnel, taken prisoner were to be treated as terrorists. They had to be handed over to the Gestapo at once and executed within 24 hours.

By the beginning of 1944, the SAS had grown from its original nucleus of 100 to a small brigade incorporating the 1st and 2nd British SAS, the latter containing a cocktail of Frenchmen, Poles with even a few ex-Foreign Legion Germans, the 3rd and 4th French Parachute Battalions and a squadron of Belgians. It had lost much of its original individualism and was, in the eyes of many of its older hands, in danger of becoming just another commando brigade. Moreover, in the opinion of many orthodox senior officers, its lack of obvious structure and discipline made it dangerous.

Perhaps it was inevitable therefore, when those SAS officers and troopers not actively involved in operations abroad were recalled home a few months prior to D-Day, several influential opponents of irregular warfare began to ask whether the Regiment even had a role in the future liberation of Europe.

Above: SAS officers relax prior to a briefing.

Initially it was decided to ignore the obvious expertise of the SAS in small-unit warfare, and to deploy it in a conventional airborne role, dropping behind the enemy lines shortly before the D-Day landings to impede the progress of enemy reinforcements in reaching the Normandy beaches. Despite the strenuous objections of the Regiment itself, manifested in the resignation of Bill Sterling (a founder member and commanding officer of 2SAS, this view might have prevailed had it not been for the timely intervention of Sandy Scratchley, an expert in irregular warfare, who had the ear of the Prime Minister. He argued that the Regiment's expertise in sabotage made it a far better strategic than tactical weapon. Distancing it as far as possible from the Special Operations Executive (S.O.E.), which ran agents in occupied Europe and with which it was often confused by the uninitiated, Scratchley argued convincingly that the SAS was an integral and highly disciplined, if 'different', part of the army which could only hope to perform its duties if left largely alone and free from external interference.

Fortunately Scratchley's views prevailed. The Regiment was now to operate deep inside occupied France, Belgium and Holland to provide a disciplined corps for the Resistance while striking at targets of opportunity and providing target information for the R.A.F. The size of each party would vary according to circumstances from a lone trooper to a half-squadron. In the case of the larger drops, a small reconnaissance party would parachute first, sometimes blind, sometimes with the aid of flares and torches provided by the local Resistance. If it were able to report favourably, it would be quickly reinforced by the rest of the party, supplemented where necessary by a number of specially converted armoured Jeeps.

It was conceded finally that the SAS be employed strategically reporting directly either to Montgomery's 21st Army Headquarters when established on the mainland or to Eisenhower's own Supreme Headquarters at S.H.A.E.F.

Left: A heavily armed SAS patrol advances through a village somewhere in North East France.

Below left: An SAS trooper relaxes, pipe in mouth, while he loads a Browning machine gun magazine.

Bottom: Twin Browning machine guns mounted on the front of SAS jeeps afforded devastating firepower to the attackers.

Perhaps as a sop to those generals who still regarded the role of the SAS as subordinate to the Airborne Division, 18 parties were dropped in Brittany on D-Day minus 1 (5 June 1944). They carried orders to assist the Resistance in attacking lines of communication, so hindering the movement of enemy reserves towards Normandy. Such raids, however, were unpopular with the Regiment, as they frequently resulted in savage reprisals against the local civilian population. Subsequent raids were of a more permanent nature, designed primarily to create semi-permanent operational bases.

Between D-Day (6 June 1944) and the end of November, the SAS mounted some 780 air sorties of which 600 were successful. Two six-pounders, 9,820 containers, and 75 armoured jeeps were dropped in support. Most drops took place from heights of less than 100m (328 ft) with six aircraft being lost in the process. Of the 2,000 SAS participants, 330 became casualties. Enemy killed or severely wounded numbered 7,753; 4,764 were taken prisoner and 18,000 cut off. Motor vehicles destroyed numbered 7,600, with 29 locomotives and 89 railway goods wagons. The railway was cut in 164 places.

It is perhaps easier to assess the full potential of the SAS in France by studying in detail a few of the more spectacular raids. The earliest drops to be made were in Brittany, Forêt d'Orlèans, Vienne, north of Poitiers and Nièvre, west of Dijon. The first, codenamed *Houndsworth,* took place on a massive scale in the Dijon area. An advanced party was dropped on D-Day minus 1 and, working in conjunction with a *Jedburgh* team, consisting of guides and local liaison officers controlled by Headquarters Special Forces, quickly increased to a total of 153 officers and men supported by 14 Jeeps. The force was intended to be larger but tragically an entire reinforcement troop of 18 men was killed on 18 June when an aircraft went out of control and crashed.

The force attempted to control a massive area of some 13,000 sq kms (5,020 sq miles) but found that the area was too big

and the major targets were too distant. Nonetheless *Houndsworth* accounted for an estimated 220 German dead, including a general killed when his vehicle ran over a landmine, for the loss of one officer killed and four troopers injured. The railway was cut no less than 22 times between Dijon, Lyons and Paris with six trains and 70 assorted vehicles destroyed. Sixteen allied aircrew and a female agent dropped into France by S.O.E. were rescued, a Gestapo agent posing as a Belgian uncovered, and 3,000 local Maquis armed.

Rommel's headquarters were located and infiltrated. Permission was sought from London to attempt an assassination, and sniper rifles were requested as a matter of urgency. The request was turned down out of hand and the rifles never sent. Rommel survived, only to commit suicide when implicated in a plot on Hitler's life a few months later.

Not all raids were as successful as *Houndsworth. Bulbasket* took place between 6 June and 7 July 1944. Fifty-five troops from 1SAS supported by elements of the Phantom Regiment, were dropped in the area south of Châteauroux. Initially all went well. They were able to cut the railway lines between Limoges, Vierzon, Poitiers and Tours a dozen times besides inflicting

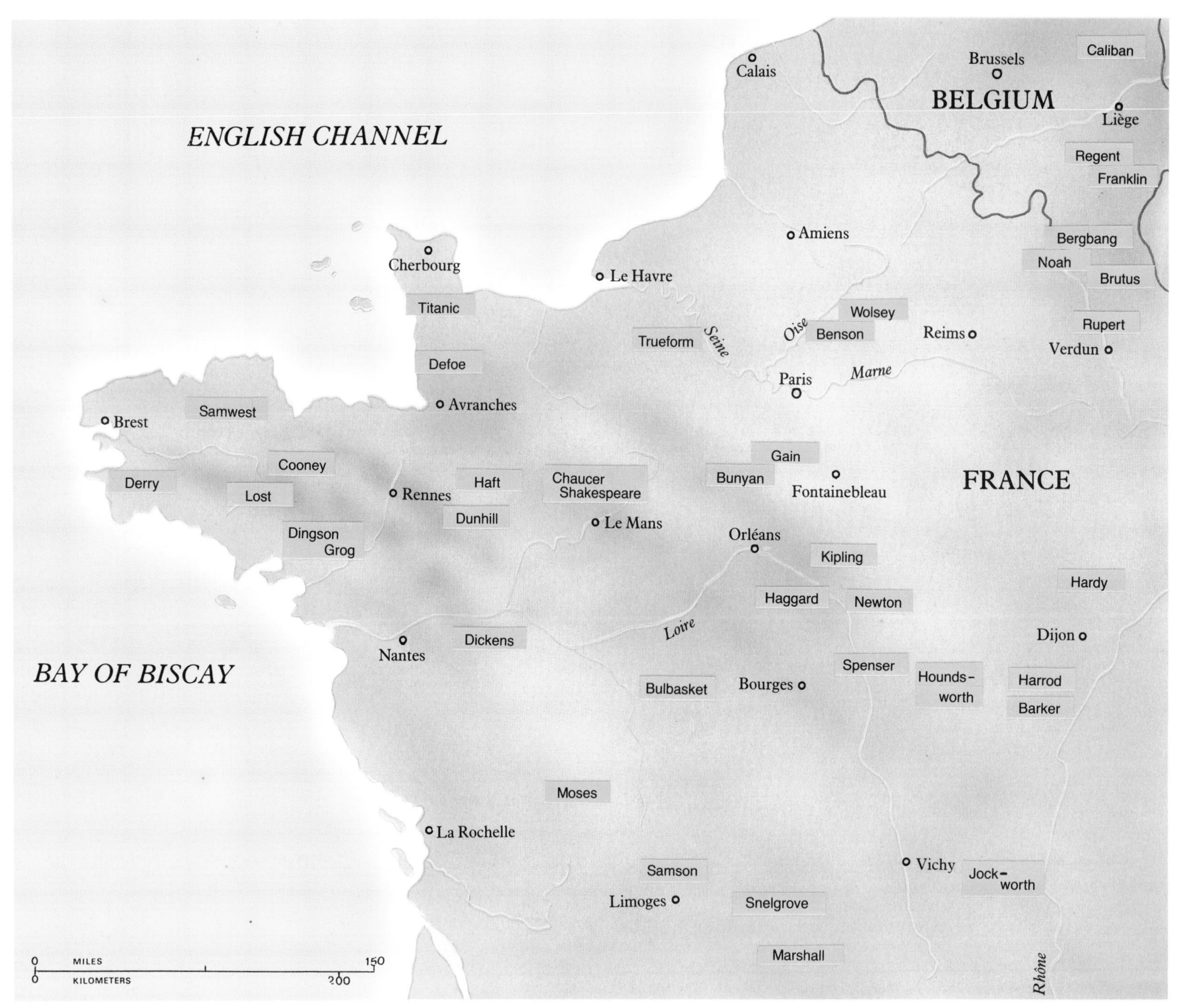

In 1940, during Britain's darkest hour, Churchill ordered the top secret S.O.E. 'to set Europe ablaze'. In compliance, agents were parachuted on to the Continent to establish 'resistance', to organize escape lines and to undertake increasingly daring acts of sabotage. As D-Day approached these agents were joined by Jedburgh teams drawn from American, British and French officers, and by SAS units. The role of the SAS was two-fold to gain intelligence and to organize the local resistants and Maquis into coherent fighting units ready to rise up in open revolt when their day came. SAS teams of varying sizes were dropped throughout France and the Low Countries, the largest groups concentrating in the sparsely populated mountains north and east of Limoges. Ultimately, the effect of these troops, working together with their civilian French Allies , was totally out of proportion to their size. Hitler was so incensed by their success that he ordered the summary execution of all captured SAS troopers.

20 casualties on the enemy. Success, however, turned to tragedy when the SAS base was treacherously compromised by unknown elements of the local population. The base was attacked, resulting in 37 casualties of whom 33 were captured and executed. It has since been alleged that some of those executed had given themselves up when surrounded. Ignorant of Hitler's Commando Directive and only lightly armed, they had assumed that they would be treated according to the terms of Geneva Convention, preferring the idea of a prisoner of war camp to death. In any case, *Bulbasket* represents one of the worst atrocities of the post-invasion war.

Operation *Gain,* involving ten officers and fifty men under the command of Major Ian Fenwick, took place between 14 June and 15 August in the area of Fontainebleau south-west of Paris and met with considerably more success. Using armoured jeeps equipped with 0.5in Vickers machine guns the team tore about the countryside of Rambouillet, Orléans and Chartres, attacking targets of opportunity, mixing with German convoys and knocking out enemy trucks. Taking tremendous risks the team succeeded in severely compromising communications within the vital Orléans Gap. Frequently surrounded and heavily outnumbered, on several occasions Fenwick and his men only escaped with the selfless help of French Resistance workers. Initially luck befriended the bold but, as so often happens, eventually it ran out. Fenwick, searching for a missing vehicle crew, was killed with three others when his vehicle ran into an ambush at Chambon. Typically he and his men died refusing to surrender, with all vehicle guns blazing. Fourteen SAS members who were subsequently captured were dealt with as terrorists, maltreated and in most cases shot.

The incredible bravery of the French citizenry, not all of whom were Resistance members, in helping the SAS should not be overlooked, nor should the fate which befell many of them as a consequence. Operation *Loyton,* comprising 91 men and six Jeeps under command of Lieutenant Colonel Franks, was dropped several weeks behind schedule in the Vosges region of Eastern France. Instead of finding the comparatively quiet sector anticipated, the SAS found themselves in the middle of the major German withdrawal route. The local Maquis, badly led, ill-armed and riddled with informers, refused to help, leaving the troopers to make their own way as best they could back to the safety of the advancing Allied lines. During the retreat, the SAS were constantly hounded by specially trained counter-insurgency troops introduced specifically for the purpose.

Above: Local Maquis in Quillebeuf, including a sympathetic policeman, greet the arrival of British troops.

Below: Members of the Maquis clean their weapons before going into action in the Breton area.

Two were killed and 31 captured and executed. One village, Moussey, offered protection to the escaping Britons. In revenge, the Germans removed the entire male population — 210 men and boys — to concentration camps. Two-thirds died in internment. Of the 70 who returned after the war many subsequently died of the effects of starvation and torture.

Parachute operations became all but impossible as the winter of 1944 set in and the front line moved further east. The Belgian SAS Squadron and a detachment of the 4th French Parachute Battalion undertook deep reconnaissance missions behind the enemy lines but otherwise special forces activity virtually ceased until the following spring.

In all, the SAS undertook 42 missions in France throughout the second half of 1944. Although many were costly in terms of lives, none was a failure. Whole German divisions were diverted from the front to counter the elusive paratroopers. Communications were thrown into chaos. No more than 2,000 SAS personnel were employed in France yet their contribution to the ultimate Allied victory was immense.

Training, boldness and an element of luck once again combined to prove the truth of the motto *Who Dares Wins.*

Above: French hostages shot in reprisal for acts of sabotage undertaken by Maquis units.

Below: French Red Cross workers identify the bodies of resistants massacred by the Germans before their withdrawal from Paris.

Below: Members of 1SAS helping 43 Division clear snipers along its route of advance.

The Inchon Landings, U.S. Marine Corps in Korea, 1950

The decision to execute a large-scale amphibious landing at Inchon was one of the most audacious and inspired of twentieth century warfare. It confirmed General Douglas MacArthur's place as one of the great commanders in modern history and did much to prevent the total humiliation of the United Nations.

North Korea's invasion of the South on 25 June 1950 had caught the defenders unprepared. Within days they had been forced to withdraw in disorder to Pusan in the south-eastern corner of the peninsula. They had been driven from the capital of Seoul and from every other major city. American units on garrison duty in Japan had been hastily dispatched to the area and had succeeded in creating a weak perimeter around Pusan. Various United Nations member nations had agreed to send military assistance but it would be some while before intent could become reality and for the immediate future the United States and South Korea would have to stand alone. It was transparently clear that unless pressure could be brought to bear on the North Koreans forcing their withdrawal, the chances of non-Communist survival were slim.

Desperate times call for desperate measures and inspired leadership. Commanders who excel in set piece battle are often reduced to impotency by the unexpected and are totally incapable of waging irregular or unorthodox warfare. They nonetheless fully understand the need for political patronage and can be relied upon to do nothing detrimental to the furtherance of their career. Others regard victory as reward in itself and are less inclined to court those whom they regard as interfering fools. Such men rarely attain their full potential in the military but when they do they are devastating.

Such a man was General Douglas MacArthur. Recalled to active duty at the age of 61 in 1941, he had done much to engineer the Allied victory in the Pacific and, since the Japanese surrender in 1945, had ruled that country almost absolutely. Described by Liddell Hart as one who enjoyed, 'strong personality, strategic grasp, tactical skill, operative mobility and vision' he was a class above his peers and the ideal man to assume command of the forces in Korea at that crucial time.

MacArthur reasoned that the key to success lay in the recapturing of Seoul, close to the pre-war frontier on the 38th Parallel, and at once set about making plans for an amphibious landing at Inchon to the west of the capital. The North Koreans had little logistic support and had stretched their supply lines, most of which passed through Seoul, to breaking point. If he could recapture and hold the city he would bolster the shattered morale of the South Korean people who were rapidly coming to regard defeat and annihilation as inevitable. More fundamentally he would deny the enemy the arms and materiel essential for continued victory and almost certainly force his withdrawal.

Conceived on 29 June MacArthur's daring plan, now codenamed Operation *Blue Heart,* was prepared in every detail and ready for submission to the Joint Chiefs of Staff Committee (J.C.S.) by 4 July. It envisaged a landing by the 1st U.S. Cavalry Division: then in Japan, on 22 July, the first date when the tides at Inchon would be favourable. The very complexity of the operation proved to be its downfall and *Blue Hearts* was cancelled on 10 July when the sheer impossibility of meeting so tight a timescale was finally admitted. Disappointed but not disillusioned, MacArthur regarded the setback as no more than a postponement of his plans, which he continued to improve.

By now thoroughly alarmed at the possibility of defeat and with Congress now fully behind him, President Truman

U.S. Marines of the first Division watch as Marine aircraft napalm a Chinese Communist road block.

ordered the dispatch of the entire United States based 1st Marine Division, specialists in amphibious landings, to Korea on 25 July. The first of its three regiments, already en route for Korea, reached Pusan a week later and on 12 August the Joint Strategic Plans and Operations Group (J.S.P.O.G.) of MacArthur's Far Eastern Command in Tokyo began the preparation of detailed plans for the landing.

The problems facing Operation *Chromite*, as it was now entitled, were immense. In the words of one of the J.S.P.O.G. intelligence staff officers involved in the planning 'We drew up a list of every conceivable natural and geographic handicap and Inchon had 'em all'. To reach the harbour itself the Marines would first have to negotiate Flying Fish Channel, a long narrow seaway scattered with reefs, islands and rocks which twisted and turned in such a way that large ships would not be able to approach close to the shoreline. To compound the problem the tides at Inchon were the second highest in the world, which meant that at low tide the harbour was cut off by some 5km (3.12 miles) of unnavigable mud flats, creeks and streams. The assault ships would only have three hours of sufficiently high water on one day per month to enable them to operate. A delay for whatever reason would leave them stranded and vulnerable, totally defenceless against the surrounding Communist shore batteries. The multi-national (and therefore multi-lingual) fleet of warships, essential for the suppression of enemy coastal artillery, would have to lie far offshore, firing at extreme range. They had not operated together before and had therefore to be regarded as something of an unknown quantity.

Even without these obvious and to many insuperable difficulties, Inchon was not an ideal place for an amphibious landing. Instead of gently sloping beaches of firm sand, the port was surrounded by rocky sea walls designed to halt the encroaching mud. The landing therefore would have to take place not on to beaches as had always been the case in World War II, but at harbour walls 3.6m (3.9yds) high, which would have to be scaled under fire by ladders and which led directly into the town. All possible landing sites were clearly visible from enemy held positions in the hills and were in range of artillery batteries located on the small island of Walmi-do in the centre of the harbour.

Finally, the acquisition of detailed preliminary intelligence, regarded as essential for such a mission, would be difficult to obtain as excessive overt reconnaissance in the area might alert the North Koreans to American intentions. Eventually it was decided to infiltrate the

area with South Korean agents and to land a U.S. Navy lieutenant to conduct a one-man reconnaissance of the target to gather as much information as practical about the tides, enemy strengths, dispositions and defences. Despite a series of close encounters this remarkable young man succeeded in avoiding compromise for the fifteen days during which he remained hidden. Not only did he manage to transmit a series of crucial short-wave radio messages to his headquarters, but on the night of the landings actually succeeded in activating a small lighthouse in the harbour mouth to act as a beacon to the approaching landing craft.

Anxieties regarding these physical difficulties only served to confirm the view of many that the plan was madness. Not only was it doomed from the outset but it would take the United States' finest fighting troops in the theatre away from the Pusan Perimeter which was then under considerable pressure. Even when Intelligence reported that there were no more than 2,000 enemy troops in the area and fewer than 5,000 in Seoul itself, the plan enjoyed little initial support. Indeed had it not been for MacArthur's all pervading optimism and sheer strength of personality, it would almost certainly have been rejected by the Joint Chiefs of Staff. When ordered to a conference in Tokyo on 23 August MacArthur was forced to concede to the Chief of Naval Operations and army Chief of Staff present that the entire plan was based on intuition without a fraction of logical basis. Yet during a 45 minute exposition, delivered without the aid of a single note and throughout which he continued to smoke his pipe, MacArthur won his personal battle and the landings were approved. The plans were finalized on 4 September and the landings scheduled for eleven days later.

Command of the operation was entrusted to Admiral Arthur Struble, Commander-in-Chief of the U.S. Seventh Fleet, with control on the ground delegated to Major General Edward Almond, Commander of the X U.S. Corps.

It was decided to commit 1st Marine Division and 7th U.S. Infantry Division to the landing, an overall total of 70,000 officers and men. The 1st Marine Division (comprising the 1st, 5th and 7th Marine Regiments) had already been committed to the war and was therefore in an advanced state of readiness. The 1st and 7th Regiments, the latter less one battalion, reached Japan from America between 22

Left: Marines load their M-47 tanks en route to Inchon beachhead.

Above: Allied warships bombard Communist positions along the Inchon waterfront prior to the Marine Corps' landing.

Below: Marines use scaling ladders during the amphibious assault against the Inchon harbour installations.

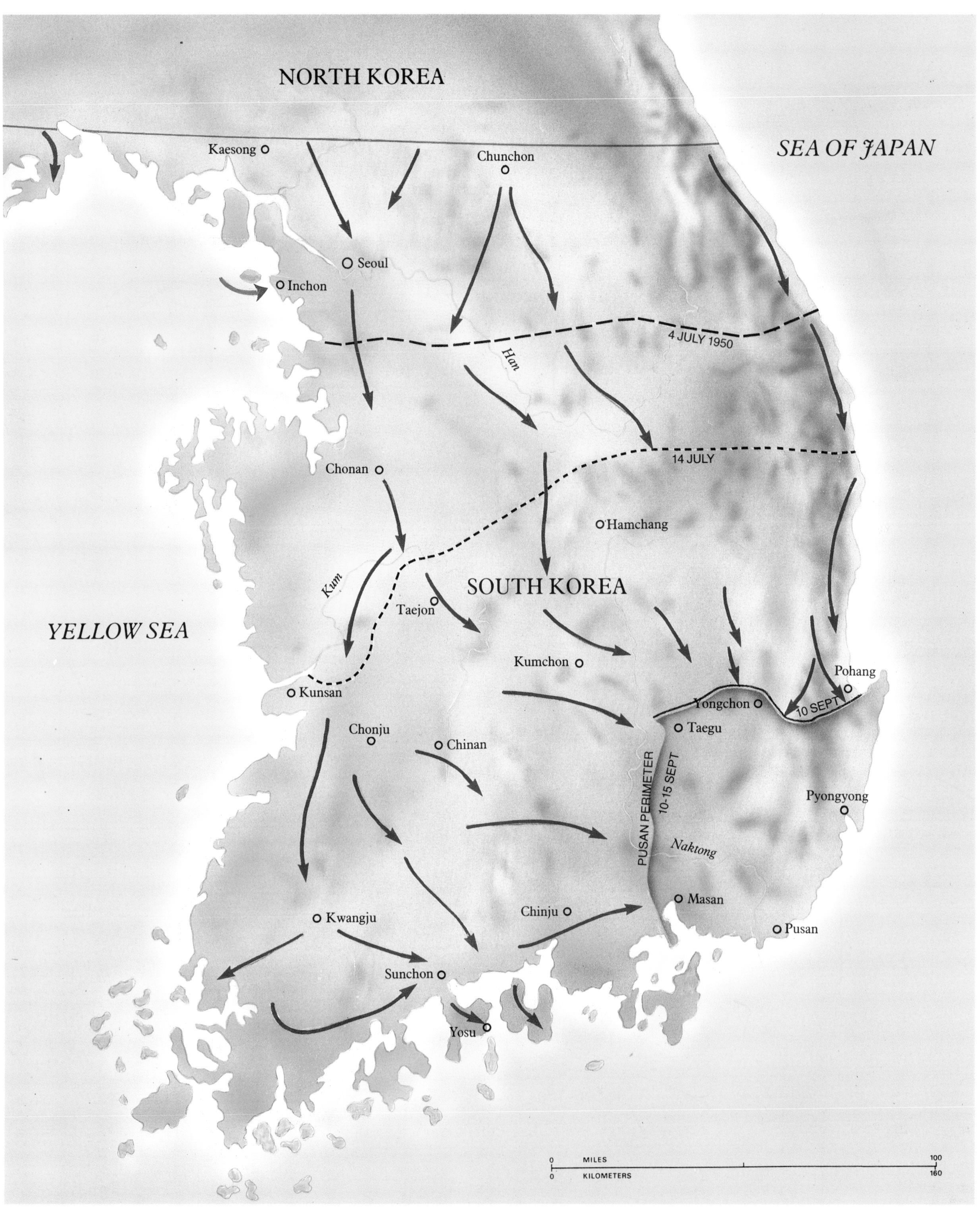
NORTH KOREA
SEA OF JAPAN
Kaesong
Chunchon
Seoul
Inchon
4 JULY 1950
Han
14 JULY
Chonan
Hamchang
Kum
SOUTH KOREA
Taejon
YELLOW SEA
Kumchon
Pohang
Kunsan
Yongchon
10 SEPT
Taegu
Chonju
Chinan
PUSAN PERIMETER
10-15 SEPT
Pyongyong
Naktong
Masan
Chinju
Kwangju
Pusan
Sunchon
Yosu
MILES
KILOMETERS
0
100
0
160

North Korea's invasion of the South on 25 June 1950 caught the defenders unprepared. By 4 July the Communists had taken Seoul, Inchon and the lower reaches of the Han river. By 14 July they had advanced to Kunsan and by early September had forced the South Koreans and their American allies to withdraw into the Pusan peninsular. General Douglas MacArthur, appreciating the need to take the war to the enemy, formulated a plan which, if successful, would not only land a force of Marines behind the enemy lines at Inchon but would lead to the speedy recapture of Seoul. The landings were a complete success. The 1st and 5th Marines formed a beachhead, took Kimpo Airfield, crossed the Han river and moved into the northern outskirts of Seoul, having sustained comparatively few losses. The North Koreans were thrown into complete disarray. One of there main lines of communication having been destroyed. Almost at once the now vastly reinforced Allies began a breakout from Pusan pushing the enemy back beyond his own borders.

Above: Four LSTs offload men and equipment on to Inchon beach. Initial losses were incredibly low.

Left: U.S.S. Begor lies at anchor off Hungnam, ready to load the last U.N. landing craft.

August and 6 September. The 5th Regiment, already deployed at Pusan, was extricated from the mainland fighting on 6 September and was joined three days later by the missing battalion of the 7th Regiment which until then had been serving with the U.S. Sixth Fleet in the Mediterranean.

The 7th Infantry Division, until then on garrison duty in Japan, was in a less enviable state. The only major unit in South-East Asia not committed to the war, it had been constantly drained of its best troops by the three divisions in combat and was dangerously under-strength. When warned off for the Inchon landings on 26 July it reported a deficiency of 290 officers and more than 8,000 men. All reinforcements to the area were at once posted in and a total of 390 officers and 5,400 men, mostly from training establishments and of the highest calibre, rushed over from the United States. Even so the Division was still considered too small for the tasks allotted until a further 8,000 Korean civilians were conscripted, given rudimentary basic training and committed to its strength.

It was decided that the Marines would make the initial landing on 15 September and advance directly on Seoul. The 3rd Battalion, 5th Marines would land on Walmi-do, designated *Green Beach*, on the morning tide to mop up pockets of resistance not otherwise neutralized by the bombardment. The 1st and 2nd Battalions would land in Inchon itself *(Red Beach)* and the 1st Marines to the south of the town *(Blue Beach)* on the evening tide. They would be followed a day later by the 7th Infantry Division which would deploy south and east of the city. Two days before the first assault warships from the U.S. Navy, the Royal Navy, the Royal Australian,

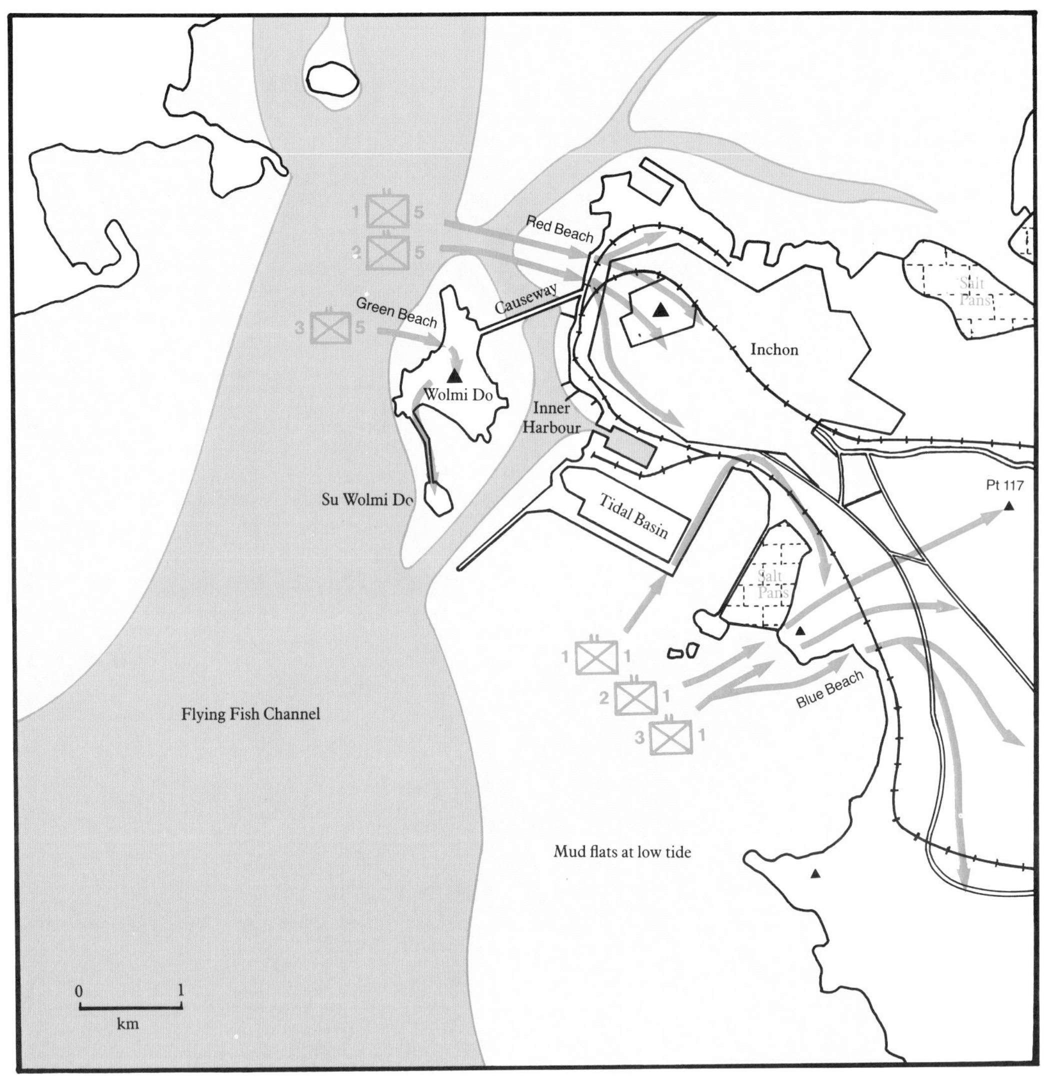

The landings at Inchon were a huge, if calculated, risk. The only approach to the harbour was through Flying Fish Channel, a long narrow seaway scattered with reefs, islands and rocks. To compound the problem the tides at Inchon were the second highest in the world, which meant that at low tide the harbour was cut off by some 5km (3.1 miles) of unnavigable mud flats, creeks and streams. The assault ships would have no more than three hours of sufficiently high water on one day a month to enable them to operate. The 3/5th Marines spearheaded the attack by landing on and securing the island of Walmi-do at the mouth of the harbour {Green Beach}. *Thereafter 1/5th and 2/5th Marines scaled the harbour walls* {Red Beach} *while the 1st Marine Regiment stormed ashore along* {Blue Beach} *to the south. The landing was a complete success. By the end of D-day the U.S. Marine Corps had achieved its every objective for the loss of only 20 men killed, 1 missing and 174 wounded.*

Canadian and New Zealand Navies, from France and from South Korea itself would bombard enemy positions near Inchon and on Walmi-do in an attempt to neutralize the Communist batteries. Concurrent bombardments and air raids would be undertaken against sites well to the north and south of Inchon in an attempt to mask American intentions.

The 3/5th Marines arrived on schedule 1.6 km (1 mile) off Walmi-do at 5.30 a.m. and transferred to their landing craft without incident. The first echelon set off for its objective at 6.25 a.m. reaching the island unopposed eight minutes later. Within half an hour their M-47 tanks had landed and by 7.30 a.m. the island was secure at a cost of only 17 wounded. Thereafter the battalion dug in and remained marooned for the rest of the day as the tide went out.

At 3.30 p.m. troops of the 1st and 5th marines loaded into their landing craft and began to make for the shore in the knowledge that the enemy was now fully alerted and would almost certainly be expecting them. Nonetheless, when the leading element of the 5th Marines began to scale the harbour walls (euphemistically designated *Red Beach*) at 5.33 p.m., they encountered only sporadic and largely ineffective resistance. By midnight they had secured the high ground overlooking Inchon and were able to declare the port in their hands.

The 1st Marines landed on *Blue Beach* at 5.00 p.m. Having encountered some initial problems caused more by the pitch darkness and smoke of battle than the enemy they reached their main objective, the main road from Inchon to Seoul, at 1.30 a.m. on the morning of 16 September.

By the end of D-Day the U.S. Marine Corps had achieved every objective for the loss of 20 men killed, 1 missing and 174 wounded.The next day the 1st and 5th Marines linked up to establish a perimeter 10km (6.25 miles) inland from the landing sites, enabling the 7th Infantry Brigade to come ashore unopposed.

During the next few days the 5th Marines took Kimpo airfield, crossed the Han River and moved into the northern outskirts of Seoul. The 1st Marines captured the town of Yongdungpo on the west banks of the Han River while the 7th Marines, not committed on the first day, cut the railway lines in and out of Seoul. The 32nd Infantry Regiment moved into the southern suburbs of the capital which fell to the United States forces on 22 September. The 3/187th Airborne Regiment together with a South Korean Marine Regiment landed and fanned out to the north, consolidating the Allied position. Four days after the fall of Seoul, X Corps linked up with the Eighth Army advancing from Pusan. Confused,

Above: U.S.M.C. 105mm artillery dug in in support of the advancing infantry.

Left: U.S. Marines advance from the beachhead under the protective cover of friendly artillery and air power.

Left: General MacArthur confers with Major General Harris and Vice Admiral Doyle aboard U.S.S. Rochester *during the Inchon landings.*

disorientated and disillusioned, their morale shattered, the North Korean invaders pulled back to their own borders.

The Glorious Glosters, Imjin River, 1951

From its source some 32km (20 miles) inland from Wonsan on the east coast of North Korea, the Imjin River flows south some 128km (80 miles). At the point where it crosses the 38th Parallel just north of the village of Choksong, on the road running 48km (30 miles) south to Seoul, the Imjin describes a meandering bend to the south-west on the last lap of its route to the Yellow Sea. It was here, between the south-westerly bend of the Imjin River and Choksong, that the *Glorious Glosters* stubbornly held their position for four days (22-25 April 1951) in one of the hardest-fought battles in the whole of the Korean War.

The conflict had been ongoing since 25 June 1950, when Communist North Korean forces surged across the 38th Parallel at 11 points and ignored the request of the United Nations Security Council to withdraw. Two days later the Security Council appealed to member states of the United Nations to supply forces for the support of the American-backed Republic of Korea. Before these forces could arrive in strength, however, the North Korean invaders had occupied nearly the whole of the Korean peninsula. By the first week of September 1950 the South Korean and United Nations forces had been penned into a disconcertingly small beachhead around Pusan, at Korea's southern tip.

Under the command of American General Douglas MacArthur, the U.N. forces struck back on 13 September 1950 with an amphibious landing at Inchon, 320km (200 miles) up the west coast behind the North Korean lines. By the end of the month the North Koreans had been forced back beyond the 38th Parallel. The U.N. General Assembly decreed that there should be a united, Democratic Korea on 7 October but the North Koreans ignored MacArthur's demand for their surrender. MacArthur ordered the crossing of the 38th Parallel into North Korea on 9 October and used his massive advantage of sea power to launch another amphibious landing, at Wonsan. By the end of October the United Nations forces had reached the Yalu River, on the Korean-Manchurian frontier.

The third phase of the Korean War began in November 1950 with North Korean counter-offensive, this time massively reinforced by Communist Chinese troops. By the end of the year the United Nations forces had been pushed south to the 38th Parallel, the South Korean capital, Seoul, was captured for the second time by the Communists on 4 January 1951. The strategic impasse of the war was now becoming defined. The further south the Communists advanced, the more certain they were of being ground to a halt by intensifying United Nations air attacks. However, the further north the United Nations forces advanced out of the territorial funnel of the Korean peninsula, their forward units became more and more exposed to outflanking Communist ground attacks in overwhelming strength, beyond the range of round-the-clock air cover and supply.

The fourth phase began at the end of January 1951 when MacArthur attacked again, eventually recapturing Seoul on 14 March. His second offensive north of the 38th Parallel, which began on 3 April, had been going barely a week when President Truman replaced him with General Matthew B. Ridgway, whose first concern was meeting the new Communist offensive of April 1951. As before, the prime objective of this offensive was Seoul — and in the path to Seoul lay the British blocking force covering the Imjin river bend at Choksong.

Defence of the Imjin River crossing was in the hands of the 1st Battalion, Gloucestershire Regiment, called *The Glosters,* commanded by Lieutenant-Colonel James Carne. Knowing that his 800-strong force had no chance of meeting a major attack without being outflanked

British troops attend Church Parade. Only one Padre taken prisoner by the North Koreans survived.

and swamped by Chinese manpower, Carne made no attempt to hold the line of the river along its south bank. He chose instead to deploy his four companies on the hills flanking Choksong, about 2,400m (11/2 miles) south of the Imjin. As long as the battalion held these hills, it would be able to offer each other mutual support. He hoped to be able to hold this position long enough for air support and a ground relief force to be provided.

After repeated sightings of Chinese reconnaissance parties during the daylight hours of 22 April, Carne sensed that a major attack was imminent. He ordered a 50 percent stand to that night, with a 16-strong fighting patrol posted as an ambush party south of *Gloster Crossing* the ford across the Imjin.

First honours in the Imjin River battle went to this ambush party on the night of 22-23 April, when no less than four Chinese attempts to force a crossing were repulsed with resulting heavy losses. Only when the men of the ambush party were down to three rounds a rifle and less than half a magazine for the Sten sub-machine and Bren light machine-guns, did the ambush party, from the *Glosters'* C Company, fall back from the south bank of the Imjin. Unknown to the defenders, however, the Chinese had forced a second crossing 4km (21/2 miles) downstream of *Gloster Crossing* — the *Western Crossing*, as the hard-pressed defenders called it.

The original Chinese plan for a two-pronged strike across the Imjin would have launched simultaneous blows at A Company on *Castle Hill* and D Company on the other side of the Seoul road. This

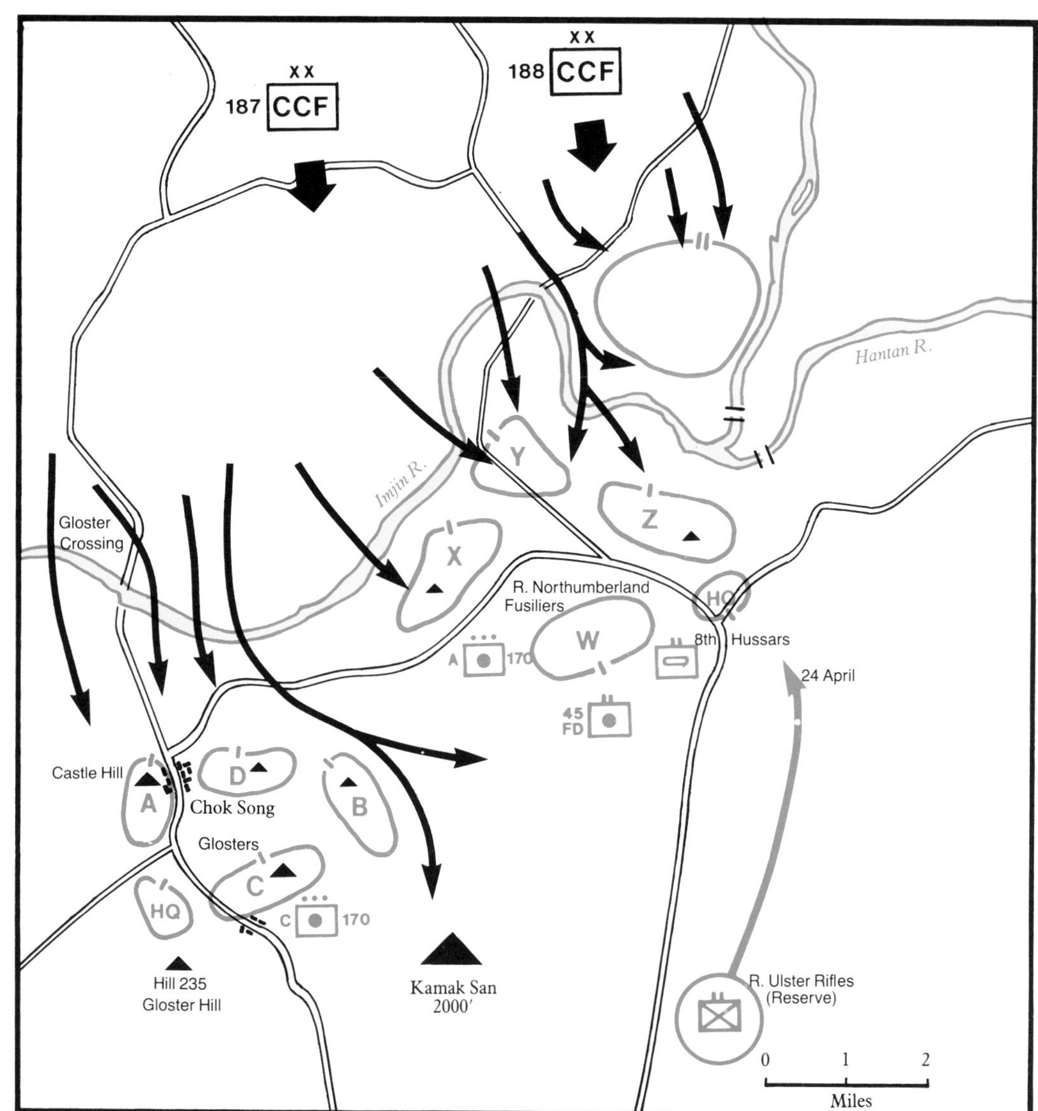

Lt. Colonel Carne was awarded the Victoria Cross for his actions while commanding the Glosters in Korea.

The 800 officers of the 1st Battalion Gloucestershire Regiment - The Glosters *- knew that they were doomed as soon as they received their mission. Lieutenant-Colonel James Carne and his troops were ordered to hold their position on the Imjin river against an estimated force of 80,000 Chinese and North Koreans advancing from the north. During the second day of intensive fighting the battalion received the dreaded news that the anticipated relieving force had run into difficulties and a day later was advised that it would no longer be coming. Unperturbed, the battalion fought on valiantly refusing to surrender ground until finally ordered to withdraw. Only five officers and 41 men made it to safety with 19 officers and 505 men taken prisoner. Two Victoria Crosses, three D.S.O.s and six M.C.s were awarded to individuals. The entire battalion was honoured with the United States Presidential Citation.*

plan was thrown badly out of gear by the repulse of the Chinese at *Gloster Crossing.* It took several hours for the left-flank Chinese to push south of the Imjin and attack D Company, which managed to hold its position. By dawn on 23 April however, A Company, after a desperate resistance, had been forced off *Castle Hill* — the highest point of the *Glosters'* forward defences — by seemingly inexhaustible waves of Chinese attackers.

Even though Carne wasted no time in ordering the recapture of Castle Hill and its retention at all costs, Chinese reinforcements continued to pour across *Gloster* and *Western Crossings* throughout the daylight hours of 23 April, and there was nothing the British could do to stop them. By nightfall Carne was forced to weigh the certain destruction of two rifle companies against the risk of falling back from his forward positions and regrouping further to the south. He chose the latter option, which would still permit his depleted platoons to block the Choksong-Seoul Road, although this entailed abandoning Choksong village and pulling back the right-flanking B Company about 1,370m (1,500 yds) to conform with the withdrawal of A and D Companies.

The initial brunt of the fighting on the night of 23-24 April fell on B Company, whose original position had not been located by the Chinese until daybreak on 23 April. A full day behind schedule thanks to the resistance put up by the *Glosters* on the previous night, the Chinese suffered further heavy losses in over two hours of unavailing attacks. By 3.00 a.m. on 24th April, the pressure was telling again. The Chinese overran much of C Company's position, driving a wedge between C and B Companies and dominating the shallow valley in which Battalion Headquarters lay. Carne immediately evacuated his valley headquarters and ordered another exhausting move of position by C and D Companies. This regrouping was covered by B Company, which held its position throughout the night until the remainder of the battalion could come to its aid on the morning of 24 April. When the survivors of B Company, out of ammunition, finally rejoined their comrades, they numbered no more than 20 men — enough, when merged with the remnants of C Company, to make up a single strong platoon.

At daybreak on 24 April, the *Glosters* took stock of their immediate needs. In order of priority, these were replenishment ammunition, fresh batteries to maintain radio contact with Brigade, and food. Supplies of all three were to be found in the valley where Battalion Headquarters had stood the day before — a valley now denied to the Chinese, if only temporarily, by the fire of the *Glosters* from their new positions. With great determination, three foraging

Above and left: The Imjin River and plain taken from the Glosters' position.

Young soldiers man a Bren gun position along the Naktong River front.

parties succeeded in bringing out the needed supplies with the aid of Korean porters and their back-pack wooden A-frames. These replenishments would, it was hoped, enable the *Glosters* to hold out until their looked-for relief by an advancing Filipino battalion and the Centurion tanks of the 8th Hussars, which were expected to arrive by nightfall.

A serious blow to the *Glosters*' fire-power was the loss of the battalion's medium heavy mortar whose barrel plates had to be abandoned during the previous night's regrouping. This reduced the *Glosters* to small-arms fire and 25-pounder artillery support — a state of affairs which became desperate when, in the late afternoon of 24 April, the prospect of relief was abruptly snatched away. Over the radio link came the news that the Filipinos' advance, and that of the 8th Hussars, had been halted by heavy Chinese reinforcements. As long as the *Glosters* held their position, the Chinese would be denied at least one of the two roads leading to Seoul. For the moment, however, the only help which Brigade could offer was an air-drop of supplies and supporting air strikes for 25 April.

With his command now reduced to less than 400 effectives with many wounded, and ammunition for no more than 12 hours of moderate-scale small arms fighting, Carne made it clear that the *Glosters* could no longer be considered an effective fighting force. He added, however, 'If it is required that we shall stay here, in spite of this, we shall continue to hold.' For the night of 24-25 April he proposed to concentrate his entire remaining force on the long ridge known as Hill 235 — still overlooking the Choksong-Seoul road.

Throughout the third night of the battle the *Glosters* nursed their dwindling stocks of ammunition and continued to take a heavy toll of their assailants. The Chinese, it seemed, had learned nothing from their previous costly attacks. The noisy approach of each new assault gave the defenders plenty of warning, not to mention the raucous bugle calls which attended each move. The latter prompted a unique retaliation when the *Glosters*' Drum-Major, who had a bugle in his haversack 'returned fire' with a selection of all the British bugle calls of the day bar one — Retreat. Although the Chinese returned to the attack, they did so with no further bugle calls that night.

The morning of 25 April dawned with the *Glosters* approaching their last gasp. Twice pushed off Hill 235, they retook it with artillery support from the last 25-pounders still in action and held it against five more attempted counter-attacks — then a sixth. The Chinese were massing for their seventh assault on Hill 235 when, seemingly at the eleventh hour, the promised air support arrived. Seven F-80 attacked with petrol filled bombs, rockets, and machine-gun fire which was followed by the welcome sighting of three transport aircraft. It was now 9.30 a.m. With an air drop of supplies on the way, and a relieving column of armour and infantry expected within the hour, an end to the ordeal seemed imminent.

Then, suddenly, the supply aircraft turned and flew away. At his command post, Carne heard that the relief column was not coming. Instead it was covering the withdrawal of 3rd Division to a new defence line south of Uijongbu, 24km (15 miles) to the south. The *Glosters* had done their work on the Imjin; now they must fight their way out to the south-west and make contact with the 1st Republic of Korean (ROK) Division. After making the last of many hard decisions during the battle — that the wounded would have to be left behind — Carne ordered the remnants of his gallant command to break out by companies.

The Imjin River battle was over, but for most of the surviving *Glosters* a new ordeal was about to begin: two years in brutal conditions as prisoners of war. Only five officers and 41 men, mostly from D Company, made it through the hills to

Above: Hill 235 where the Glosters made their last stand and upon which the drum major blew 'Reveille' as a final act of defiance.

Right: British vehicles wrecked by the retreating Glosters at the base of D Company's hill-top position.

rejoin 29th Brigade. All the others — 19 officers and 505 men — became prisoners of war, 34 of them dying in captivity. Their release was not secured until the Panmunjom peace agreement of 1953.

The *Glosters'* feat was an inspiration not only to the United Nations forces in Korea but to the Free World as a whole. The battalion received two awards of the Victoria Cross — to Carne and Lieutenant P.K.E. Edwards, who died leading an attack to retake *Castle Hill* — three D.S.O.s, six M.C.s, and a host of other awards. For it's achievement on the Imjin and its contribution to halting the Chinese offensive, the entire battalion was honoured with the United States Presidential Unit Citation.

Above: Men of the 1st Glosters on board H.M.S. Fowey *at Pusan prior to sailing for home on 20 November, 1951.*

Right: A deserted slit trench of one of the Gloster's forward positions overlooking the Imjin.

Bloody Ridge, U.S. 9th Infantry in Korea, 1951

Bloody Ridge does not exist on any map. It was the name given by *Stars and Stripes* to a particularly vicious close combat battle fought between the men of the 9th Infantry Regiment, 2nd Infantry Division, Eighth U.S. Army and the North Koreans for control of an ill-defined group of hills in the central highlands.

The engagement took place in August 1951 during the preliminary Kaesong armistice negotiations. At the time both sides were vying for territory in a series of independent, often futile actions along the unstable front line with a view to gaining their negotiators an advantage. Journalists were ordered to report activity generally so as not to give detailed information to the enemy. Indeed, they were so circumspect in their analysis of the battle which they christened *Bloody Ridge* that it is said that the men of the 9th Infantry who took part in it were unable to recognize their own exploits!

Bloody Ridge consists of three hills – 983, 940 and 773 – with their connecting ridges. Four razor-back ridges converge on the western extremity to form Hill 983, a sharp and well-defined point, and the highest peak on the ridgeline. To the east, separated from Hill 983 by a steep draw, lies the centre section of the complex approximately 1,000m (1,100 yds) long climaxing in a peak at Hill 940. To the east of that, a further 914m (1,000 yds) along the ridgeway, lies Hill 773.

At the time, *Bloody Ridge* was securely held by the North Koreans who had wasted no time in constructing a seemingly impregnable network of interlocking trenches, bunkers and sangars capable of withstanding an artillery barrage. The available woodland had been used intelligently to provide excellent camouflage, making accurate aerial reconnaissance particularly difficult.

The ridge had been the subject of concentrated fighting well before the Americans arrived in the sector. On 17 August a South Korean division had attempted to take advantage of the uncharacteristically foggy morning to launch a frontal assault against the entrenched enemy. After eight days of bitter fighting, they had secured their objective only to lose it the very next day. In all they had suffered over 1,000 casualties, including nearly 300 killed or missing, and had gained nothing.

Initial probing assaults by the 9th Infantry Regiment were no more successful. The 2nd Battalion managed to seize Hill 940 on the morning of 27 August but were unable to consolidate and were forced to withdraw that same afternoon. The 3rd Battalion, attacking from the east on the following day, faired no better. It failed even to reach its objective on Hill 773 and was forced back to its start line by an unexpected nocturnal counter-attack.

Inexplicably, the regimental commander now compounded his losses by ordering the 1st and 2nd Battalions to make a near suicidal frontal assault north against Hill 940. Not surprisingly, they were stopped in their tracks with heavy losses, particularly among the officers, and were only able to extract themselves with difficulty under the cover of massed 105mm howitzer fire supplied by the seven artillery battalions deployed in support.

The final survivors did not make it to safety until 4.00 a.m. and even then were not allowed to rest. Lieutenant Colonel Gaylord Bishop in command of the 1st Battalion ordered his men to remain on alert in case of attack but did allow them the luxury of their first meal in twenty-four hours. When the anticipated dawn attack failed to materialize, the exhausted and dispirited men were trucked to an assembly area to the south where they were introduced to their battle casualty replacements and given two hours to prepare themselves for another attack.

It is never a good time to introduce fresh reinforcements into a combat-hardened unit. Cliques form among the 'old soldiers' and mutual resentment quickly sets in. It is particularly dangerous to attempt to do this in the lull of a battle. Troops need time to get to know each other, to bond as a group and to build up trust. Every soldier must know that the man next to him will not freeze in his first engagement, that he can be relied upon under fire. The introduction of raw recruits into the 1st Battalion at this critical stage therefore did nothing to improve morale.

An American built and Commonwealth manned pontoon bridge under construction across the Imjin River.

At midday on 31 August the battalion was again carried back the short way to the battle area, this time to attack Hill 773 from the east. Having debussed some way from their objective they formed into company lines, with Company C in the lead, to continue on foot. At the eastern tip of the ridgeline they veered left, deployed into single file and began their unenviable climb towards the unseen enemy. While this was going on Colonel Bishop had positioned himself in an observation post on high ground held by the 38th Infantry Regiment further to the east. In so doing he had hoped to be able to maintain overall control but had failed to take into account the morning fog and haze then prevailing in the area. He was soon out of touch with his leading elements who were forced to climb blind.

Advancing to contact, proceeding steadily towards the enemy perhaps for several hours until brought under effective fire, is never easy. It is particularly difficult with exhausted troops who know that when the fighting begins they will be caught on a narrow ridge from which they cannot easily deploy. Not surprisingly therefore, Company C began to lose momentum, stopping frequently to allow the scouts to ensure safe passage ahead.

When eventually Company C came under fire, from an unseen machine gun dug in some 150m (165 yds) to its front, it sustained immediate casualties including its commander, Lieutenant Orlando Campisi, and one of his section leaders. During the subsequent firefight both of the remaining officers were wounded leaving the company leaderless and foundering. Fortunately the radio operator, Corporal John Traux, remained uninjured and was able to advise the still unsighted Bishop of the dilemma. Bishop at once ordered Company B, reinforced by elements of Company D, to move through Company C's position and continue the advance. Lieutenant Mallard, the battalion adjutant, was ordered to assume command of Company C and, in the absence of supporting artillery fire frustrated by the fog, to give the maximum amount of cover as was practical to the attackers.

Above: Sangars such as this, placed on top of each of the hills, held up the American advance.

Below: South Korean troops man a U.S. manufactured heavy machine gun. Poor visibility reduced the effectiveness of such weapons on Bloody Ridge.

Company B had hardly begun to move before it too began to founder. Lieutenant Joseph Burkett, in command of 1st Platoon, was ordered to spearhead the continued advance. He was given a radio with which to keep in touch with the Company and was told that the four machine guns available would provide covering fire but was otherwise given little direction. Ignorant of the North Korean dispositions (no one from Company C had been able to give him any real estimate of the direction of the enemy fire which had earlier caused them so much trouble) and with 16 of his 22 men inexperienced replacements, Burkett's main aim was simply to keep his platoon intact. Warily he advanced the 140m (153 yds) to the first of a series of knolls. Having ordered the bulk of his men to form a defensive position he proceeded with three of his 'veterans' to the top of the knoll, some 10m (32.8 ft) above, in search of the enemy.

Left: A machine gun post laying down covering fire.

Burkett now used his limited supply of grenades to excellent effect. Sheltering below the rim of the knoll he hurled a missile as far as he was able on to the top. As it exploded he and his colleagues stormed over the top to find the area unoccupied.

As the four stalwarts moved warily towards the next knoll some 50m (54yds) away the enemy fire, although still random and sporadic, began to increase in intensity. Suddenly the supporting fire from the four machine guns stopped. Burkett attempted straight away to radio company headquarters to order an immediate resumption but found to his disgust that the radio was dead. Hurling it to the ground in anger (an action that could have done

Below: The U.S. infantry mans a gun pit. The rifle bayonet would not normally be fitted.

Left: Infantrymen in the front line rest during a lull in the battle.

nothing to improve the morale of his men) he ordered his platoon forward. Only later did he learn that the machine gunners had stopped firing because the fog was by then completely obscuring the forward troops who were beginning to move dangerously close to the line of fire.

As the advance continued Burkett was forced to concentrate more on the action ahead and less on the state of his men behind. The raw soldiers began to string out along the ridge destroying the final vestiges of order.

Suddenly Burkett spotted a well-camouflaged bunker ahead. The occupants began to hurl grenade after grenade at the Americans. Most fell harmlessly but others did not, landing among the petrified young

Below: A heavy mortar battery fires on Communist positions in the hills in support of the infantry.

conscripts most of whom just lay still, as if rooted to the spot, making no attempt to try to escape the explosions.

Three B.A.R. (Browning Automatic Rifle) teams were now sent forward by Captain Krzyzowski of Company B to assist the by now static 1st Platoon in the clearance of the bunker. When these proved unsuccessful Burkett at last abandoned attempts at frontal assault. Instead, he studied the terrain surrounding the bunker to seek an unsighted approach route. Through the fog he ascertained that both the bunker and his platoon were positioned on the north side of the ridge. He and a squad leader, Sergeant Charles Hartman, therefore slid silently down the south side of the ridge and proceeded to crawl to an area even with the bunker opposite. Once in position they hurled grenades into the enemy post, forcing the enemy into the open where they could be more easily neutralized by fire from the B.A.R.s. Having taken the bunker at tremendous cost, (both Burkett and Hartman were, in fact, injured in the final engagement), the remnants of the platoon were ordered to pull back to the company perimeter. This allowed the enemy to regain much of the hard-won initiative.

The next morning, 1st September, brought the men of 1st Battalion a much-needed break. The sky was clear and bright, the fog cleared at dawn and the artillery positions were able to report that they could at last register on the enemy targets. Company A was ordered to take the lead with Lieutenant Mallard's Company C in support.

Company A advanced under cover of an artillery barrage without incident until the leading elements reached Burkett's bunker which surprisingly had not been reoccupied by a grateful enemy. When the company commander, Lieutenant Elden Foulk, and two of his platoon commanders were injured, the impetus again sapped and Company A came to a halt in the very ground occupied the day before by its colleagues in Burkett's platoon.

Colonel Bishop, still entrenched on his far away hill, now ordered Company B forward to take the place of Company A. After a five minute grenade engagement the bunker, severely damaged in the previous day's fighting, was overrun. By 10.00 a.m., Bishop was able to report that his men at last held the three prominent knolls leading to Hill 773 still some 250m (273 yds) away.

At 2.00 p.m., after only minimal rest and now down to 50 men, Company B resumed its advance towards the Hill. Having negotiated the first 100m (120 yds) without incident the hapless Americans came under concerted grenade attack from

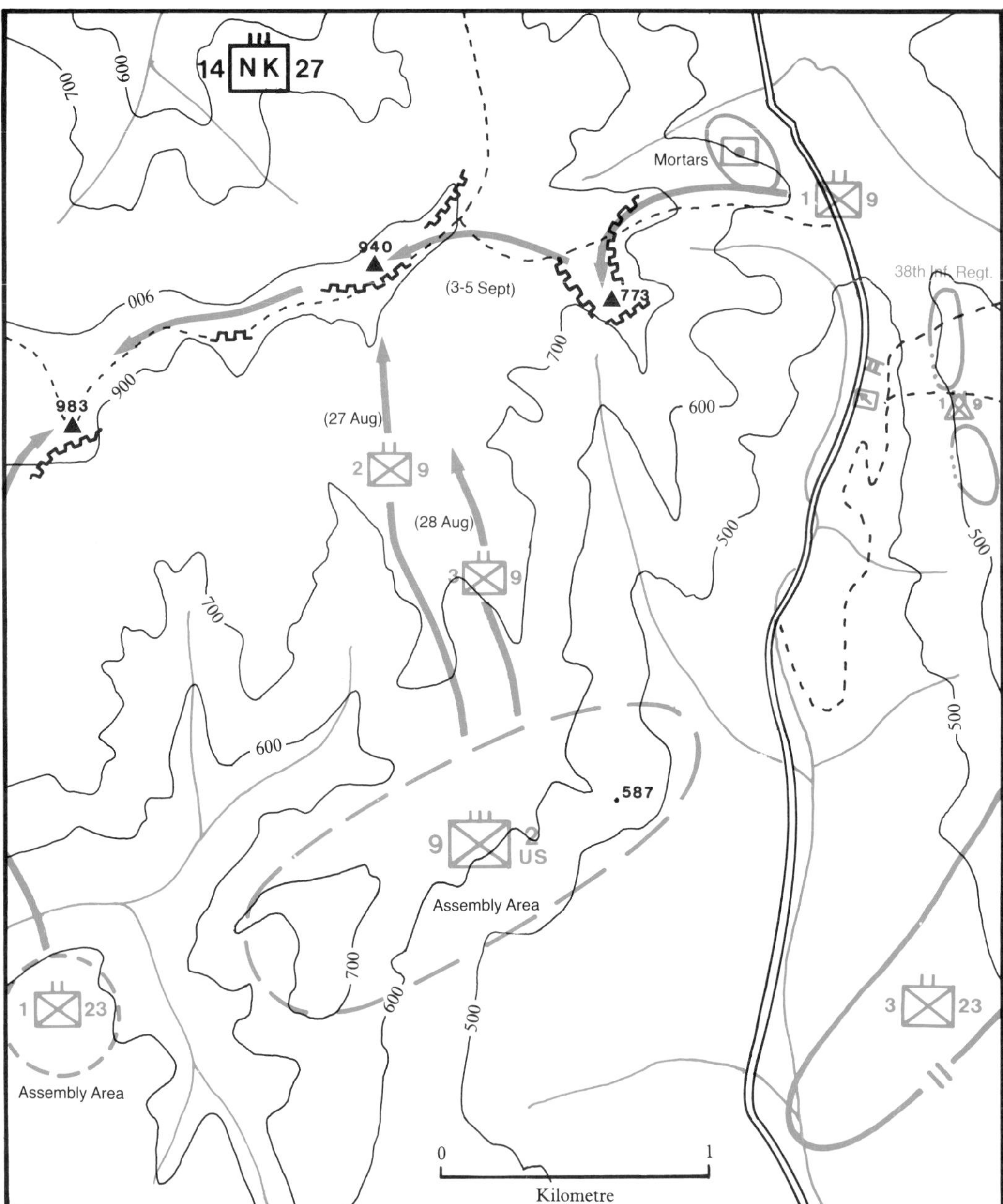

Bloody Ridge vividly portrayed the bravery but ill-preparedness of the American troops in Korea. The commanding officer took no direct part in the fighting, preferring to direct the battle from the neighbouring ridge. Leadership was often lacking and raw recruits were drafted into the lead units during the very crux of the assault, so adding to the confusion. Positions which might easily have been by-passed were instead attacked frontally, often with horrific results. When air support and artillery were muted by lack of visibility the infantry continued its attack against the dug-in enemy regardless, compounding its own casualty figures in the process. In the end the North Korean survivors simply abandoned Bloody Ridge to the Americans, melting away to strengthen the next prominent position to the north.

three independent bunkers. To compound their problems, a machine gun opened sporadic fire from Hill 940 to the left. Five men fell injured and yet again the advance faltered. By now, however, the company commanders seemed to have established a more consistent policy towards static enemy positions. Bazookas (3.5in rocket launchers) were brought forward and quickly destroyed the first bunker while concentrated fire from the battalion's 60mm mortars was brought to bear on the hilltop. Following Burkett's pattern of the previous day P.F.C. Edward Jenkins then crawled forward on the opposite side of the ridge to within throwing distance of the two remaining bunkers, silencing both with well-placed grenades. As darkness approached, the 22 remaining members of Company A and 20 members of Company B pulled back to a battalion defensive perimeter. Early the next morning six replacement officers and 150 men joined the battalion, immediately destroying the trust and camaraderie which had built up among the survivors of the previous three days.

On 2 September, 9th Regiment at last began to make concerted use of its available potential. A tank and quad .50 flakwagon were deployed on the road to engage enemy positions on Hill 940. At the same time, Lieutenant Mallard was ordered to establish an observation post on the most westerly of the captured knolls. From there, he was to direct both the tank and the two companies of heavy mortars which to date had played little part in the battle, artillery fire was directed independently on to Hill 940 and airstrikes were put in against the west end of the ridge. Only now did the battalion group begin to function fully as a unit. There was no formal attack on 2 September although a few fighting patrols were mounted to probe the enemy defences.

Hostilities on the next morning commenced at 10.30 a.m. with an air strike directed by Lieutenant Robert

Below: A bazooka team from the 9th Infantry fire at point-blank range into a Communist sangar.

assumed command of Company A in lieu of the injured Lieutenant Faulk. Two flights of four aircraft each dropped a total of eight napalm and eight anti-personnel bombs on their targets, causing the enemy considerable losses.

Shortly after 1.00 p.m. Company C, now up to 85 men strong, resumed the attack. The riflemen were divided into three platoons. Two were made up of experienced soldiers, some of whom had only joined the battalion three days earlier. The third platoon consisted entirely of novices. Both 'experienced' platoons were pushed forward against a new ring of bunkers and were cut to pieces. At last flame-throwers, the ideal close-quarter anti-bunker weapon, were brought forward. Supported by the third platoon they soon made short work of the enemy positions allowing the remnants of the

A G.I. digs in next to a wrecked tank. During the fluid battles of 1951 such positions frequently changed hands.

Lacaze, a battalion officer who had recently company to move forward and secure the peak of Hill 773.

Two days later Colonel Bishop's battalion occupied Hills 940 and 983without opposition. The enemy had simply melted away to strengthen the next prominent position in the north, which would itself ultimately have to be taken.

To the politicians 1/9th Infantry had captured a 'crucial' hill and had therefore gained a victory although few successes could have been more Pyrrhic. Many lessons should have been learned on *Bloody Ridge* but unfortunately were not.Commanders have to be close to the battle not on a neighbouring hill. No battle can be won without planning and all available resources must be exploited at all times. Officers cannot hope to command respectuntil they have earned it. It is therefore ridiculous drafting young sub-lieutenants into a battle and giving them immediate they have earned it. It is therefore ridiculous drafting young sub-lieutenants into a battle and giving them immediate command tasks; their men will simply ignore them. Similarly, it is pointless drafting raw recruits into a combat engaged unit. They will not mix, fit in or be of any real use.

The men of 1/9th infantry were unquestionably as brave as they were ill-directed. More planning and thorough prior reconnaissance would certainly have led to a speedier victory and, more importantly, to a considerable reduction in casualties.

Malaya,
The Commonwealth v Marxism, 1948–1960

It took Europe's maritime powers 400 years to build the empires which crumbled in the aftermath of World War II. Militant Communism, exported first from the Soviet Union and then from China, took a mere 30 years to establish an iron control over Poland, Rumania, Bulgaria, Hungry, Czechoslovakia, East Germany, the Republic of China, North Korea, and the majority of South-East Asia. Between 1945 and 1950, Communist-controlled territory expanded at the rate of 155sq km (60 square miles) per hour.

For many years, Communism seemed to be an unstoppable world force — impervious to political manoeuvre and submersion and unbeatable by military force, particularly in guerrilla warfare for which Communist idealism was a potent fuel. A half success was scored in Korea between 1950 and 1953, but the Korean War ended with North Korea triumphantly Communist, ready and willing to take over the South. The shattering defeat of the French in Indo-China by the guerrillas of the Viet Minh left Vietnam similarly partitioned, on the verge of a protracted war which ended in the most humiliating defeat in the history of the United States. Vietnam remains the classic victory of Communist expansion through guerrilla infiltration, indoctrination, terror and ultimately by military supremacy, completely discounting the efforts of the most powerful military nation on earth.

Between 1948 and 1960, however, the British in Malaya showed that Communist guerrillas could be taken on at their own game and comprehensively defeated — not merely in terms of policing and firepower, but in the battle for the hearts and minds of the people. At first sight this appears all the more unlikely because it had been in Malaya, with the shattering defeat by the invading Japanese in 1941-42, that the prestige of Imperial Britain had suffered its heaviest, most humiliating reverse.

During the war, the British in India had supported the Malayan Communist Party (M.C.P.) and its leader Chin Peng as an anti-Japanese guerrilla force. Almost entirely Chinese, the M.C.P. fought not only to expel the Japanese but to achieve equality for the minority Chinese population in postwar Malaya. When this was denied by Clement Atlee's postwar British government in the face of Malay opposition, Chen Ping re-formed his guerrillas as the Malayan Races Liberation Army (M.R.L.A.) and began a campaign of intensifying terrorism in June 1948.

The M.R.L.A.'s objective was the undermining of every aspect of normal life under British colonial rule in the Federated Malay States. M.R.L.A. tactics included the murder of estate owners, colonial officials, and police, the destruction and sabotage of estates, mines, and factories, and intimidating the rural population into cooperation. The guerrillas, referred to originally as bandits but later as C.T.s (Communist Terrorists), used their wartime weapons caches and jungle fighting expertise to operate from jungle bases. An organization of underground sympathizers in the countryside, the Min Yuen, supplied Chen Ping's guerrillas with money, intelligence, food, and medicines. By means of material destruction, terror, and the effective wrecking of Malaya's economy, Chen Ping planned to create so much chaos that the British would abandon the country and let the Communists take over.

For the first two years, 1948-1950, the M.R.L.A.'s campaign proceeded without

Above: A Communist prisoner taken in Malaya. Many such individuals were 'turned' by the British policy of hearts and minds.

Below: British national servicemen patrolling deep in the Malayan jungle.

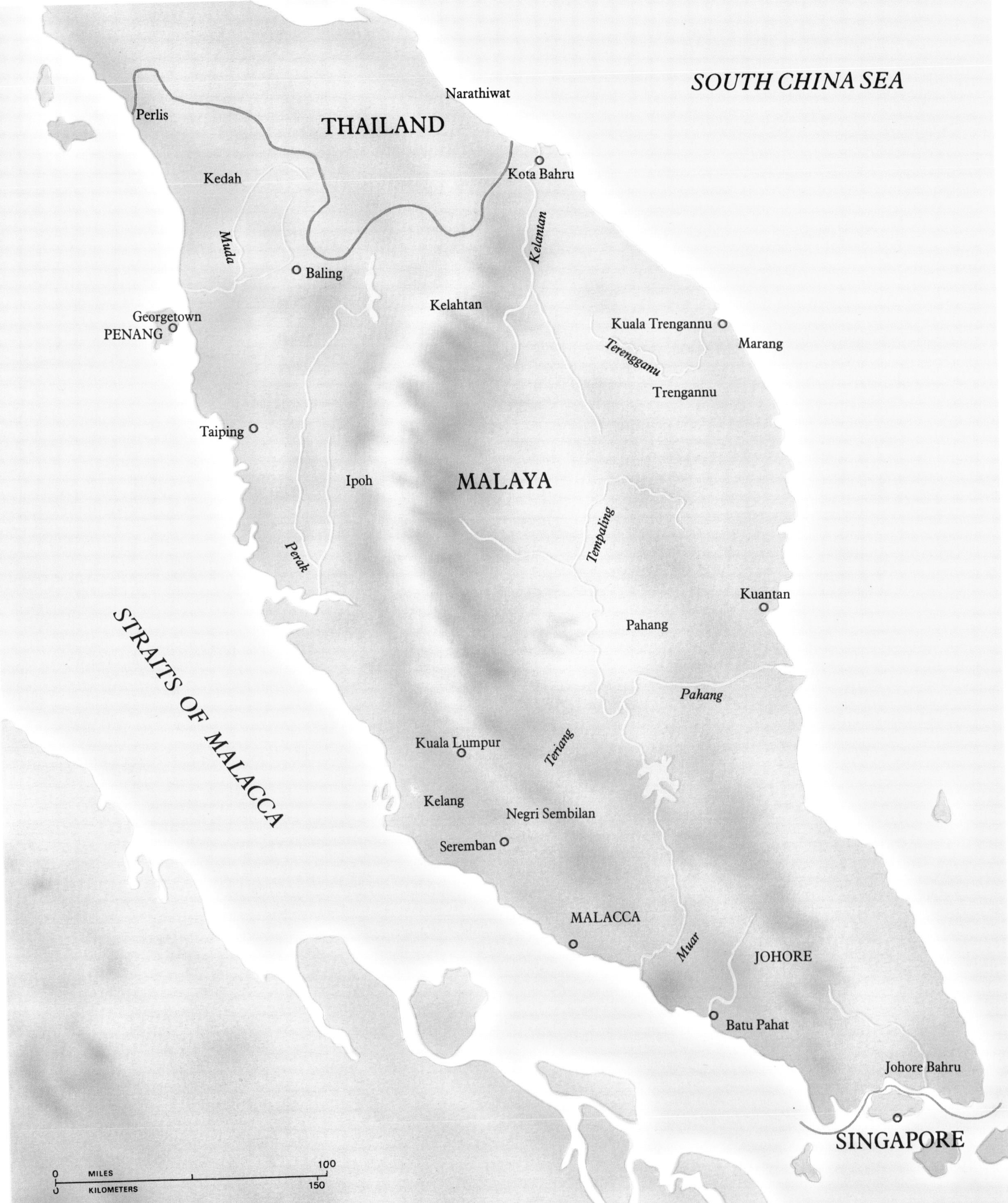
SOUTH CHINA SEA
Narathiwat
Perlis
THAILAND
Kota Bahru
Kedah
Muda
Kelantan
Baling
Kelahtan
Georgetown
PENANG
Kuala Trengannu
Marang
Terengganu
Trengannu
Taiping
Ipoh
MALAYA
Tempaling
Perak
Kuantan
STRAITS OF MALACCA
Pahang
Pahang
Kuala Lumpur
Teriang
Kelang
Negri Sembilan
Seremban
MALACCA
Muar
JOHORE
Batu Pahat
Johore Bahru
SINGAPORE
0 MILES 100
0 KILOMETERS 150

Between 1948 and 1962 the British Government turned the near certainty of a Communist takeover in Malaya into a victory for democracy. Painstaking steps were taken to turn the hearts and minds of the Chinese minority against the Communist Terrorists (CTs) whom they had once supported. Tough controls over the sale and movement of food were introduced in an attempt to eliminate supplies reaching the CTs with every crop recorded in minute detail. The SAS were reformed and introduced into the jungle to pursue and destroy the enemy in his own lairs. Up to 25,000 British troops with 15,000 Gurkhas were employed in supporting search and destroy missions. In 1957, when Malaysia finally gained its independence, there were no more than 1,500 CTs still operating, of whom 309 were killed that year and 209 surrendered. In 1960 the insurrection was finally abandoned, the remaining terrorists fled to Thailand.

Below: British soldiers check a village. The troops are relaxed, suggesting that the village is friendly.

Above: An Australian soldier carrying an Owen sub-machine gun on patrol.

any serious check from the British. The will to defeat the C.T.s was not lacking on the British side; what was needed was an effective strategy and its firm implementation. Merely to police roads, garrison towns and villages, and make random arrests was not enough, and the postwar British forces in Malaya were trained for little else. They certainly lacked the experience, as postwar National Servicemen, to seek out and destroy the C.T.s in the jungle. All this was to change, however, in April 1950 when Lieutenant-General Sir Harold Briggs was appointed as Director of Operations. From the methodical assessment which he brought to the problem of Communist terrorism, Briggs produced the master plan for the defeat of the M.R.L.A.

In essence, the Briggs Plan took Mao Tse-Tung's theories of guerrilla war and turned them against the guerrillas, starting with 'the sea of the people in which the guerrillas would swim like fish'. Guaranteed normality and security in the daily life of the people would effectively leave the C.T. 'fish' high and dry. Malaya must be combed, sector by sector from south to north, in a rigorous collaboration between the military, the police, and the civil administration. 'New Villages' would be built for the protection of the population most at risk: those who lived on the edge of the jungle. To starve the C.T.s, Briggs proposed tough controls over the sale and movement of food, with every purchase and every crop harvested recorded in minute detail. This strategy must not appear to be a tyrannical British imposition; Malay political and community leaders must be involved in the process. Thus the Malays who joined the fight against the C.T.s would be building for their own independence — an independence in which Communism would have no part.

Field Marshal Lord Harding, Commander-in-Chief in Singapore, warmly endorsed the Briggs Plan but made one vital recommendation to the British government — that the civilian High Commissioner be replaced by a general with full powers over the armed forces, the police, and the civil administration. The evident need for drastic action was rammed home in October 1951 when the C.T.s assassinated the High Commissioner, Sir Henry Gurney, in an ambush. In the same month the Attlee government fell, and one of the first acts of Churchill's new Conservative government was to appoint General Sir Gerald Templer to the post recommended by Harding.

Templer arrived in Malaya in February 1952 not only with a unique combination of powers but with instructions that in due course Malaya was to become self-governing — a deadly long-term weapon against the aspirations of the M.R.L.A. A dynamic personality in his own right, Templer wasted no time in putting the Briggs Plan into action. He turned all operational details over to Major-General Sir Rob Lockhart, who by the spring of 1952 commanded a total of 45,000 men in 24 battalions, 25,000 of them British. To man the special hunter-killer platoons intended to seek out and destroy the C.T.s in the jungle, there were 15,000 Gurkhas; 22SAS Regiment was revived — also on Harding's recommendation — under its wartime leader, Major David Stirling. Together wiith police and Malay Home Guard units, Templer and Lockhart had some 250,000 men to turn against the M.R.L.A. which, in any given year, never exceeded a total strength of about 6,000 C.T.s.

The new energy and practicality which Templer brought to the war against the M.R.L.A. was almost immediately effective. The stringent new food regulations, in which every tin of food sold had to be punctured by the seller to prevent

Above: An SAS patrol awaiting inspection in a jungle clearing at Ulu Langat, near Kuala Lumpur.

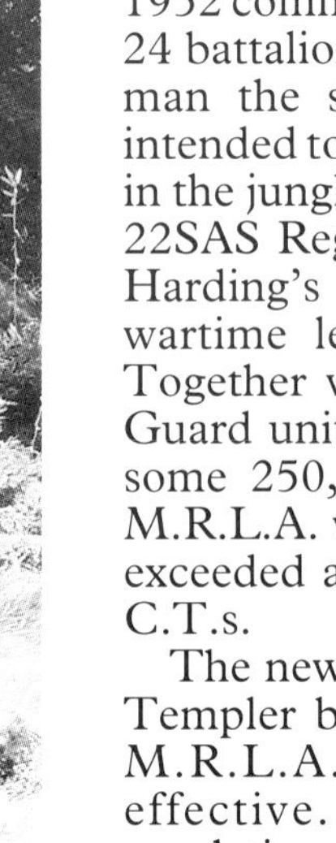

Below: A Whirlwind 2 helicopter lands in a jungle clearing. Patrols were often inserted by this method.

SAS troopers emplaning before making a drop into the jungle in North Perak.

hoarding, had by the end of 1953 reduced the M.R.L.A to a position where it was forced to spend an estimated 90 percent of its time organizing food supplies. The New Villages, equipped with shops, medical centres, schools, electricity, and water, were not only easier to defend and popular with their inhabitants, they were obvious investments in Malay's future, of a nature which the M.R.L.A. could not hope to emulate.

The aggressive new style of jungle patrolling was backed up with helicopter supply flights to extend the duration of patrols, with stepped up air surveillance and coastal patrolling by light naval craft. Templer's implementation of the Briggs Plan made maximum use of Malay's natural geography, which was another factor working against the M.R.L.A. The narrowness of the Malayan peninsula made it impossible for the C.T.s to emulate the Viet Minh in Indo-China and, when faced with an excessive frontal threat, faded away into the hinterland.

The patrolling was backed up by intelligence work in unheard of depth. Dossiers were built up of all C.T. leaders and their groups, and the clearing of new White Areas, freed of Communist influence, was accelerated by the insertion of intelligence and psychological warfare teams. Massive rewards were offered for information, the biggest being £30,000 for Chen Ping himself. One of Templer's most thorough techniques was tested in the town of Tanjong Malim, a centre of intensive operations, and was supervised by Templer in person. The inhabitants of the town were mustered, addressed, and requested to give information. When this was not immediately forthcoming a 22-hour curfew restricted the inhabitants to their homes, where they were required to complete detailed written questionnaires on their knowledge of C.T. activities. The result was a startling amount of information, and Templer used the technique again and again.

By the end of its first year, Templer's implementation of the Briggs Plan was already showing dramatic results. The 1951 figures for victims of C.T. killings had been 1,195 for the security forces and 1,024 for the civilian population. Comparable figures for 1952 were respectively 664 and 632, dropping in 1953 to 209 and 143. It was the same story with the total for C.T. incidents, the intensity of which was the only means which the M.R.L.A. had for displaying its ability to strike at the British. There were 2,333 major incidents in 1951, dropping to 1,389 in 1952 and 258 in 1953; minor incidents declined from 3,749 in 1951, to 2,338 in 1952 and 912 in 1953.

If Templer's methods brought about a drastic reduction in the M.R.L.A's freedom of operations and effectiveness, they also carved steadily into the M.R.L.A.'s manpower at a steady 1,000 C.T.s killed per year between 1951 and 1953 — excluding the unknown number of C.T. casualties who died unrecorded in the jungle. More significantly, they increased the number of C.T. surrenders: men who could no longer stand the ever more wretched, starved conditions which the British and their Malay supporters were forcing on the would be 'liberators'. The 1953 figure for C.T. surrenders was 372 — another encouraging sign of the success of Templer's strategy.

Chen Ping's only real hope was a mounting tide of popular discontent at the British regulations and restrictions necessary to make the Briggs Plan work, but this was a tide which never even began to flow. The reason was the encouraging progress made under Templer's direction on the political front. In 1953, Tunku Abdul Rahman's United Malays' National Organization was expanded to include Chinese and Indian organizations and became the Alliance Party. Its aim was political independence under British guarantee. After electoral successes for the Tunku in 1955, Chen Ping asked for a meeting at which the Tunku's only offer was unconditional surrender. Chen Ping returned to the jungle, to continue a struggle which he now knew to be hopeless.

Templer's last achievement before returning to Britain in October 1954 was to hand back the reins of the civil administration, but this was achieved without any let up of the military pressure on the M.R.L.A. In 1957, when the new state of Malaysia finally gained its Independence (31 August) only about 1,500 C.T.s were still operating in the country; 331 were killed that year,. and 209 surrendered. Figures for C.T. incidents in 1957 were 40 major and 150 minor; security force and police casualties were 44, civilian casualties 31. By 1960, when Chen Ping finally abandoned the struggle and withdrew into Thailand, he only had about 500 effectives left. In that year the terrorist uprising was finally squashed and the Malayan Emergency declared over. It had lasted 12 years, but its decisive months had been from February 1952 to October 1954 when Templer and his lieutenants, military and civilian, had written a unique chapter in military history.

Top: The first Malayan squadron of the Federation Armoured Corps move slowly along a jungle track wary of Communist ambush.

Above: A Gurkha patrol cuts its way through the intense undergrowth of the Malayan jungle.

Left: Between 1948 and 1950 there were 700 separate attacks against the railway. A few resulted in spectacular derailments.

Dien Bien Phu, The French Withdrawal, 1954

Dien Bien Phu was one of the most famous and important battles of the twentieth century. It heralded the demise of the French Empire in Indo-China and marked the beginning of the end of Western influence in that area: it was as much a battle between ideologies as armies.

Before Dien Bien Phu, French mastery of Tonkin, the northern province of modern Vietnam, had never been absolute. Localized guerrilla actions, and even rebellions, had been common and had always been suppressed with uncompromising brutality. An unsuccessful uprising at Yen Bay in 1929, however, had served to establish a pattern of resistance which had led a year later to the creation of the Indo-Chinese Communist Party (I.C.C.P.)

For ten years the I.C.C.P. had bided its time, its founder, Nguyen ai Quoc (soon to be known to the world as Ho Chi Minh), shunning open confrontation. Instead he had established a network of clandestine cells throughout the provinces of Tonkin, and Annan to the south, to be activated should French influence in the area ever wane.

In 1940, France had fallen to the Germans and Indo-China had come under control of the collaborationist Vichy Government. Exploiting the situation to the full, Ho Chi Minh had drawn together the various Vietnamese nationalist groups and in March 1941, had formed the *Viet Nam Doc Lap Dong Minh Hoi*, or *League for the Independence of Vietnam,* soon to be recognized universally as the *Viet Minh.*

Resistance activities had been increased and allied assistance sought. When the Japanese seized control of Indo-China from the then Gaullist French colonial regime in March 1945, the Viet Minh, recognizing another window of opportunity, seized the power vacuum in the countryside, expanded Communist control (often brutally), and made ready to assume political power.

On 2 September 1945 Ho Chi Minh celebrated the unexpectedly rapid surrender of the Japanese by entering Hanoi and declaring the establishment of a Democratic Republic of Vietnam. However his jubilation had been short lived. British troops soon landed at Saigon, driving the Communists out of the south, while Chinese Nationalists advanced from the north. In February 1946 Ho was forced to approach the French to seek their assistance in expelling the Chinese in exchange for which he was forced to relinquish total independence accepting instead the creation of a unified Vietnam within a greater French-controlled Indo-Chinese Federation. In March, Chinese troops were replaced in Hanoi by the French who at once set about engineering a series of provocative incidents. In November 1945 the Viet Minh were ordered to quit the major port of Haiphong and in December were expelled from Hanoi. Embittered, Ho Chi Minh retreated to his safe bases in the countryside from which he undertook a series of guerrilla operations. Subsequent attempts by the French to organize large scale search and destroy operations against the Viet Minh failed; indeed they simply alienated the local population encouraging them more and more to offer active support

Pro-French Vietnamese troops patrolling through rough terrain.

to the Communists.

In April 1949 the Viet Minh, now under command of the brilliant Vo Nguyen Giap, went on to the offensive, successfully attacking the series of outposts which the French had constructed to the north of Hanoi. In February 1950, strengthened by massive assistance from the Communist Chinese who were now in control of the North, Giap attacked the garrison at Lao Khe, close to the border. Despite the intervention of crack French parachute troops the garrison fell and with it the town of Dong Khe. Within months the French were forced to evacuate the border area, losing over 6,000 troops in the process. Subsequent attempts by Giap to organize his irregulars into conventional units for an attack on Hanoi met with less success. Quick to recover and now reinforced by a number of élite units, the French constructed a series of defended positions, known as the *De Lattre Line*, around Hanoi. These they made impregnable with the skilful deployment of overlapping artillery, airborne and fighter cover. In a series of attacks the Viet Minh lost heavily on one occasion sustaining over 3,000 casualties in a single five-day action.

In 1952 the war took a bloodier turn. The French withdrew from their most isolated bases leaving the northern areas firmly in Communist hands. Instead they mounted a series of large-scale punitive attacks against known enemy positions. Most had become bogged down and had been forced to retire without attaining their objective; many resulted in massive French losses.

In April 1953 Giap invaded Northern Laos forcing the French to commit their limited reserves to the Plain of Jars to protect the Laotian capital from the Pathet Lao guerrillas who had risen up in support

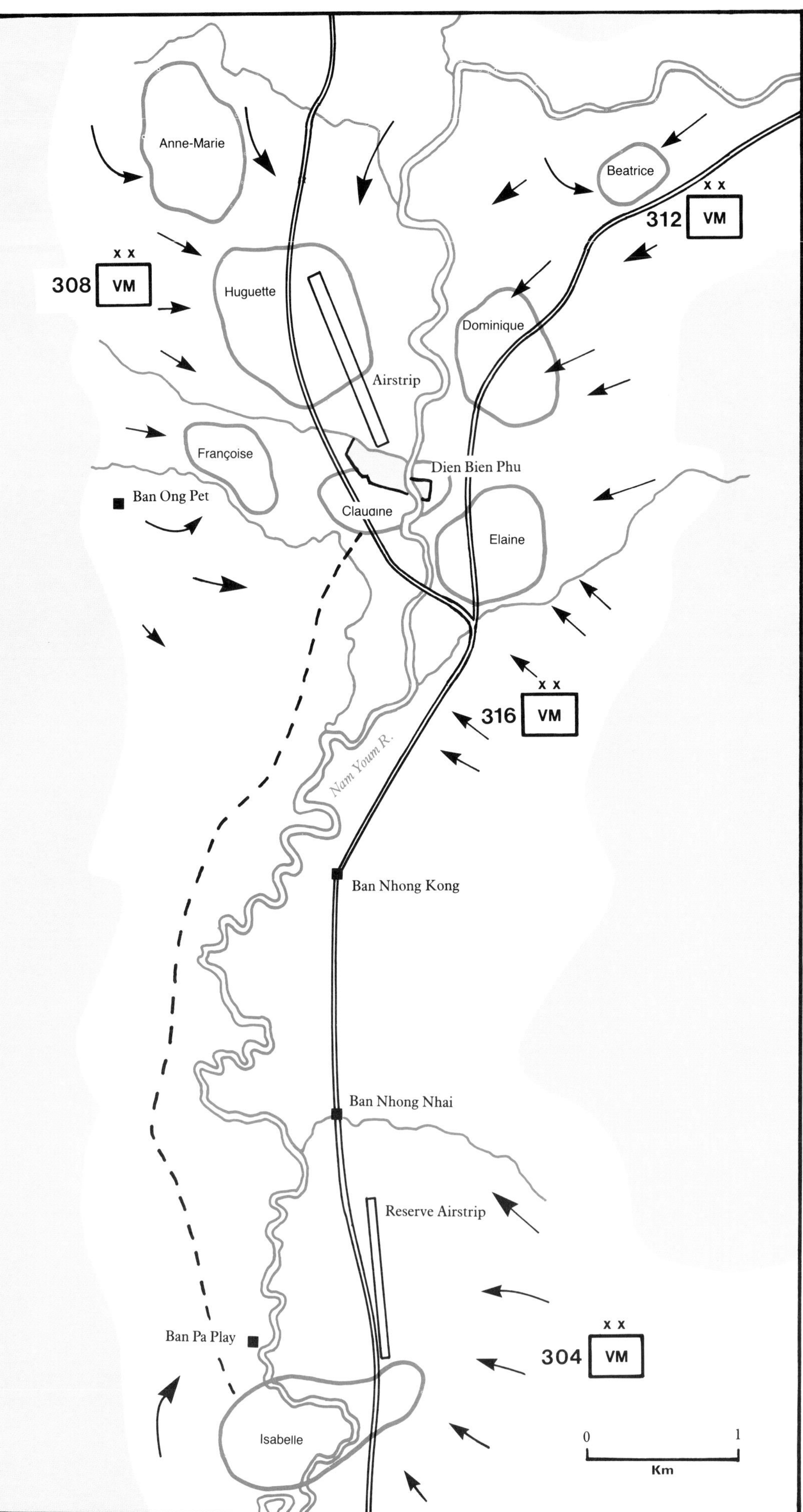

The French defences were set in a heart-shaped valley 12 miles long and eight miles wide dominated by mountains on all sides. The command bunker, hospital and main communications centre were dug into the village itself. Strongpoints, each reputedly names after one of the commander's several mistresses, were constructed to protect the headquarters from infantry, though not artillery, attack. Huguette, Claudine, Elaine *and* Dominique *were connected by a network of trenches and protected by minefields and barbed wire.* Anne-Marie, Béatrice *and* Gabrielle *were constructed as stand-alone positions closer to the perimeter, with* Isabelle *dug in isolation some four miles to the south to cover the small auxiliary airstrip. From the moment that Giap's artillery firing from the mountains began to dominate the French positions, defeat for the Colonial power became inevitable.*

Above: A high level briefing at Dien Bien Phu. Later it would become suicidal to venture into the open in daylight.

of the Viet Minh. Fearful of over-extending their fully stretched resources the Viet Minh, having secured the annual opium crop, withdrew to the comparative safety of their northern strongholds.

Inexplicably, the French interpreted this patent act of regrouping as a victory and came to reason that Giap was no longer strong enough to attack a fully protected defensive position. Accordingly, they decided to entice him into battle by creating an artificial target against which the Communists might pound themselves to oblivion. They chose the village of Dien Bien Phu, close to the Laotian border, as an ideal killing ground and in so doing condemned the bulk of the French colonial army to certain annihilation.

Despite its being held by the enemy at the time as a site for a future battle, Dien Bien Phu had a number of advantages. It straddled a Viet Minh supply route into Laos and could not therefore be ignored. It had its own primitive airstrip and was surrounded by a series of hills, each of which could be turned into an independent fortification. Situated on the edge of the T'ai Mountains, it was surrounded by a population still inherently loyal to France. It was, however, overlooked by high mountains and, but for the airstrip, was completely cut off from Hanoi, some 170 miles away.

Command of the base was delegated to Christian Marie Ferdinand de la Croix de Castries, a 52 year old veteran renowned for his bravery, skill, and determination. Wounded and captured by the Germans in 1940, he had escaped to join the Free French, seeing considerable action on the advance into Italy. Posted to Indo-China in 1946, he had quickly gained a fine reputation for valour in battle but a less savoury one as a womanizer and gambler when off duty.

The 12 mile long and eight mile wide heart-shaped valley was secured by six battalions of the French 1st and 2nd Airborne Battle Groups on 20 November 1953. Having ejected the two companies of Viet Minh stationed in the village, the French paratroopers immediately set about fortifying the perimeter by constructing a series of strong points each reputedly

Below: Viet Minh troops inspect two captured French jeeps after the fall of Dien Bien Phu.

named after one of de Castries' several mistresses. The command headquarters, the nerve centre of the defence, was dug into the village itself. Strong point *Huguette* was constructed to the west, *Claudine* to the south, *Eliane* to the east and *Dominique* to the north-east. Each was connected by a network of trenches and protected by minefields and barbed wire. Similar outposts were created beyond the central *hedgehog* commanding the approaches from the north-west, *Anne-Marie,* north-east *Béatrice,* and north, *Gabrielle. Isabelle* was dug in isolation, some four miles to the south, to cover a small auxiliary airfield. Artillery was dug in, six Bearcat fighters were stationed on the main airstrip while ten M-24 light tanks were held in reserve.

Having sought Giap's advice, Ho Chi Minh decided to accept the French challenge to battle, but under his own terms. He did not rush his nearest available troops into early combat to be destroyed piecemeal as the French had anticipated, but instead put into operation one of the finest logistical moves of modern history. True to the maxim, '*strike to win, strike only when success is certain, or do not strike at all*', he decided to commit 50,000 troops to the Dien Bien Phu. Giap ordered the mobilization of two armies, one a peasant force of 20,000 men, women and children to hack new jungle routes for weapons and supplies, the other his regular army which

Above: French paratroopers land to reinforce the Dien Bien Phu. All would later suffer death or imprisonment.

Below: Thousands of bicycles were presed into service to transport food and ammunition to the Viet Minh troops surrounding the French base.

was forcemarched twenty miles a day towards its objective. Throughout the North untold thousands of other peasants were ordered to bring in enough rice to last the Army for several months. 'Brigades of iron horses' – bicycles – were drafted in to transport the rice forward. To add to Giap's administrative difficulties, his forces could only move at night, avoiding the main roads because of the continuous French air patrols. Remorselessly they gathered around the French defences, slowly but surely gaining in strength until, by the advent of 1954, they had the base completely cut off and surrounded.

By now the French high command had learned that it was not dealing with the two divisions anticipated but with four. The possibility of evacuation was mooted but soon discounted as impractical. Instead, the garrison was increased to 15,000, half of them Algerians, Vietnamese and Legionnaires, and ordered to hold out at all cost.

Unknown to the French, who had 28 American 105mm howitzers at Dien Bien Phu, the Viet Cong were vastly superior in artillery. During the months of preparation and unseen by French aerial reconnaissance, they had man-handled over 200 'steel elephants' through the jungle and now had 48 Soviet and Chinese 105mm howitzers and 150 lighter artillery pieces at their disposal. By super-human effort involving nothing more sophisticated than flesh and muscle, relay teams roped to the guns had pulled them inch by inch – half a mile a day – through 50 miles of jungle.

Immediately prior to the attack, Giap had a three-to-one advantage in firepower and manpower. His artillery, itself perfectly secreted in caves and trenches, overlooked the enemy. In the space of weeks Dien Bien Phu had been turned from an impregnable fortress to a prison.

The attack itself began a little after 5.00 p.m. on 13 March 1954. The French had been forewarned of the attack but were nonetheless taken completely by surprise at its ferocity. All 200 of Giap's artillery pieces were brought to bear in an hour long barrage against the airfield and command centres. *Béatrice,* one of the closest outposts to the central section, was stormed and overwhelmed by an entire division; 500 of its 700 defenders were killed or captured.

Gabrielle and *Anne-Marie* were attacked by 'human wave' infantry and fell on the two successive days. By 16 March the airstrip was exposed and virtually unusable, making the evacuation of the wounded precarious in the extreme. (Limited flights did still manage to take off until 27 March when a hospital transport was destroyed

Above: An Orders Group precedes a French airborne counter-attack against a forward Viet Minh position.

Below: Viet Minh artillery shells the airfield. Note the fox-hole in the foreground.

on the runway.) Colonel Charles Piroth, the French artillery commander, his guns unable to counter the enemy ordnance in the hills, committed suicide.

On 16 March Lieutenant-Colonel Bigeard, at the head of his veteran parachute battalion, jumped into Dien Bien Phu in a desperate attempt to restore order. He found de Castries in a state of shocked impotence, wholly incapable of exercising further realistic command. With the support of his fellow paratrooper, Lieutenant Colonel Langlais, he steadily wrested control of the battle from the exhausted de Castries.

The Viet Minh renewed their attacks on 30/31 March, concentrating on *Dominique, Eliane* and *Huguette.* By now, however, the French had recovered much of their composure and losses were heavy. In one counter-attack, Bigeard, supported by all 120 mortars in the garrison and every artillery piece able to bear, recaptured the eastern sector of *Eliane* in vicious hand-to-hand fighting which reduced his battalion to less than 200 combatants. After four days of bitter close quarter combat, Giap withdrew his men to regroup. Both sides had lost at least 2,000 men and conditions had become hellish. The French had only four surgeons, all of whom were injured, and only a few nurses, including Genevieve de Galard, the only woman in the garrison, to tend to their mounting numbers of wounded. The Viet Minh had only one surgeon and no hospitals. As Giap later admitted, he began to doubt his own plans and had it not been for the high morale of his men, might have ordered a withdrawal.

De Castries used the lull to reorganize his defences, regrouping his forces into a position little more than a mile in diameter. *Claudine, Eliane* and parts of *Dominique* and *Huguette* were reinforced leaving *Isabelle* isolated to the south. New strongpoints, *Sparrowhawk* to the north of the command bunker and *Juno* to the south were hastily constructed to complete the new perimeter.

Between 4 April and 1 May, Giap switched from a policy of suicidal massed assaults to a steady encroachment, constructing an elaborate web of trenches from which to launch his final assault. On 2 May he mounted his attack from all sides, closing in relentlessly during three days of the bloodiest fighting witnessed so far. Parts of *Dominique, Eliane* and *Huguette* were overrun, exposing the central defensive area.

On 6 May, Giap ordered a massive barrage against the remaining strong points and the next morning attacked with predominantly fresh troops. By midday on 7 May, the 55th day of the siege, the French position had become hopeless. Five hours later, a Viet Minh advance unit stormed the command post forcing de Castries to surrender the main complex. Twenty-four hours later *Isabelle,* the sole remaining French position, surrendered leaving the tattered remnants of the village firmly in Viet Minh control. Over 9,500 French troops began a forced march into captivity which few were to survive. In an uncharacteristic act of generosity, Giap allowed the French to send a small flotilla of hospital aircraft to the airstrip to transport the non-walking wounded, together with the gallant Genevieve de Galand, to safety.

Although Giap had not escaped lightly, losing an estimated 20,000 men in battle, he had destroyed the last vestiges of French colonial power in the region. He had won the battle before the first bullets had even been fired, however, for Dien Bien Phu was more than anything a battle of timing and logistics. In moving a fully equipped army into the T'ai mountains, Giap had performed a totally unexpected act. He had recognized the French challenge for what it was, analyzed its weaknesses and exploited them to the full. It is unlikely that any other commander, before or since, could have brought about so complete a victory under such seemingly impossible conditions.

Top: Over 200 Communist artillery pieces were manhandled 50 miles through the jungle to give Giap overwhelming superiority in firepower.

Above: Viet Minh infantry was committed en masse against the French strongpoints. Losses were horrendous, but victory inevitable.

Sharon's Drive Through Sinai, October, 1956

The Israeli Defence Force is unique in the annals of modern warfare. Comprised of immigrant men and women from every corner of the globe, it has succeeded in amalgamating the finest traits of the best fighting forces in existence.

Part of Israel's success is borne of desperation. Since her inception in 1948 each of her several wars has been for survival, and against heavy odds. In 1948, 1956, and again in 1973, defeat would unquestionably have led to annihilation. Even today the consequences of defeat in any future war would be unthinkable. Israel has never allowed herself the luxury of passengers. Every citizen has had to contribute, in the majority of cases through military service. Hers is perhaps the purest form of citizen army in the world with its small cadre of regular soldiers, its conscripts and echelons of reservists.

The 1956 Campaign in the Sinai epitomizes perfectly the strengths and, such as they are, the weaknesses of the Israeli war machine. At the time Israel was threatened by a three-pronged attack from the combined forces of Egypt, Syria and Jordan. During the previous months, Egypt had sponsored a number of commando raids into Israeli territory. Israel had responded by launching a large-scale raid into Gaza in which over 30 Egyptian soldiers had been killed. Gamal Nasser, the newly elected president of Egypt, had retaliated by blockading the Straits of Tiran, at the mouth of the Gulf of Aqaba, and by denying Israeli shipping passage through the recently nationalized Suez Canal. War seemed unavoidable and Israel determined up on a pre-emptive attack.

Britain and France were simultaneously planning action against Egypt. In September 1955 Nasser had signed an arms deal with Czechoslovakia for the provision of Soviet aircraft, artillery and tanks. Enraged by so blatant an extension of the Cold War, Britain and the United States had withdrawn from all international projects including the construction of the highly prestigious Nile Aswan Dam.

Infuriated by what he had regarded as undue influence in Egyptian domestic affairs, Nasser had retaliated by declaring martial law in the canal zone and by nationalizing, without compensation, the Suez Canal Company. At the same time he had offered arms and sanctuary to the Algerian nationalists, then waging a brutal war of independence against France. Britain and France had responded by concentrating their élite marine and airborne units in the Eastern Mediterranean as a far from subtle prelude to the retaking of the Canal. Israel entered into a secret agreement with Britain and France and prepared for war.

The Israeli Army was not large. Since 1948 it had been reduced to a regular force of 12,000 men although these could be rapidly expanded to over 50,000 by mobilizing the first reserve, all of whom had received prior military training as conscripts and had not long been released to civilian life. A further 200,000 reserves were also available if need be.

British manufactured Centurion tanks gave the Israelis a considerable edge over the older Egyptian T-34s.

Above: A squadron of U.S. manufactured M-47 tanks advances through the Sinai desert.

Left: Israeli paratroopers dropped on to the eastern approaches to the Mitla Pass and later on to the airfield at Tor.

The Israeli Air Force was better prepared. Under the leadership of Dan Tolkovski, who had assumed command in 1953, it had purchased a number of modern fighters and had recently entered into a massive arms deal with France. It had recently taken possession of a consignment of Noratlas transports capable of operating from very short airstrips, of Meteor NF13 fighters and of Dessault Ouragan jet fighters. Most importantly, it had obtained a batch of the revolutionary new French 1120km/hr (696 mph) Mystère IVA fighters universally considered far superior to the Soviet-manufactured MiG-15s and MiG-17s supplied to Egypt under the auspices of the Czech arms deal.

Israel decided to call up her first reserves

and 100,000 other reservists to swell her military ranks to 150,000 personnel. Orders were given for a secret mobilization on 26 October 1956 only three days before the intended assault. Key officers and NCOs were alerted by telephone or telegram and then disseminated the mobilization order by word of mouth. Within twelve hours twelve brigade groups had been readied for action to be joined later by four additional brigades, 150,000 men and women in all.

The Israelis resolved from the outset to concentrate their forces in the Sinai where it was anticipated that the enemy's attention would be almost totally distracted by the Franco-British threat. To mask their armoured buildup in the Negev Desert, they began by moving an airborne brigade to the Jordanian border, having initially placed the area under curfew. Convinced of an intended Israeli attack in the east and ignorant of the buildup along the Egyptian border, the Arab coalition did nothing to strengthen its forces in the west. They were therefore completely unprepared when shortly before nightfall on 29 October, General Sharon smashed his way into the Sinai at the head of an armoured brigade.

A section of the Egyptian infantry dismounts from the protection of an armoured personnel carrier prior to going into action.

The overall Israeli plan was as daring as it was simple. As Sharon advanced, a parachute battalion would drop close to and secure the Mitla Pass, a key bottleneck on the invasion route. The force would then split, a subordinate group heading south along the Gulf coast towards Sharm-el-Sheikh, the other major force striking directly across the Sinai towards the Gulf of Suez. A third independent force would attack across the northern Sinai towards Abu Ageila and the Suez Canal. Having attained a foothold in Egypt the Israelis would halt to enable Ben-Gurion and the politicians to review the situation. If Egyptian resistance were proving more stalwart than expected, or if the major powers had decided to intervene, the forces would be pulled back to Israel with minimal loss of face. If, however, Egyptian resistance had collapsed and the major powers had remained uncommitted, the Israeli forces would roll forward to seize the Suez Canal and the strategically important Gaza Strip.

Ultimately Egypt collapsed while the world looked on unable to assist, its entire attention being consumed by the imminent Franco-British incursion into Suez and by the anti-Communist Warsaw rising about to be mercilessly suppressed by Soviet forces.

As the war progressed, Britain and France demanded jointly that both Egypt and Israel withdraw from the canal in response to a cease-fire ordered by the United Nations. This was seen as nothing more than an excuse for their invasion fleet to put to sea and only served to encourage the now aggressive Israelis.

Initially boldness won out and the plan went well. Sharon advanced rapidly on Thamad securing it against minimum opposition before dawn on 30 October. The airborne drop from two Dakotas was executed without incident some 24 km (15 miles) from the Pass, consolidated quickly and moved with little difficulty towards its objective. A second force, advancing behind Sharon's tanks, crossed the border to deploy north, taking the town of Qusseima and

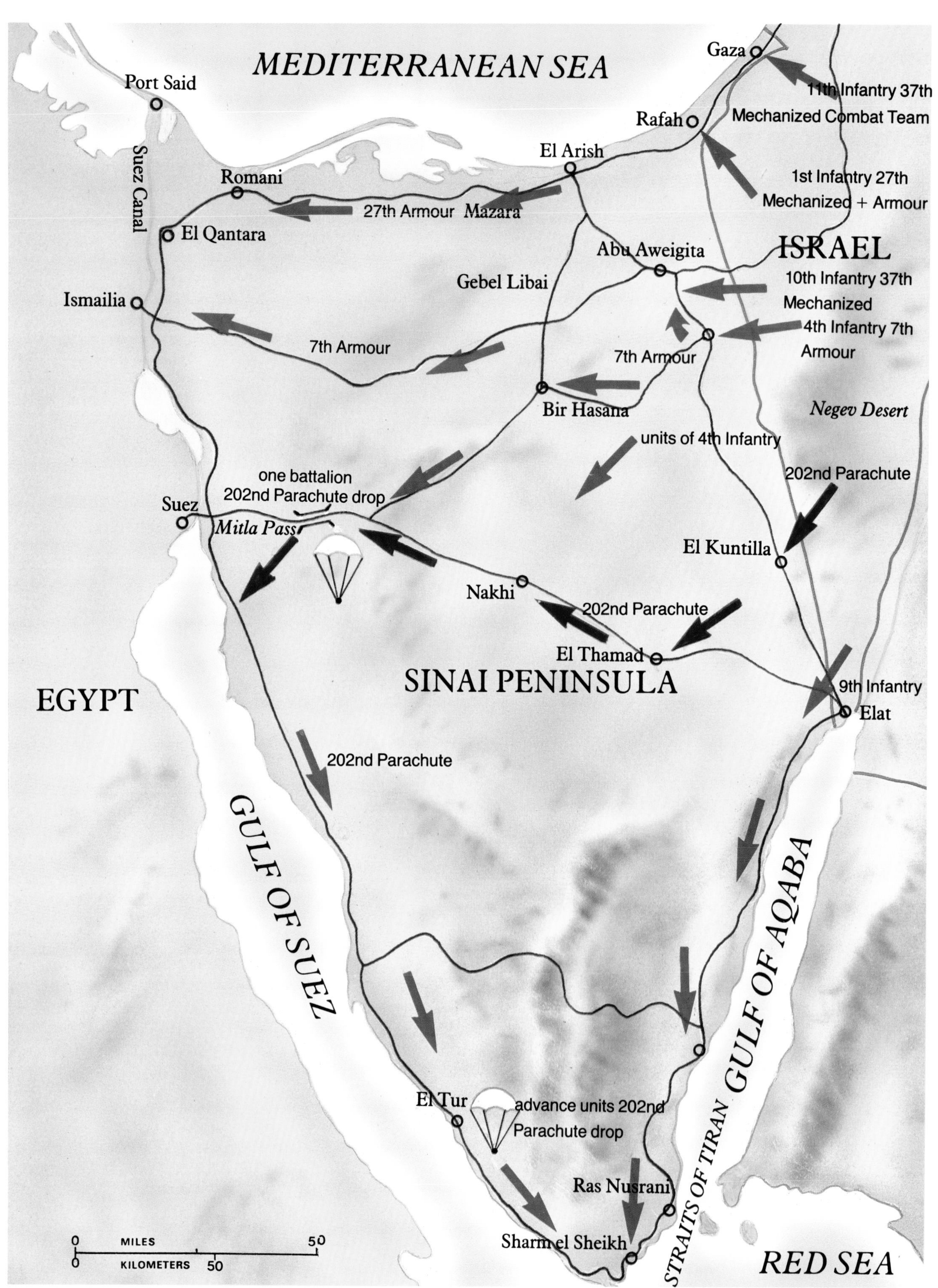
MEDITERRANEAN SEA
Gaza
11th Infantry 37th
Mechanized Combat Team
Port Said
Rafah
El Arish
Suez Canal
Romani
1st Infantry 27th
Mechanized + Armour
27th Armour
Mazara
El Qantara
Abu Aweigita
ISRAEL
Gebel Libai
10th Infantry 37th
Mechanized
Ismailia
4th Infantry 7th
Armour
7th Armour
7th Armour
Bir Hasana
Negev Desert
units of 4th Infantry
one battalion
202nd Parachute drop
202nd Parachute
Suez
Mitla Pass
El Kuntilla
Nakhi
202nd Parachute
El Thamad
SINAI PENINSULA
9th Infantry
EGYPT
Elat
202nd Parachute
GULF OF SUEZ
GULF OF AQABA
El Tur
advance units 202nd
Parachute drop
STRAITS OF TIRAN
Ras Nusrani
Sharm el Sheikh
RED SEA
0 MILES 50
0 KILOMETERS 50

opening a second potential route to the Mitla Pass.

It was at this point however, that matters began to take a turn for the worse. Sharon's column, resting while it awaited fuel and ammunition resupply from the air, was caught in the open and strafed by Egyptian fighter aircraft. More seriously, the paratroopers were delayed when they fell victim to artillery fire and air attack while still some distance from the Pass.

To compound Israeli difficulties, intelligence sources began to report the movement of Egyptian units from Suez towards the Mitla Pass. Determined to pre-empt them, Sharon ordered his armour forward at maximum speed. He was unexpectedly delayed at Nakhl, where he was forced to deploy his batteries of 25 pounders to dislodge the stubborn defenders who had been reinforced by the survivors from Thamad, but nonetheless managed to link up with the hard-pressed paratroopers by nightfall. At daybreak on the next morning, 31 October, after a short but fierce firefight, the combined force succeeded in securing the Mitla Pass, thus successfully completing the first and most crucial phase of the entire operation.

The three-pronged Israeli invasion of Sinai was highly successful, reaching its objectives with minimum cost. It was marked with dash, elan and – above all – luck. The overall plan was as daring as it was simple. As Sharon advanced, a parachute battalion dropped close to, and secured, the Mitla Pass - a key bottleneck on the invasion route. The force then split, a subordinate group heading south along the Gulf coast towards Sharm-el-Sheikh, the other major force striking directly across the Sinai towards the Gulf of Suez. A second independent force then attacked across the northern Sinai towards Abu Ageila and the Suez Canal. Finally a third force moved south from Elat along the Gulf of Aqaba to link up with their colleagues in Sharm-el-Sheikh. In less than a week the Israelis gained a complete victory against all the odds, wresting the entire Sinai from the Egyptians and destroying one-third of their army.

The northern column, comprising an armoured brigade led by Colonel Ben-Avi and an infantry brigade under Colonel Harpaaz, crossed the border soon after Sharon and met with equal success. Having taken Kusseima against little opposition they swept north to engage the major Egyptian defences at Abu Agheila. When initial attempts to turn the Egyptian flanks were frustrated, the bulk of Ben-Avi's armour was brought forward to confront the enemy's T-34s tanks. During the ensuing 16-hour battle, an Israeli reconnaissance company succeeded in infiltrating through the Egyptian lines, cutting the defenders off from their reinforcements. With Abu Agheila effectively neutralized, a mechanized detachment from Harpaaz's brigade was dispatched south to reinforce Sharon. By the morning of 31 October the entire lower Sinai east of Mitla was firmly in Israeli hands.

The second phase of Operation *Kadesh,* the codename for the invasion, began on 1 November. That morning a motorized infantry brigade under Colonel Yoffe crossed the border near Eilat, turned south and headed at speed along the Sinai coast road towards Sharm el Sheikh. Resupply was provided with typical Israeli ingenuity. Landing craft were brought overland from the Mediterranean on specially built transporters and stored secretly in Eilat before the commencement of hostilities. From there they were used to ferry ammunition and supplies forward to pre-arranged points along the advancing troops' route.

Just as victory seemed assured, it became apparent that the Egyptians were in fact far from beaten. An armoured brigade and infantry regiment dispatched from Ismailia to relieve the beleaguered defenders still holding out at Abu Agheila nearly succeeded in their objective. Although scattered by the Israeli Air Force in the region of Bir Gifgafa, elements regrouped to attack the Israeli blocking positions. The Egyptians in Abu Agheila then launched a sudden and altogether unexpected night armoured counter-attack into the Israeli rear. For a few desperate hours it seemed that the Egyptians might seize the initiative and in so doing sever one of the vital supply lines to Sharon's troops to the west. Indeed, it was not until General Moshe Dayan's personal intervention that the battle for Abu Agheila swung in favour of the Israelis. An all out assault, launched on the night of 1/2 November against dogged resistance, finally broke the Egyptian will to fight. Defeated though far from dishonoured, they melted away into the desert leaving the town securely in Israeli hands.

During 1 November Brigadier Laskov, at the head of his armoured corps, joined the battle. Bypassing Abu Agheila he struck north to take Raafah and immediately thereafter drove west along the coast to threaten the major Egyptian supply dump at El Arish. Having captured this valuable prize intact at the cost of minimum casualties, he continued his momentum west until nightfall when his leading troops were able to bivouac just short of the Suez Canal.

Simultaneously, Sharon's veterans on the Mitla Pass broke out of their defensive positions, pushed aside a derisory Egyptian counter-attack and sped towards Port Tewfiq at the southern end of the canal. Rather than embarrass the Franco-British allies, who had by now issued their withdrawal ultimatum to both adversaries, they halted 15km (9.5 miles) short of their objective, dug in and awaited events.

By the morning of 2 November the canal, and with it the northern Sinai, were firmly in Israeli hands. A mechanized infantry brigade was then dispatched into the Gaza Strip to clear it of its remaining and by now thoroughly demoralized Egyptian defenders. An airborne battalion was dropped on the Red Sea airfield of Tor, Sharon's exhausted but jubilant brigade moved south to link up with them and then continued south to Sharm el Sheikh to meet the advance guard of Yoffe's brigade from Eilat.

In less than a week Israel had gained a complete victory against all the odds. Her troops had wrested the entire Sinai from the Egyptians, destroyed one-third of Egypt's army and with Anglo-French Air support, neutralized her air force. The cost to the Israeli Defence Forces had been 200 killed and four prisoners lost.

The Israeli forces had now come of age but had already come to exhibit a number of dangerous traits. They were too willing to push ahead regardless, often without full reconnaissance and the guarantee of resupply. Their officers led by inspiration from the front with little worry for their own safety, or for the overall effect on their men's morale should they be killed. Armour was regarded as the unquestioned king of the desert without recourse to the growing potency of anti-tank weaponry.

With the exception of the gallant defenders of Abu Agheila, the Egyptians did not fight well. Had they done so the outcome of the Sinai campaign might have been different and some of these mistakes realized. In her subsequent campaigns, Israel, although always ultimately victorious, would pay the price of too much inspired passion and too little regard for the consequences of her actions.

The Battle for Jebel Akhdar, Oman, 1959

Between 1959 and 1967 the SAS fought three 'low intensity' campaigns of which the general public knew little. They were, nonetheless, important in the history of the Regiment, transforming it from a jungle force to the finest counter-insurgency unit in the world.

The first of these mini-campaigns was for control of Jebel Akhdar in northern Oman. Translated from Arabic Jebel Akhdar means 'Green Mountain.' It rises for over 2,000m (6,500 ft) straight out of the desert, although it has several peaks which are far higher. Its plateau can be approached only by a series of narrow, twisting and easily defensible tracks. It is the perfect setting for a tribal insurrection.

In 1954 Sulaiman Ibn Himyar, chief of the Bani Riyam, began to challenge the authority of the Sultan of Muscat and Oman with whom Britain had treaty obligations. With the support of the local Imam, Ghalib ibn Ali, and Galib's brother, the ambitious and powerful Talib, Sulaiman led two of the southern Jebel tribes, the Bani Himya and Bani Riyam, into open revolt. In 1957 Britain dispatched an infantry brigade from Kenya to restore order. Nazwa, the regional capital and an important communications centre, was secured and Sulaiman's fort and power base in the village of Tanuf was destroyed by R.A.F. bombing. Rather than surrender to an uncertain fate, Sulaiman and Talib fled into the Jebel from where they continued to attack isolated Government posts. Britain dispatched reinforcements from the Royal Marines and Trucial Oman Scouts to assist the Sultan's somewhat primitive domestic forces in containing the problem. By 1958, however, it had become clear that nothing less than a full assault on the Jebel stronghold itself would suffice to restore order.

Britain was in a dilemma. Her incursion into Suez in 1956 had had a catastrophic effect on Anglo-Arab relations even within the comparatively friendly Gulf, and she wished to do nothing to make matters worse. However she realized the necessity for maintaining her influence with the oil rich states of Kuwait, Bahrain and Qatar on which she was becoming increasingly reliant for her domestic needs. The Macmillan Government had managed to withhold from the popular press the destruction of Tanuf, with its attendant civilian deaths, and now reasoned that if it were to send a large force to the area the full extent of its earlier involvement would become known with disastrous political consequences. After an appeal from the Foreign Office Macmillan decided publicly to do nothing but in secret reality to send the SAS to the area.

Members of A Squadron 22SAS distributing 'largesse' to local tribesmen. 'Hearts and Minds' was crucial to British success.

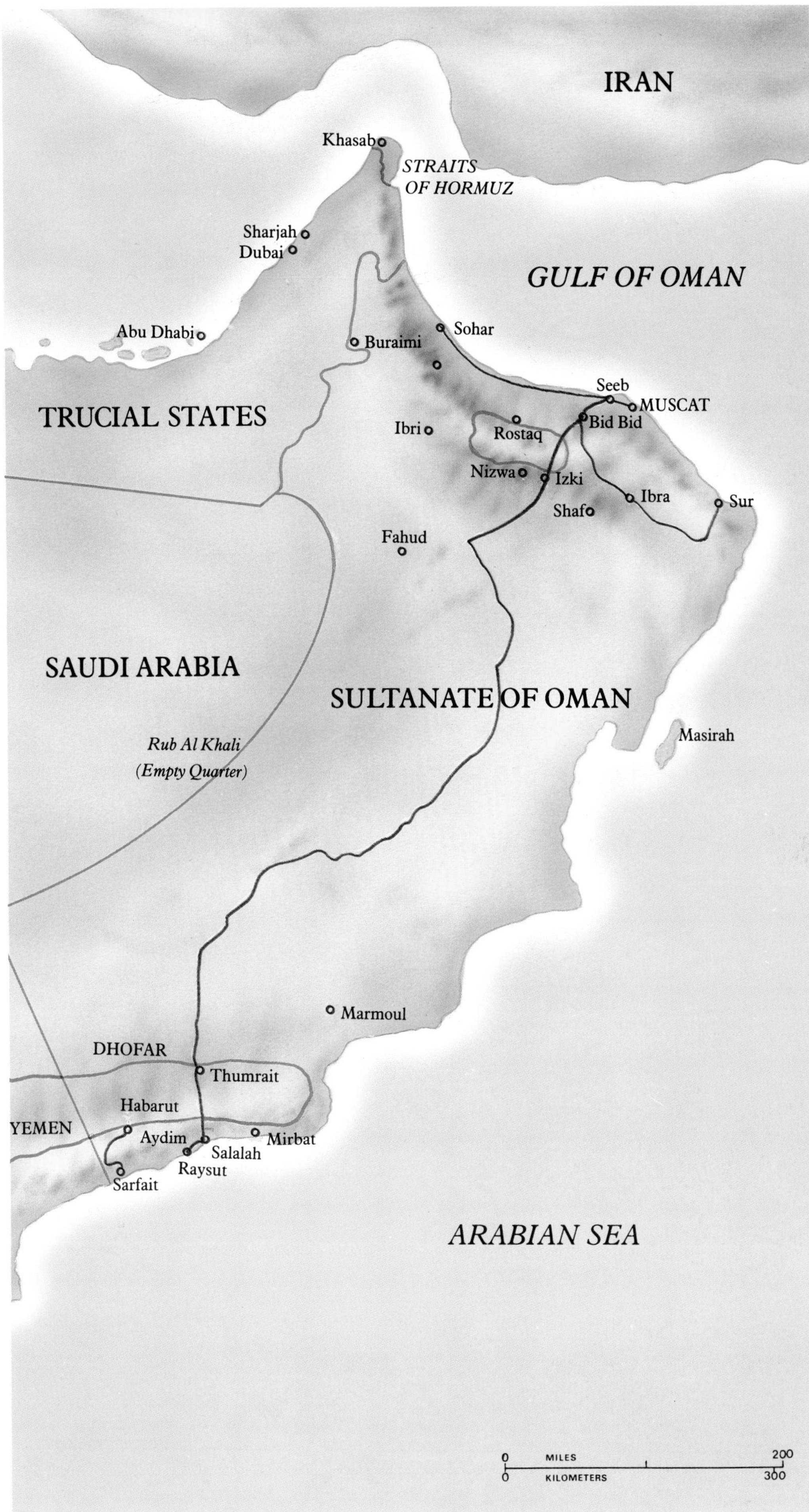

The Sultanate of Oman covers an area approximately the size of the United Kingdom, possessing 1,600km (1,000 miles) of coastline and a population of about 1,500,000. A mountain range runs from the northern frontier with the UAE (formerly the Trucial States), southeast to meet the sea at Muscat and contains the Jebel Akhdar rising to over 2,000m (2,160ft) from the flat plains below. Many of the local population centres are quite fertile and comparatively self-sufficient with extensive date gardens dependent upon the ancient falaj *water system. The whole of southern Oman is generally known as the Dhofar. The border with the Yemen runs across arid gravel desert in the north and through rugged mountains in the south. The Dhofar itself can be divided into three distinct regions, the narrow coastal plain around Salalah, the Jebel Qarra range surrounding it and the flat Negd desert running between the Jebel and the Empty Quarter.*

Lieutenant-Colonel Deane-Drummond, then commanding 22 SAS, delegated the task of neutralizing the rebels to the 70 offices and men of D Squadron, under command of Major John Watts. The small team arrived in the Oman amid the greatest secrecy straight from the jungles of Malaya on 18 November 1958 and, without even waiting to acclimatize, set about at once winning the hearts and minds of the indiginous population.

Psychological warfare, in which the British were world-renowned experts, had been used to great effect against the Communist guerrillas in Malaya and the Mau Mau in Kenya. In the latter instance Kikuyu tribesmen, having surrendered or been captured, had not been imprisoned but instead had been 'turned', formed into counter gangs and sent into action against their former allies.

Small SAS teams were deployed to the villages surrounding the Jebel. Once in position they watched, waited and above all listened for any scrap of useful intelligence. Armed with this information, much of it often unwittingly given, they began to build up a pattern of the enemy's movements on and off the plateau. Where possible ambushes were set and Talib's irregulars were either killed or captured.

Ever a realist, Deane-Drummond appreciated that however psychological operations might weaken the enemy, they would not destroy him. That would necessitate a more conventional form of military engagement which would have to be preceded by a period of intensive and painstaking reconnaissance. After the unfortunate death of Corporal Duke Swindells at the hands of a sniper, and

Left: Sulaiman Ibn Himyar felt secure in his moutain fortress but reckoned without the intervention of the R.A.F.

Below: The ruins of Tanuf destroyed by the R.A.F. after its occupants offered support to the rebels.

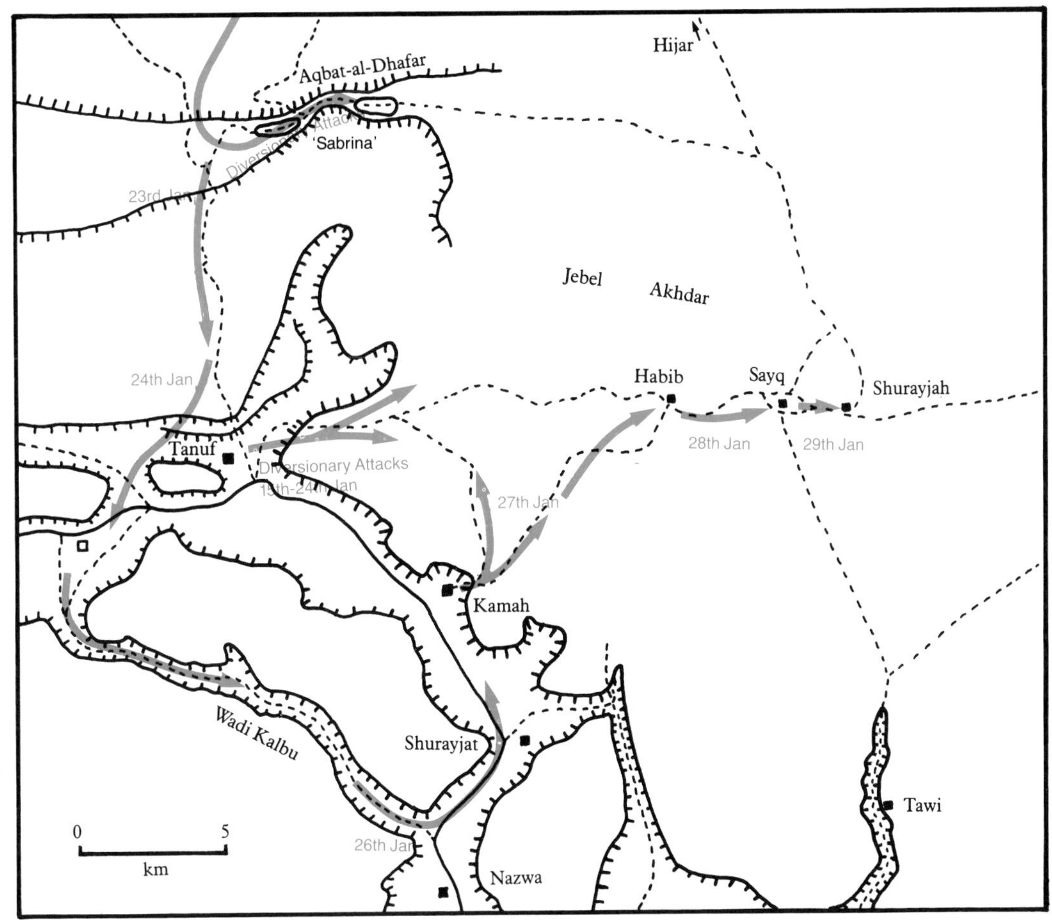

The ruins of Tanuf and the water system.

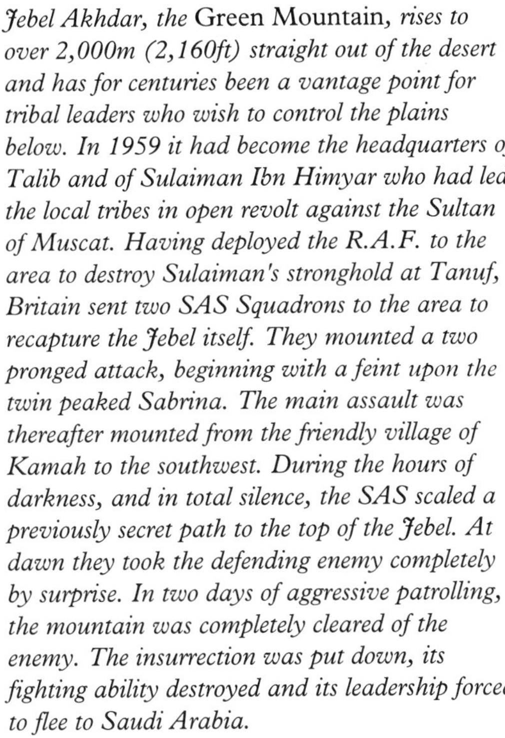

Jebel Akhdar, the Green Mountain, *rises to over 2,000m (2,160ft) straight out of the desert and has for centuries been a vantage point for tribal leaders who wish to control the plains below. In 1959 it had become the headquarters of Talib and of Sulaiman Ibn Himyar who had led the local tribes in open revolt against the Sultan of Muscat. Having deployed the R.A.F. to the area to destroy Sulaiman's stronghold at Tanuf, Britain sent two SAS Squadrons to the area to recapture the Jebel itself. They mounted a two pronged attack, beginning with a feint upon the twin peaked Sabrina. The main assault was thereafter mounted from the friendly village of Kamah to the southwest. During the hours of darkness, and in total silence, the SAS scaled a previously secret path to the top of the Jebel. At dawn they took the defending enemy completely by surprise. In two days of aggressive patrolling, the mountain was completely cleared of the enemy. The insurrection was put down, its fighting ability destroyed and its leadership forced to flee to Saudi Arabia.*

against the better judgement of the Sultan's own experienced loan-officers, patrolling was undertaken at night. Despite the obvious dangers inherent in operating at night in an alien terrain against seasoned adversaries, the policy soon met with a degree of success.

On the northern side of the Jebel two troops led by Captain Rory Walker and guided by a 'turned' local, scaled the top of the mountain at a twin peak, later nicknamed *Sabrina.* Before their presence was noticed, they succeeded in constructing a series of sangars on the plateau, some within 3,000m (3,250 yds) of the enemy's position, from which they were able to undertake a number of damaging nocturnal raids. Despite spirited counter-attacks from Talib's men, Walker's team maintained this precarious but crucial foothold on the plateau until the very end of the campaign.

While the insurgents' attention was drawn by Walker's activities to the north, an SAS deep-reconnaissance patrol in the south discovered a well-protected arms cache hidden in a cave. As soon as it was practical, Peter de la Billière, later to command the British forces in the Gulf but at that time an SAS troop commander, was ordered to attack the enemy position. Under cover of darkness his men made a long and tortuous approach through enemy held territory to within a few hundred metres of the objective. As dawn broke the unsuspecting rebels in the vicinity of the cave were greeted by a barrage of rockets and rifle fire. True to their martial heritage, the Arabs did not break and run but rather went to ground returning the British fire. Despite the assistance of a number of R.A.F. air strikes, one of which destroyed an enemy mortar with its entire team, and the accuracy of the SAS marksmanship, de la Billière was forced to execute a fighting withdrawal under the protective cover of Sergeant *Tankie* Smith's Browning machine gun. He did, however, manage to destroy the cave with much of its irreplaceable arms cache and in so doing drove yet another nail into the coffin of Talib's resistance.

By December 1958 it had become clear that the resources available to the SAS in Oman would simply not be sufficient to bring about the destruction of Talib's hardened and resolute followers before the advent of the hot weather in the following April. After some discussion it was agreed to double the SAS force available by committing a Squadron, then under command of Major John Cooper, to the

Above: The Jebel Akhdar rising behind the ruins of Tanuf.

Left: Jebel Tayin, part of the Jebel Akhdar range, rises sheer from the desert plain.

battle. Arriving in early January 1959, A Squadron was immediately deployed in support of Walker's two troops to the north of the Jebel, using an assault on the twin-peaked *Sabrina* to acclimatize.

Now that the SAS considered itself strong enough to take the battle to the very heart of the enemy, a plan truly worthy of the Regimental motto *Who Dares Wins* was devised. It was decided to mount a series of feints on the northern and western sides of the Jebel while the main force mounted its assault along previously untried routes from the friendly village of Kamah in the south-west. As a final touch muleteers sympathetic to the rebels were advised 'in confidence' that the main attack would be launched from Tanuf in an attempt to draw the main enemy forces away from the intended route.

No one doubted that the assault would be dangerous in the extreme. The main force would have to negotiate a 1,230m (4,000 ft) climb along unknown and ill-defined tracks with full packs in the dark and be in position before dawn if it were not to be cut to pieces by enemy marksmen.

Above: Today the Sultan's flag flies proudly over the ruins of Jabri Palace, a testament to the British success.

Aerial reconnaissance was able to report prior to the assault that the subterfuge had worked and that the enemy were massing in the areas of *Sabrina* and Tanuf. Nonetheless it was known that a sizeable force, more than capable of destroying the troopers if it caught them in the open, remained to be overcome.

D-Day was set for 26 January 1959. That morning both squadrons, together with a group of somewhat dubious donkey handlers provided by the Trucial Oman Scouts, congregated in Tanuf. The donkeys were dispatched to the assembly area at Kamah Camp while the SAS received a detailed operational briefing from Deane-Drummond. That night the two squadrons, having by now been reunited with their donkeys if not the bulk of the donkey handlers who had gone on strike, crossed the start-line at 8.30 p.m. At the same time 4 Troop launched a diversionary attack to cover the unavoidable noise of the climbing troops. Abandoning those few troops who were either too unfit or overladen to make their own way the SAS climbed steadily throughout the night. By 5.00 a.m. it became clear that progress had been slower than anticipated. Although A Squadron had reached its objective, three of the four troops of D Squadron were still bunched and vulnerable some way from their target. Fearful for the consequences should his men be caught in the open at sunrise Watts bravely ordered two of his troops to dump their extra kit and ammunition and push on. Unencumbered, they reached their objective and comparative safety at 6.30 a.m., just in time to receive a resupply drop from a flight of R.A.F. Valettas. As the drop was made and the enemy became fully aware of their own predicament, the third D Squadron troop bringing up the rear brought a 'captured' (previously unmanned) Browning machine-gun to bear on the enemy positions with excellent results. As the light improved, R.A.F. Venoms joined the battle, strafing the countryside in search of enemy snipers. By 2.30 p.m., as the final snipers were silenced, the SAS prepared to send out fighting patrols to reconnoitre the largely uncharted plateau. The next morning the deserted village of Habib was occupied and a group of 38 Arabs, including women and children, were detained and brought in for interrogation. True to the traditions of hearts and minds prevailing within the regiment, none was mistreated and indeed most were soon released.

On 30 January Sulaiman's cave, which he had been using as a headquarters and home since his eviction from the fort, was located. A subsequent search revealed a vast quantity of documents and a

Below: The fortress of Nakhl to the south-west of Nizus remained in friendly hands throughout the insurrection.

substantial number of weapons. A number of Talib's prisoners, who until then had been held manacled in atrocious conditions, were released and a number of his lieutenants captured and taken off the mountain to Sharaijah for interrogation.

Patrolling continued until by 31 January, the entire Jebel was secure. Although Talib, Ghalib, and Sulaiman had not been caught having made good their escape and subsequently seeking sanctuary in Saudi Arabia, the insurrection had been crushed and the Jebel, together with the Walidom of Nazwa returned to the Sultan.

Once again the SAS had proven the truth of the maxim *Who Dares Wins.* In a few short weeks they had restored the prestige of Britain in the eyes of her Gulf allies, their training, skill at arms and sheer tenacity having won through where more conventional soldiering would have failed. Perhaps not surprisingly two of the officers who played so prominent a part in the assault on Jebel Akhdar, Watts and de la Billière, would later go on to command the Regiment.

Above: A tribesman guards the parapets of the Nazwa fort. The windowless building in the background was the men's prison.

Below: Nazwa was used as the SAS adminstrative headquarters. The Jebel Akhdar looms in the background.

Retaking the Crater,
The Highlanders in Aden, 1967

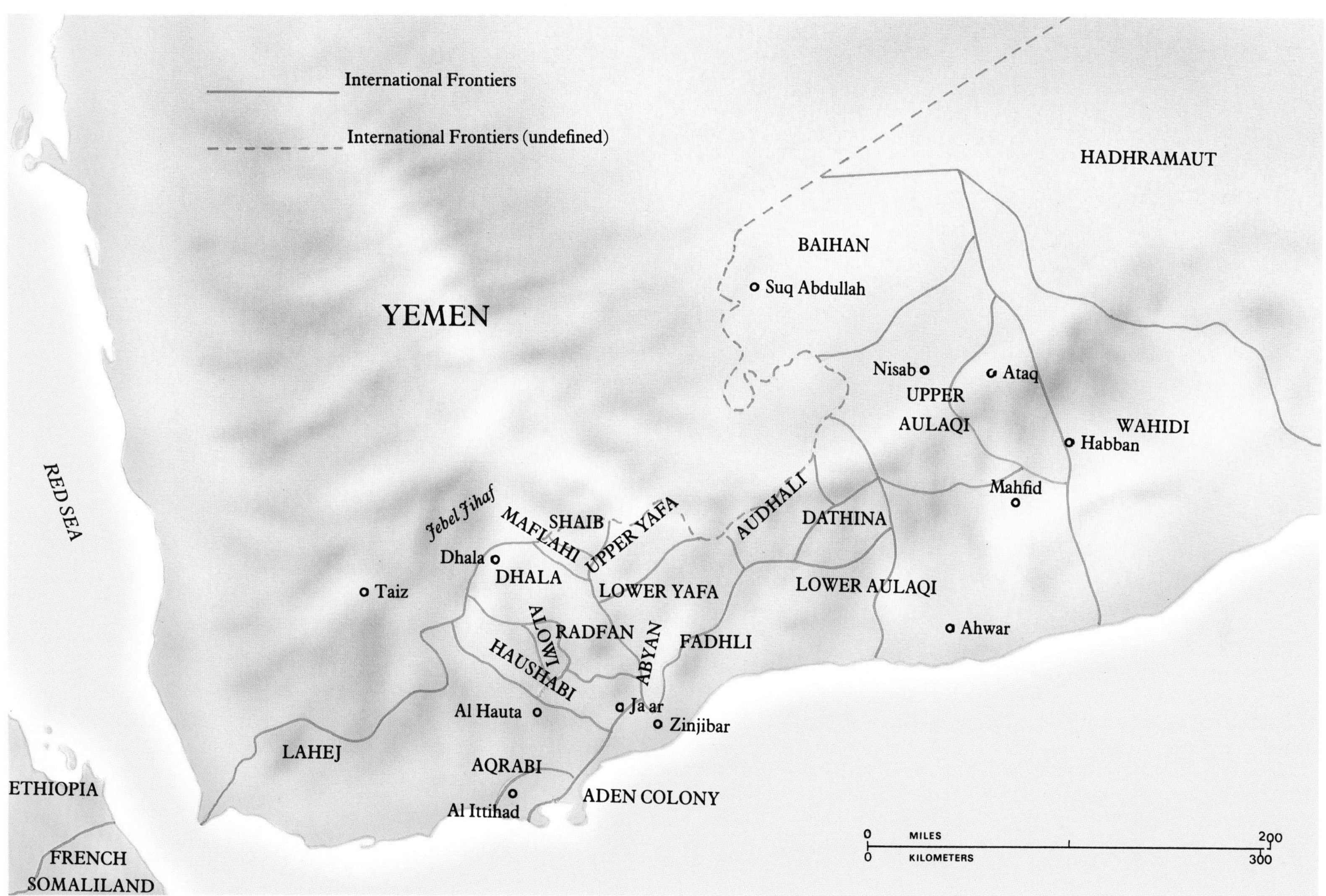

June 1967 was a traumatic and disturbing month for the Arabs. Nasser was comprehensively routed by the Israelis in a Jihad or Holy War producing a sense of bitterness and frustration throughout the Muslim world. Unable to punish Israel, many of the Middle Eastern Arabs turned on Britain and the United States, whom they accused of siding with her. The presence of British troops in Southern Arabia not only served to compound the problem but gave it scope for expression.

To make matters worse, Federal forces then in control of the region were torn apart by tribal feuding and petty jealousies.

Stirling Castle, *the operation to retake the Crater, was as daring as it was well-conceived. The plan called for a two-pronged advance into the town by Lieutenant Colonel Mitchell's Argyll and Sutherland Highlanders reinforced by companies drawn from the Commandos and the Prince of Wales' Own. Although new to the area every member of the Argylls knew the Crater well, having studied a mock-up of the area constructed in the regimental gymnasium in Plymouth. Prior to the assault, British snipers took up position on the rim of the Crater with orders to shoot any Arab bearing arms, while SAS patrols deploying from the surrounding peaks at night pinpointed the exact enemy dispositions. The advance into the Crater, on the evening of 3 July, was led by Pipe Major Kenneth Robson playing* Monymusk *– the Regimental quick march – on the pipes. By 5.30 a.m. the next morning, some ten hours after the first Highlanders entered the area, Mitchell was able to report the Crater once more under British control.*

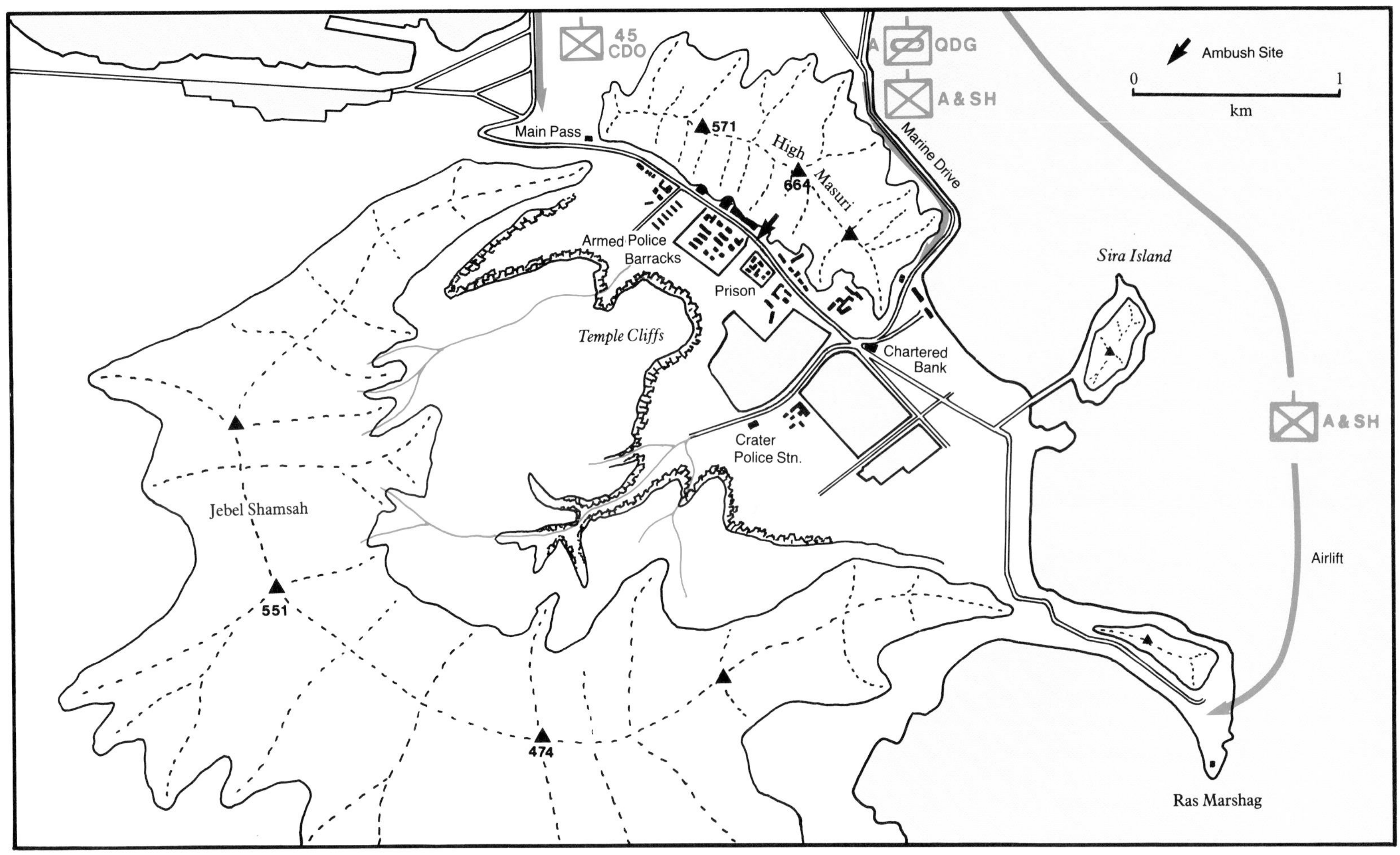

The recent reorganization of the Federal Regular Army and the Federal Guard into the South Arabian Army and South Arabian Police had led to allegations of favouritism towards the Aulaqi tribe. The appointment of Colonel Nasser Bureiq, an Aulaqi of dubious ability, to command the newly reformed army did nothing to ease the growing tension.

As a final ingredient to this recipe for disaster, the local Arab Armed Police which traditionally controlled the area was in turmoil. Aware that Britain was due to leave Aden within the year many of its members were feeling betrayed, some even falling under the influence of the growing tide of Arab nationalism. A few had even become secret members of the N.U.F., a Communist organization sponsored by Cairo and dedicated to the overthrow of colonialism.

The growing disquiet first manifested itself into physical disorder on 19 June. Three days earlier, four influential non-Aulaqgi colonels of the South Arabian Army had been suspended after complaining about the appointment of Bureiq as commander designate. Protest meetings were held throughout the S.A.A., culminating in a failed attempt on 19 June to break into the armoury of the recruit training camp at Bir Fuqum.

Aden is situated in an unlovely bay on the tip of southern Arabia. During the early stages of the twentieth century Aden had been regarded by the British as an important coaling station en route *to India. However by 1967 it had lost its strategic importance and Britain was preparing to pull out. The numerous sheikdoms and walidoms surrounding the Colony were in turmoil as rival tribes fought for sovereignty and Egyptian exported Marxism began to displace religion as the daily diet of the ordinary people. British infantry battalions patrolled the mountainous areas surrounding the Colony aggressively but could not hope to stem the pervading tide of pan-Arab nationalism. When Britain withdrew from the colony in 1968 the old order was destroyed, the wholly Marxist People's Democratic Republic of Yemen rising to take its place.*

Early next morning, amid unfounded rumours that the colonels had been sacked and arrested, S.A.A. apprentices in the neighbouring Lake Lines rioted, attacking the Officers' Mess and Guard Room. Although the riot was soon quelled internally by the Arab officers and senior NCOs, shots were heard in the South Arabian Police Barracks in Champion Lines. Jumping to the conclusion that the British were attacking their Arab compatriots, the police now mutinied, seizing weapons from the armoury. The confused and volatile police then manned the perimeter of their camp ready to fend off the anticipated British counter-attack. Minutes later, a British 3-ton lorry containing 19 soldiers of 60 Sqn, Royal Corps of Transport, hove into view. The soldiers were completely ignorant of the problems brewing in the area, indeed they were either unarmed or had their weapons unloaded. When the vehicle was 100m (110yd) from the barracks the Police opened fire without warning, killing eight British soldiers and wounding eight others.

At the same time fire was opened on the neighbouring Radfan Camp killing Second Lieutenant Young of the Lancashire Regiment.

When news of the rapidly escalating trouble reached the Federal Government, demands were made of the British forces to restore order. C Company, Kings Own Border Regiment, supported by 5 Troop, A Squadron, QDG were ordered to secure the armoury and main guard room in Champion Lines, using minimum force, so as not to inflame the situation. Despite sustaining losses, the Company succeeded in regaining control at 12.20 p.m., having used very little force, a most commendable action under the circumstances.

The scene now shifted to Crater. At 11.00 a.m., a rumour began to spread among the 140 policemen on duty in the Crater Armed Police Barracks that the British had attacked Champion Lines and were now on their way to carry the fight to them. Near panic ensued as the police rushed to the armoury to get weapons with which to defend themselves. At about the same time, terrorists in the town attacked the civil prison and released several hundred prisoners.

The force immediately responsible for Crater at this critical moment was Y Company, 1st Battalion, The Royal Northumberland Fusiliers supported by 4 Troop, A Sqn, QDG. At about midday, still unaware of the dramas at the police barracks, a Fusilier patrol entered Crater to be met by intense police hostility. Ordered to withdraw, it began to do so via a safe route which took it well away from the barracks. Unfortunately the route also took it into an area where its radios were screened by the hills, as a result of which it was unable to communicate with its headquarters.

Unaware of the reason for the radio silence and fearing that the patrol had run into trouble, the Fusilier's company commander, Major Moncur, decided to go in search. Taking eight men with him (including three men from the Argyll and Sutherland Highlanders about to take over responsibility for the Crater from the Fusiliers) he proceeded in two Land Rovers towards the Armed Police Barracks. The party was met by intense rifle and machine gun fire and all but one were killed.

After three abortive attempts to recover the bodies of their comrades, all the British troops in the Crater were ordered to withdraw to the surrounding peaks, leaving the majority of the town in terrorist hands.

Demands by the military to be allowed to take Crater at once with the use of overwhelming force were refused by the Government fearful that so drastic an action might lead to heavy civilian casualties and precipitate the total disintegration of the S.A.A.

By 21 June the British security forces had lost 22 killed and 31 wounded in what they regarded as cowardly ambushes and had been forced to leave the Crater in the hands of their comrades' murderers. Morale was low but fortunately discipline was high and no reprisals were taken against the local population.

As dawn broke many of the inhabitants of the Crater went on an orgy of looting which the Armed Police seemed either unable or unwilling to stop. The Aden Legislative Building and several banks were ransacked while the Fusiliers, impotent and furious, looked on. Throughout the day the military took action to drive the terrorists from their vantage points and sniper points within the town. Anyone seen bearing arms was shot at and at least four gunmen were killed. That night, as though in contrition, the Armed Police brought the bodies of nine of the dead British soldiers to within a few hundred metres of a forward observation post and allowed them to be retrieved. Next morning the remaining bodies were recovered with the active assistance of a particularly brave, and still loyal, Armed Police Arab officer.

Although Crater was now firmly in terrorist hands with N.U.F. flags flying everywhere, the British retained the initiative. No one could get in or out without their agreement and an increasing number of gunmen were falling victim to their snipers.

As the days progressed, the Armed Police within Crater began slowly to wrest control from the terrorists. They resumed guarding banks, re-arrested eleven of the escaped criminals and regained 399 of 400 rifles

A patrol of the 1st Bn Royal Sussex Regt. patrolling in the mountains surrounding Aden.

handed out to supporters during the panic of 20 June. More fundamentally, they remained aloof from the sniping taking place between the N.U.F. gunmen and the British.

On 28 June 1st Battalion, The Prince of Wales' Own Regiment, which recruited in Yorkshire despite its name, returned to Aden after an absence of only nine months. With the return of this additional battalion it became possible to carry out a limited redeployment allocating units more conveniently to specific areas and tasks. The Argyll and Sutherland Highlanders, which had just taken over from the Fusiliers, together with a company of 45 Commando, was given the sole duty of containing, and eventually retaking, the Crater.

While the civil authorities did everything possible to add to the N.U.F.'s complacency, even suggesting that the British might leave the Crater in Arab hands, the military planned for action. Patrols, their boots muffled by socks and their faces blackened, began slipping into Crater at night to pinpoint enemy key positions. Meanwhile, SAS patrols deploying from surrounding peaks confirmed that the Arabs were dropping their guard at night.

Although the Argylls had only been in Aden for a few days they knew every corner and building of Crater. Months earlier their commanding officer, Lieutenant Colonel Colin Mitchell, had constructed a mock-up of the area in the battalion's gymnasium in Plymouth. He had even had the building's heating turned to maximum to enhance realism. When, therefore, Mitchell received orders from Lieutenant Colonel Peter Downward, the acting brigade commander, to produce a plan for the retaking of the Crater he was able to do so with minimum difficulty.

His plan, which was accepted at once, called for a two-pronged advance into the town by the Argylls reinforced by the Commandos and a company of the Prince of Wales' Own. Report lines were agreed to control the rate of advance and contingency plans made for proceeding, halting and even withdrawing at each stage according to circumstances. The operation was code-named *Stirling Castle* in honour of the Argyll's headquarters, and timed to begin at 7.00 p.m. on 3 July.

On the afternoon of the assault a company of Argylls were moved by helicopter to the Ras Marshag area, to the south-east of the Crater and still in friendly hands. A second company, supported by A Squadron QDG, flying red and white hackles from their aerials in memory of the fallen Fusiliers, formed up ready to enter from Marine Drive. The Commandos took up position to the north leaving 1 PWO held in reserve.

Shortly before 7.00 p.m., Pipe Major Kenneth Robson began playing *Campletown Lock* on his bagpipes. At precisely 7.00 p.m., the tune changed to *Monymusk*, the regimental quick march of the Argylls, and the two lead companies began their advance into the pitch blackness of the Arabian night. Mitchell reached his first objective, the Chartered Bank, without serious incident and at once ordered sand bags to be brought forward to establish a temporary post. He moved from there to the Aden Commercial Institute, where he set up a temporary command post, and then onward to Grindleys Bank.

As the Argylls fanned out they met little resistance until by 5.30 a.m. the next day they were able to report the Crater once more under British control. As dawn broke the residents were awoken by the sound of twelve pipes and four drums sounding reveille. Later that morning Mitchell took a group of reporters on a guided tour of the Crater, much of which was still far from subdued, and in so doing earned himself the nick-name 'Mad Mitch' with which he was to rejoice for the rest of his military career.

Operation *Stirling Castle* retook the Crater at the cost of only two Arab lives and as such was justifiably labelled a great success. A few days later, Chief Superintendent Mohamed Ibrahim, commander of the Armed Police in Crater, called upon Mitchell at his headquarters to discuss terms for a surrender. Mitchell made it quite clear that his Scots would be perfectly willing to wipe out the Armed Police to the very last man if necessary. He further explained that his men believed in action not words. They were fresh from bloody fighting in Indonesia and were more than keen to avenge their murdered comrades. Hardly, surprisingly, the Armed Police surrendered their arms unconditionally.

The Argyll's success thrilled Britain in the jingoistic manner of Mafeking. Far more importantly, the Regiment was now so much in the public eye that the Government of the day found it politically impossible to include its disbandment as part of their defence cuts.

An infantry patrol awaits collection by Wessex helicopter, November, 1967.

The last British soldier to leave Aden; Lt. Colonel Morgan C.O. of 42 Commando Royal Marines.

The Paddyfield War, Vietnam, 1967–1971

Vietnam was a dirty, uncompromising war fought without scruples. The terrain, the enemy and his tactics, indeed almost everything he was faced with was alien to the young American conscript. These young soldiers, many of them not long out of school, were sent, often unwillingly, to fight for a cause that few people understood. In summer the countryside was hot, dry and dusty. During the monsoon period the same areas became either a sea of glutinous mud or else they simply disappeared under water. Rice, the staple diet of the Vietnamese, grew in abundance provided the farmers were left in peace to work the land. If they were not, or if too much of the crop was stolen by the various military factions, whole areas simply starved. Control of the paddyfields, and at least in the early stages of the war the support of the farmers who worked them, was considered crucial. However, paddyfields were not easy to patrol. The same dykes which ringed and criss-crossed the fields to make their negotiation relatively effortless in peacetime could, without much effort be mined causing them to become pathways of death during a war. Patrols could use the dykes for cover but were otherwise forced to wade through waist deep mud in order to reach their objectives safely. Progress was always slow and exhausting, particularly for United States conscript troops patently not acclimatized to the conditions.

By 1965 Washington had privately conceded that the South Vietnamese Army alone could not defeat the growing Communist threat without a massive influx of United States manpower and materiel. The draft was extended and young conscripts, with an average age of only 19, were shipped to Vietnam in increasing numbers. It soon became clear that many Stateside lessons learned by these green recruits would have to be unlearned quickly if they were to survive. However, the only classroom available for many was the battlefield itself. In fairness to the instructors the void between training theory and the practical reality of fighting was not entirely of their making. Few had experienced anti-incursion warfare. The majority were therefore forced to draw upon personal experiences gained in Korea and in some cases, even as far back as World War II. There were those who even made the fundamental mistake of drawing a non-existent parallel between the Vietnamese and Japanese on the naive basis that as Orientals they both shared the same psyche.

Above: A U.S. mechanized patrol in the Lowlands. Tracked vehicles were of little, if any, use in the Paddyfields.

Below: A U.S. Army tunnel rat about to enter a hidden Viet Cong underground shelter.

Ironically at that time both goodwill and experience abounded among the United States' allies. France had fought a protracted and bloody war against the same Communists now threatening the Saigon Government while Britain had recently defeated the Marxist insurgents in Malaya. In this case it was true that Britain's task had been somewhat easier than the one which now faced Washington. In Malaya, the enemy had been drawn almost exclusively from the ethnic Chinese minority and had therefore been easily identifiable. They had failed to coerce the majority into even passive support and their arena of operation had been definable making resupply difficult if not impossible. Above all, the insurgents had proved susceptible to the newly acquired art of psychological operations in which the British had become adroit. Nonetheless, valuable lessons were learned, particularly in the art of winning over the 'hearts and minds' of the non-combatant and largely neutral rural majority. Both France and

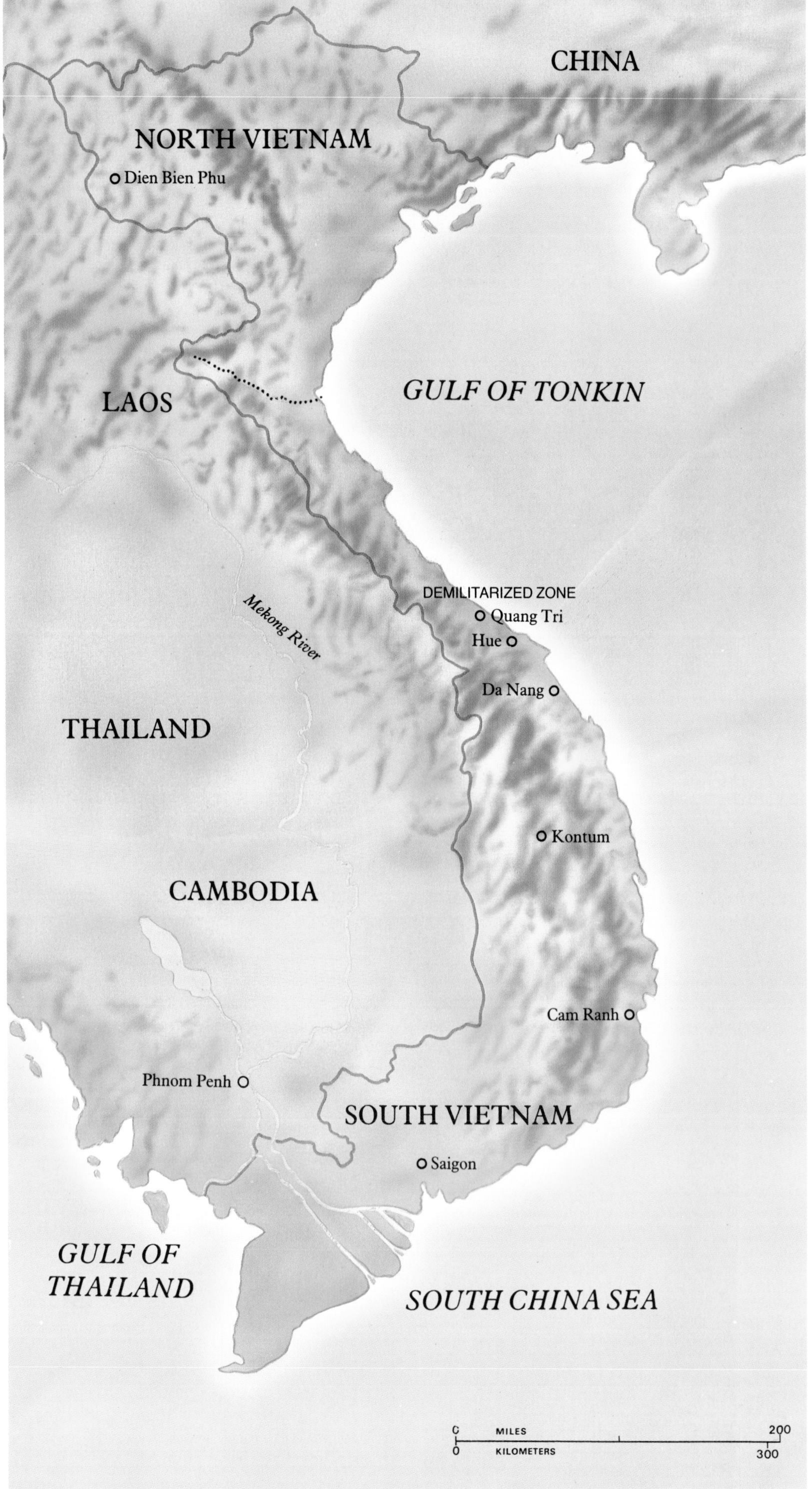

Vietnam was a ruthless, uncompromising war. Fought in the skies over the North, in the mountainous central region and in the plains and paddyfields of the South, it enveloped the entire nation, both civilian and military. In a feat of unbelievable ingenuity, the North kept its troops in the South supplied along the largely subterranean Ho Chi Minh trail which ran along the Vietnamese-Laotian border. What the NVA and Vietcong could not receive in the way of supplies they took from the local villagers in the form of taxes and tribute. The punishment for failing to help the Communists was brutal, but so was the retribution meted out upon the villagers who were found to be offering assistance. Many villages were burned to the ground by American patrols, simply on suspicion of having helped the enemy. By the early 1960s the young G.I.s were unable to tell friend from enemy, soldier from non-combatant, and in many cases had given up trying, preferring to treat all Vietnamese as potential enemies. The effects on the largely neutral civilian population were as drastic as they were inevitable.

Britain offered overt and if need be covert assistance. Their overtures were rejected by an all too self-assured Pentagon. Later, however, the United States came to realize the true worth of 'hearts and minds', whereby an attempt was made to introduce the concept to the battlefield. Tragically, by this stage, things had gone too far by. It was too late.

The United States Army's lack of experience in Vietnam was compounded throughout the war by the Establishment's blinkered adherence to the twelve-month roulment policy. Young men were called up soon after their eighteenth birthday and spent the next year in basic training. Thereafter they spent the remaining twelve months of their service in Vietnam before returning home to almost immediate discharge. Men who had come to know and trust each other during the rigours of basic training were not kept together and posted en masse in the manner of a European army. Instead they were broken up and sent out separately to their designated active service unit in order to fill gaps left by casualties or returnees. It was not unusual for them to find themselves in action within hours of landing in Vietnam. This inevitably led to friction. 'Veterans' of twelve months warfare — who in terms of professional soldiering were really only then beginning to master their trade - were suddenly replaced by green recruits resulting in unavoidable effects on squad morale. Often the newcomer was given the nastiest, most dangerous duties (for which he was least equipped) until able to prove his worth to his peers. Not surprisingly more conscripts sustained death and injury in the first quarter of their tour than in any other sector.

The position for officers was potentially even worse. Although they too served a

Top: Strongholds such as this in the Central Highlands forced the Viet Cong to concentrate their hostilities against the southern paddyfields.

Above: 3 Plt. Coy G, 2nd Bn, 4th Regt. moves across a dyke while patrolling the Ly Tin area, 8 miles north-west of Chu Lai.

Above: Rangers move through dense jungle during a patrol northeast of Xuan Loc. Few U.S. troops truly mastered these conditions.

Above: A soldier from Company H, 75th Rangers keeps a close watch as his patrol moves deep into enemy territory.

Below: Members of 505th Inf. Regt. cross a field during a search-and-destroy mission. Their vulnerability to sniper fire is obvious.

twelve month tour in Vietnam, half of this was likely to be spent in a staff appointment, leaving them with only six months in the field. The resultant scarcity of combat experienced officers led to gross over-promotion which often resulted in companies in action being led by 'Second-tour' captains with less experience than half the men under their command. In any Army which lacked a strong senior NCO cadre this frequently proved disastrous. To compound the problem many of the best young officers did not serve in Vietnam at all. A number of college students, having successfully deferred enlistment until after their graduation, subsequently volunteered

Right: The M-148 XM rifle, equipped with a 20mm grenade launcher mounted below the barrel, was a favourite weapon.

Above: As the war progressed it became more uncompromising. Villages even suspected of supporting the Vietcong were torched.

Above: Troopers from 173rd Airborne Brigade search a haystack for any sign of enemy activity within the village.

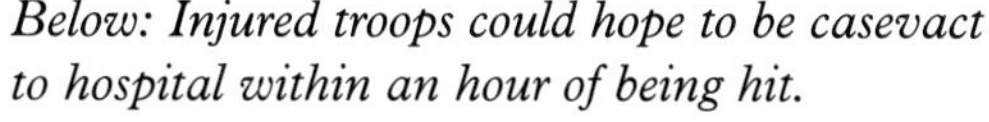

Below: Injured troops could hope to be casevact to hospital within an hour of being hit.

Below: Rangers run for cover after a helicopter insertion into Tuyen Duc Province.

for a three year short service commission in the regular army. As a result of this course of action, rather than being given a post in South-East Asia, they would find themselves in the far less dangerous position of serving in Europe. Other young men, willing to fight but scornful of the rapidly deteriorating reputation of the Army, enlisted for a three year minimum period in the Marine Corps. Most subsequently served in Vietnam, many for far longer than the year to which they would have been condemned by the Army. However, they first underwent a period of gruelling and comprehensive basic training far superior to that provided for their colleagues in the Army. Therein lay the difference, for as a direct result their competence, morale and discipline were far higher and their losses correspondingly lower. Many fit young men felt the casualty factor alone reason enough to join the Marines, possibly to the detriment of the line infantry units to which they would otherwise have been allotted.

Accordingly, the draftees who from 1965 found themselves fighting in the paddyfields were far from prepared. To compound the already extreme difficulties facing these inexperienced conscripts, the reputation and performance of each individual unit to which they were attached varied greatly. The 1st Cavalry Division (Airmobile) was by far the best but was kept in reserve as a nationwide fire brigade. It was, for this reason, rarely seen on routine patrol in the paddyfields. The 11th Armored Cavalry Regiment, the 1st/101st Airborne Division and the 173rd Airborne Brigade were also excellent but tended to recruit selectively and then only the best. If he were lucky the draftee might find himself posted to the 1st or 25th Infantry Divisions or to the 5th Infantry Division (Mech) all of which were

Above: Sgt. Brock of 4/3rd Marine Division demonstrates the concealed entrance to a newly discovered Viet Cong tunnel.

regarded as good. If he were unlucky he might find himself attached to the 11th Light Infantry, the 196th or the 198th Brigades which shared a universally appalling reputation for ill-discipline.

Wherever fate sent him the young rookie would soon learn the first and most frustrating lesson of counter-insurgency warfare; that friend, foe and disinterested farmer all look exactly alike. This was particularly true in the Mekong Delta, the geographical centre of the paddyfields, where the population divided politically rather than socially and generalizations became dangerous. Without uniforms it was difficult to tell a Viet Cong fighter from a 'loyal' Vietnamese, particularly when

Right: A UH-1D Medivac helicopter takes off on a mission to recover an injured member of 101st Airborne Division from the DMZ.

the latter might have been a Viet Cong sympathizer, and failure to do so occasionally resulted in a bullet in the back. Villagers were subjected to thorough search and destroy missions which became more random and brutal as the war progressed, civilian casualties seeming to be less important than the need for enemy head counts. If suspected contraband was discovered — and it was left to the excitable and hyped patrol on the ground to decide what *was* suspect — the entire village was, more often than not, put to the torch. If weapons were found, field interrogations — illegal under the Geneva Conventions — and even summary execution, occasionally followed. The cruellest of all recorded examples of 'summary justice' occurred in the village of My Lai on 16 March 1968, when American soldiers from Company C, 1/20th Infantry massacred over 300 old men, women and children on suspicion of pro-communist involvement. My Lai epitomizes the type of disaster which can occur when sending untrained

Above: Marines observe a distant treeline across a faceless paddyfield during a sweep of the Mekong Delta.

Below: A Chinook helicopter unloads artillery shells north-west of Tuy Hoa during a search-and-destroy mission in the Phu Yen Province.

raw troops into a guerrilla environment against a virtually anonymous enemy. Neutrals were often mistaken for guerrillas by the 'hyped' troops.

As time went on, particularly after the 1968 Tet Offensive and the 1969 announcement of U.S. troop withdrawals, the Army in Vietnam declined dramatically. President Johnson's refusal to involve more than a handful of National Guardsmen or Army Reservists in the fighting had the effect of alienating the conscripted soldiers. More and more people began to question the direction and morality of the war. Conscientious objectors and draft dodgers were lauded on school and college campuses. Parents joined their children in anti-war demonstrations throughout the land. For the first time in American history returning troops were openly abused in the streets. Drug abuse, racial fights, even the occasional 'fragging' of unpopular officers, became the regular diet of those left to patrol the paddyfields and villages of Vietnam. The Vietnamese became 'gooks' and all 'gooks' became the enemy. 'Search and destroy' became 'ignore and survive' as gradually the entire countryside was wrested from Government control.

The United States Army was soundly beaten in the paddyfields of Vietnam. For years the cause of her defeat was largely ignored by the American population as a whole, but not by the Pentagon which analyzed its mistakes in detail. For a number of years the Army went into decline both socially and professionally as it sought a solution to its malaise. The concept of a special force deploying, gained in popularity with the establishment as U.S. policy moved away from large scale to localized confrontation. The conventional Army slimmed down and reappraised its training techniques. The Army which emerged recently to lead the Alliance in the Middle East was altogether leaner, meaner and in all respects, far more efficient than the Army in Vietnam. Most importantly, it was wholly professional, its regular units having been supplemented where necessary by Reservist and National Guard volunteers. Perhaps now, the spectre of the paddyfields which hung over America for the past twenty years, has at last been laid to rest.

Viet Cong prisoners captured in a tunnel complex by elements of 173 Airborne Brigade in the Thanh Dien Forest.

The Battle for the Imperial Palace, Hue, 1968

Vietnamese troops parade to mark the Tenth Anniversary of the fall of Saigon.

By the winter of 1967/68 it had become clear to the Communists that the war for South Vietnam was not going according to plan. A huge increase in American military commitment over the previous two years had caused the North Vietnamese to lose the initiative. Their supply lines were being cut denying them a regular flow of food and ammunition and they were sustaining increasingly heavy casualties in the field. More fundamentally they were losing the respect and trust of the once largely sympathetic Southern rural population. Without an immediate victory there appeared to be little hope for the future.

The North conceded that she would not be able to defeat the United States in open battle. She therefore sought to carry the war to domestic America. Reasoning that America's weakness lay not in her military firepower but in her civilian resolve, Hanoi determined to turn public opinion against the war. For the first time in history the realities of combat were being brought nightly to the living rooms of the American public courtesy of live television. Young G. I.s were dying in the sight of their loved ones and inevitably the whole morality of intervention was coming under increasing scrutiny. If U.S. prestige could be dented it was anticipated that popular support for the war would crumble, leaving Washington with no alternative but to withdraw.

It was decided to launch the offensive on the morning of 31 January during the Tet festival. Traditionally Tet, the Vietnamese New Year, was marked by an informal cease-fire. The bulk of the South Vietnamese Army would be on leave and security would be lax making the smuggling of weapons into the target areas comparatively simple.

Plans were put into effect for the execution of a series of simultaneous mass

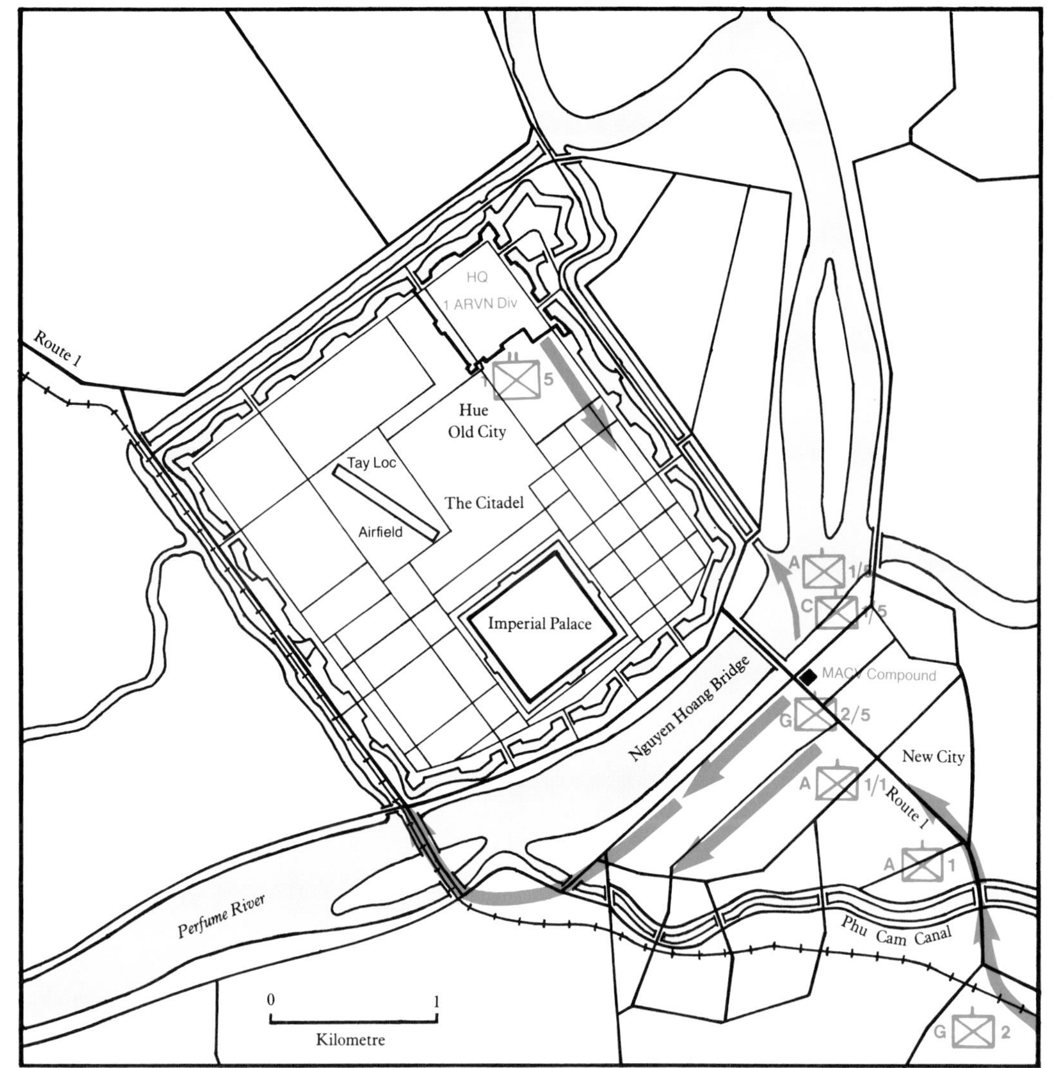

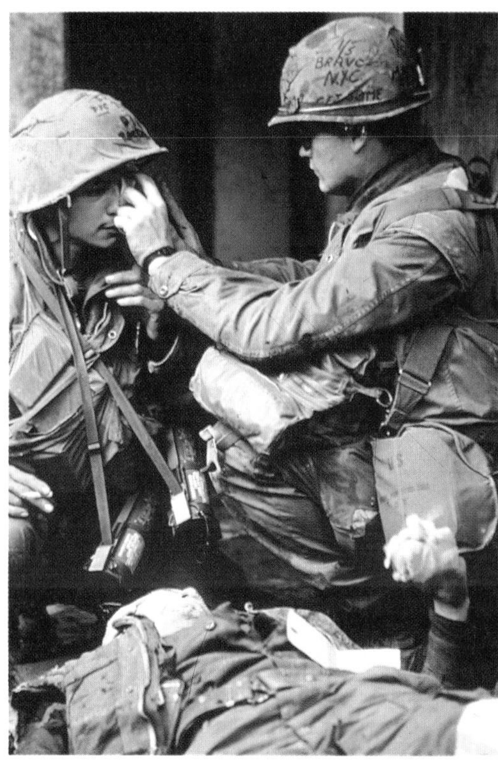

Above: Wounded marines receive aid during the battle for Hue.

Below: Marines advance into Hue past the bodies of dead Viet Cong guerrillas.

On 31 January joint NVA/VC forces seized most of Hue, the ancient capital of Vietnam. The U.S. Marine troops sent to regain control were veterans of jungle warfare with no knowledge of how to fight in an urban environment. Although slow but steady progress was made, and the ruins of the city eventually retaken, losses were high. Whereas the MACV compound in the New City was quickly relieved by Company G, 2/5th Marines a subsequent attempt to cross the Nguyen Hoang Bridge into the Old City was bloodily repulsed. Thereafter it took the Marines eight days of vicious, often hand-to-hand fighting, with the assistance of a company of M-48 tanks, to regain control of the New City. The fight for the Old City was worse. For six days the 1/5th Marines battled their way south from the ARVN headquarters in the north-east of the Citadel to the Perfume River. United States artillery and air power were used almost indiscriminately, to such an extent that the heart of Hue was almost totally destroyed by its supposed liberators. There were 5,000 civilians killed, 10,000 homes destroyed and 116,000 citizens made homeless.

attacks against designated cities and Government centres throughout the South. Regular troops of the North Vietnamese Army were fed down the Ho Chi Minh Trail and local Vietcong units alerted. Feint attacks were launched against remote outposts in an attempt to draw American reserves away from the intended targets.

The attack when it was launched came as a complete surprise to the Allies. In the space of less than 24 hours a total of 84,000 Communist troops assaulted the capital city of Saigon together with 36 of the South's provincial capitals, five of its six autonomous cities and 64 of its 242 district capitals.

Nowhere was the fighting fiercer than in the old provincial capital of Hue, a city which until then had been spared the worst excesses of war. At 3.40 am on 31 January Communist infantrymen crossed the Perfume River under cover of mortar fire from the mountains to the west. They quickly seized the Citadel, with its massive walls over 20 feet high and up to 200 feet thick, and fanned out into the new city. Within minutes they had successfully cut Route 1, the major highway running north to the border. By dawn the Communists had taken all but a handful of buildings in the city and were defiantly flying from the southern wall of the Citadel.

Shocked by the sheer audacity of the attack the Allied forces in the locality found themselves completely unprepared. They had known for some weeks that the Communists were concentrating massive reinforcements in the area but had assumed incorrectly that these were being husbanded for the assault on Khe Sanh to the west.

The 1st ARVN Division maintained its headquarters in the north-east sector of the Citadel and garrisoned a small MACV base for advisers just south of the river but was otherwise bivouacked in its entirety outside of the city limits. More alarmingly Marine Task Force X-Ray, destined to provide U.S. Tactical support, was critically below strength.

Brigadier General Lahue, in command of the 1st and 5th Marine Regiments comprising the task force, was the first to react. Realizing at once that his first priority was to relieve the U.S. advisers in the MACV outpost he dispatched Company A, 1/1st Marines north along Highway 1 towards the new city. Having crossed the Phu Cam Canal without incident the company was almost immediately pinned down by concentrated fire and it was not until reinforcements arrived in the form of Company G, 2/5th Marines supported by four M-48 tanks of the 3rd Marine Tank Battalion that the now much enhanced force was able to reach its objective.

Having relieved their exhausted comrades in the MACV compound at approximately 3.00 pm the Marines continued to put their superior training to excellent advantage. The area surrounding the compound was secured, a temporary helicopter landing zone established on the riverbank and the southern end of the Nguyen Hoang Bridge leading directly into the Citadel was seized.

Above: Marines from Coy A 1/1st Regt fire from a window during a search-and-destroy mission in the battle for Hue.

Tragically, the Marines' total lack of familiarity with urban warfare now began to tell. Despite the obvious foreboding of its commander, Company G was ordered across the bridge to probe the extent of the enemy positions. However, after having breached the outer wall of the Citadel, the men of Company G became hopelessly entangled in the nightmare of narrow streets beyond, suffering severe casualties in the process. That night, to the sheer relief of the Marines, North Vietnamese engineers destroyed the bridge, precluding the possibility of any future suicidal probes.

During the next few days the Marines, experts in jungle warfare, were destined to learn the vicious and uncompromising realities of street fighting. On 3 February 2/5th Marines supported by 1/1st Marines on their left were ordered to clear the New City west of the MACV compound. They were soon reminded of the lessons learned so savagely by Company G less than three days before. Virtually every building in the 11 blocks comprising the axis of advance had been transformed into a fortress. Denied air and artillery support by the monsoon conditions then prevailing, the Marines, never fully at one with the bayonet, were forced to resort to hand-to-hand fighting. For several days small knots of Marines could be seen moving from one house to the next seeking shelter from the constant enemy gunfire whenever and wherever possible. Initial attempts to minimize the use of armoured support in an attempt to maintain the structure of the city intact were soon abandoned. Troops with M-48 medium battle tanks and Ontos

Below: U.S. Ambassador Bunker views the damage to the U.S. Embassy after the Tet Offensive.

tank-busters were brought forward to pound the areas of strongest resistance although this frequently resulted in the destruction by the Marines of the very Government buildings they had been sent to save. On 11 February, after eight days of bloody fighting, 2/5th finally secured its objective by reaching the confluence of the canal and Perfume River. Two days later it crossed the river into the western suburbs of the Old City to await the arrival of the 1st Cavalry and 101st Airborne Divisions fighting their way in from the north.

By this stage the nucleus of the battle had passed firmly to the Old City. Although the 1st ARVN Division had succeeded in relieving its headquarters complex and retaking much of the northern part of the Old City, the Citadel itself together with the Imperial Palace and much of the surrounding area remained in enemy hands. United States Marine assistance was sought by the South Vietnamese and granted in the form of 1/5th Marines recently withdrawn from operations in the Phu Loc area. On 12 February Companies A and C 1/5th were moved by landing craft from the MACV complex in the New City along the moat to the east of the Citadel and ordered to link up with Company B already in situ in the ARVN headquarters complex having been flown in by helicopter the day before. On the morning of 13 February, Company A was ordered to advance along the eastern wall unit until it reached a large tower which it was to secure. Within minutes the Marines came under heavy fire sustaining two dead and 30 wounded. Totally inexperienced in urban warfare (the 1/5th had taken no part in the fighting for the New City) the Company was forced to withdraw without coming close to attaining its objective. Company C, committed to the battle that afternoon, fared no better.

For 36 hours the hand-to-hand fighting continued relentlessly until eventually Company D, originally held in battalion reserve, was brought forward and managed to gain a foothold in the tower. Even then the battle was far from over. Firing from hastily prepared positions in the ramparts, the enemy continued to harry the tired and by now frustrated Marines. Having secured the tower the 1/5th was ordered to continue its almost suicidal advance south along the Citadel wall for a further four days until it reached the river at which time the insurgents were effectively cut off from all hope of escape. Inexplicably no attempt was made to reinforce or relieve the hapless battalion until it had been fought to a virtual standstill, nor were its tactics varied. The obvious fact that the M-48 tanks and Ontos tank-busters which had proved to be crucial in the earlier battle for the New City could not operate in the narrow lanes of the Old City was simply ignored as inconvenient. Higher command reverted to the dubious twin gods of air power and artillery to clear a route for the advancing Marines regardless of the fact that neither could provide the pin-point accuracy essential for the support of house-clearance operations. United States heavy ordnance turned Hue into rubble and in so doing gave the Communists precisely the kind of propaganda victory which they sought.

Above: Tan Son Nhut, devastated by retaliating U.S. fire during the Tet offensive.

Ironically the Imperial Palace, the last Communist stronghold to fall, was liberated not by the Marines but by the ARVN *Black Panther* Company imported specially in a forlorn attempt to bolster the flagging morale of the South Vietnamese forces.

In three weeks of bloody and almost continuous fighting in and around Hue over 10,000 homes were destroyed and 116,000 civilians out of a population of 140,000 were made homeless. An estimated 5,000 civilians, many of them government employees, were murdered by the Communists who in turn lost 5,113 confirmed dead. The South Vietnamese Army suffered 384 dead, the United States Marines 147 dead and 857 wounded.

The Marines had fought magnificently to win the battle for Hue but in so doing had inadvertently paved the way for ultimate defeat. The minutiae of combat had exploded before an incredulous and horrified audience in America. The single-minded bravery and determination of the Communist enemy, a factory already recognized by the military, had become apparent to the armchair strategists back home. Victory over an alien ideology, the sole purpose for prosecuting the war, was no longer regarded as a certainty.

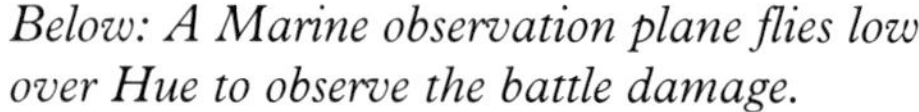

Below: A Marine observation plane flies low over Hue to observe the battle damage.

Khe Sanh,
The U.S. Marines in Vietnam, 1968

In 1954 French forces were surrounded by the Viet Minh at Dien Bien Phu and forced to surrender. Their fate had sealed the end of French colonial ambitions in Indo-China. Fourteen years later a smaller force of U.S. Marines found itself in similar circumstances at Khe Sanh. The entire United States nation took the battle to its hearts and determined that this time the Vietnamese would not succeed. President Johnson had a scale model of Khe Sanh constructed in the White House and demanded of his commanders in the field that the base be held at all costs. It is even suggested that he considered the use of tactical nuclear weapons against the besieging enemy as a last resort. Ultimately the Vietnamese were unsuccessful and were forced to withdraw, having sustained enormous casualties. The 6,000 Marines involved in the battle owed their success in no small part to their tenacity and training. Above, all, however, Khe Sanh was a victory for air power.

Khe Sanh Combat Base was regarded by the United States as strategically very important. Built on a low plateau around an airstrip, it commanded Route 9 and offered some protection to the ancient city of Hue to the south east. More fundamentally it acted as a covert base for special forces teams operating across the Laotian and North Vietnamese borders.

Khe Sanh base had first been constructed in 1962 by the U.S. Special Forces as a centre for one of its Montagnard Civilian Irregular Defence Groups but had been taken over by the Marines four years later. Since then it had been expanded and by 1968 consisted of a series of hills to the west and north of a low plateau. Of these the most important were Hills 881 North, 881 South and 861, so designated after

Below: Marine vehicles parked in the open at Khe Sanh. Those which could not be protected were destroyed in the seige.

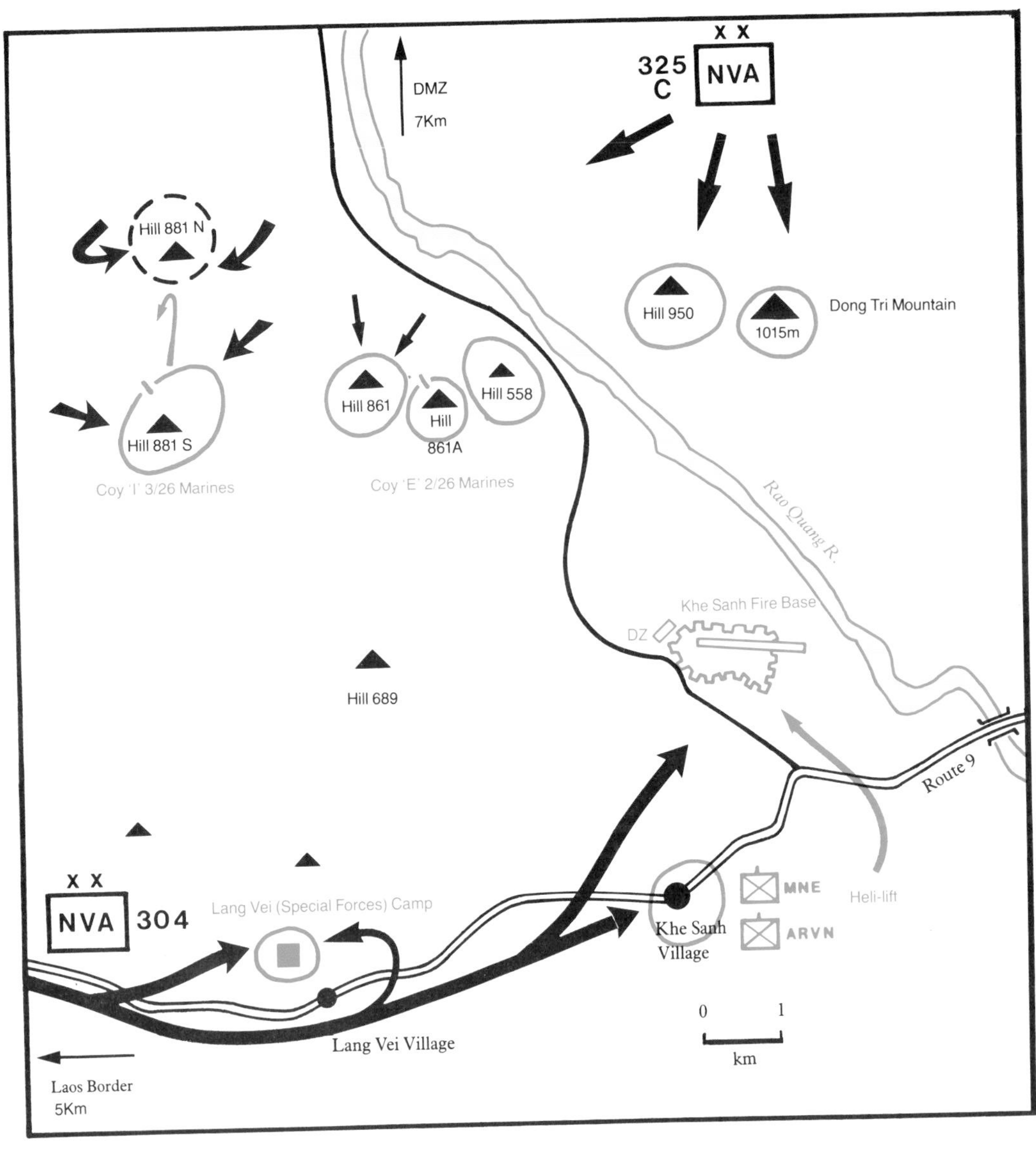

The siege of Khe Sanh lasted for 77 days and ended in an American victory. The defending forces, aware of the French mistakes at Dien Bien Phu, determined to hold the high ground surrounding the firebase at all costs. Hill 881 North fell at an early stage of the siege, as did the Special Forces base at Long Vei, but the other strongpoints held firm. Massed attacks by troops of the 304th and 325th NVA Divisions were cut to pieces by U.S. artillery and mortar fire often supported by fighter ground attack and B-52 airstrikes. Unlike Dien Bien Phu the airbase remained open at all times enabling the Marine defenders to casevac their injured and receive regular resupplies. The Khe Sanh airbase was formally relieved on 6 April 1968 when elements of the 3rd ARVN Airborne Taskforce were airlifted in and linked up with the 37th Rangers. Less than three months later it was quietly evacuated.

their height in metres. All overlooked the plateau and commanded the Rao Quan River approaches, a likely Vietnamese attack route from the north-west. The Marines fully appreciated that were these hills to fall into enemy hands they would be ideally placed to bombard Khe Sanh making aerial resupply impossible. Nonetheless they were not heavily manned until December 1967, by which time Special Forces and Marine patrols were reporting a massive build up in the area. Unknown to American intelligence the North Vietnamese had moved two full divisions across the Laotian border and were planning an all out attack on the base to coincide with the Tet Offensive.

In January 1968 the Marines, now reinforced by the three battalions of the 26th Marines under command of Colonel David Lownds, established new defensive positions on Hills 558 and 861A, to the east and north-west of 861, and began to prepare for the imminent battle.

The long awaited attack began on 17 January when Vietnamese regulars from 325C Division ambushed a patrol from Company I, 3/26th Marines in the area of 881 North. Two days later another patrol was attacked in the same area sustaining heavy casualties. Initial attempts by Captain Dabney's Company I to clear the area of the enemy on 20 January were frustrated when a deserter reported that the main airbase itself was due to be attacked by two full divisions during the early hours of the next morning. Dabney was ordered to break off the assault and to retire to the comparative safety of 881 South leaving 881 North temporarily in enemy hands.

Just after midnight on 21 January the anticipated main attack began when some 300 North Vietnamese breached the perimeter wire, attacked Hill 861,

Troops working on the airstrip in Khe Sanh. Note the protective sandbags close by.

penetrated the Marine defences and captured the helicopter landing zone. At 5.30 a.m., hundreds of rockets, artillery shells and mortar rounds suddenly rained down on the main combat base igniting one of the principal ammunition dumps. Simultaneously, Khe Sanh village itself, to the south of the base, was attacked by strong enemy forces necessitating the evacuation by helicopter of a number of Marine advisers. As the North Vietnamese consolidated their early gains the siege of Khe Sanh, which was destined to last for 77 days, began.

It soon became clear that despite their overwhelming superiority in numbers the North Vietnamese simply did not have the resources or will to mount a successful frontal assault against the closely interlocked American fire bases. For most of the time they were content to batter the base with 82mm and 120mm mortars positioned in an arc some 2,500 to 3,000m (2,708 to 3,250 yds) to the north-west, with 122mm rockets deployed on Hill 881 North and with long-range 122mm D-30 and 152mm D-1 artillery firing from concealed positions across the Laotian border. In all an average of 2,500 rounds of assorted artillery per week, 27,500 rounds in all, were fired into an area little more than half a square kilometre in size.

Despite the ferocity of the artillery bombardment, so long as the American and South Vietnamese defenders kept their nerve and remained underground they were comparatively safe. Having overcome their initial detestation for digging, (many Marines regarded burrowing as beneath their dignity), they had eventually constructed an excellent complex of intertwining bunkers and fire trenches which afforded excellent protection against all but direct hits. It had even become possible to create a somewhat basic nocturnal routine by which repairs were effected and supplies distributed under cover of darkness. The only troops to remain above ground during daylight were the limited number required to mount a few localized patrols and man the sentry positions.

When the Vietnamese did undertake assaults they were rarely well coordinated and invariably resulted in heavy losses. Typical of these was the attack mounted against Hill 861A on 5 February. At 3.05 a.m., after a short mortar bombardment which did little other than alert the Americans of their intentions, the Vietnamese launched wave after wave of unprotected infantrymen against the perimeter wire. Most were cut to pieces in the flat beaten zone surrounding

the American positions. Those few who succeeded in breaching the outer defences were quickly neutralized by Company E, 2/26nd Marines under command of Captain Earle Breeding. The surviving Communists withdrew only to try again some three hours later – this time in daylight. As was inevitable, they were annihilated by artillery and mortar fire brought down on their positions from fire bases on the neighbouring hills. The 81mm mortars on Hill 881 South alone fired over 1,000 rounds into the enemy positions. As the Vietnamese turned and fled the Marines counted 109 enemy dead for the loss of the remarkably low number of seven Americans killed.

Attacks against the main perimeter fared no better. On 8 February regular troops from the Vietnamese 325th Division, some of them veterans of the Dien Bien Phu campaign, executed a daylight raid against American positions on the south-western extremity of the base. Initially their action met with success. The Americans, perhaps complacent after their successes on Hill 861A only three days earlier, had not expected another frontal attack so quickly and had momentarily dropped their guard. Company A, 1/9th Marines was cut off, surrounded and nearly overwhelmed. Had it not been for the timely arrival of reinforcements provided by the rest of the Company, disaster might have ensued. As it was, the Communists were forced to withdraw across open ground where they came under American artillery fire. Over 150 Vietnamese were killed for the loss of 21 Marines dead and 26 wounded.

Precisely why the Vietnamese failed to use their overwhelming superiority in numbers to better effect remains a mystery. Had they launched a series of simultaneous attacks along the entire American front the Marines would have been unable to concentrate their artillery. A number of the outlying hills would almost certainly have fallen leaving the defence of the airfield itself untenable. Equally inexplicably, the Vietnamese had light tanks in the area but failed to commit them. On 6/7 February 11 Soviet-built PT-76 tanks spearheaded a successful attack against the Special Forces base at Lang Vei only five miles from Khe Sanh, but were not deployed again. True, five of them had been destroyed by the Special Forces but losses had never been regarded as important by the Communists. The appearance of the surviving tanks outside of the perimeter would have had a devastating effect on American morale yet they remained impotent on the outskirts of the battle, their potential squandered.

From the very beginning of the siege President Johnson had determined that Khe Sanh would be held at all costs. In late January the garrison was augmented by 1/9th Marines with their additional 105mm artillery pieces and by the crack 37th ARVN Ranger Battalion increasing its size to nearly 6,700 men. A previously unknown aggressive patrolling, particularly towards the south, became the order of the day.

Logistics, particularly in the area of resupply, became a nightmare. Everything from food and water to fuel and ammunition had to be flown in through monsoon conditions into a hail of often accurate enemy fire. Heavy equipment was carried in U.S. Air Force C-130 Hercules and C-123 Provider transport aircraft supported by Marine CH-46, Army CH-53 and UH-1E helicopters. It did not take the North Vietnamese long to register their artillery on to the airstrip and they soon became adroit at bringing down fire on to the dispersal areas as soon as aircraft engines were heard in the distance. It was for this reason U.S. losses were heavy. A C-130 carrying fuel to the main base received a direct hit and exploded while at least five helicopters were lost attempting to resupply Hill 881.

As casualties mounted, new techniques evolved to counter the enemy artillery. Pilots of C-130 aircraft perfected the art of precision ultra low-level parachute drops while the helicopter crews learned to reduce their turn-around time to less than the enemy's average response time of 19 seconds.

Coordinated support from fighter ground attack aircraft and strategic bombers paid a great part in Khe Sanh's survival. Within hours of the beginning of the siege, President Johnson authorized the implementation of Operation *Niagara*, the stated aim of which was 'destroy enemy forces in the Khe Sanh area, interdict enemy supply lines and base areas ... and provide a maximum tactical air support of friendly forces'. Guided by veteran Tactical Air Controllers flying 0-1 Bird Dog light aircraft wave after wave of U.S. Air Force and Marine fighter bombers armed either with rockets or with a lethal cocktail of conventional bombs and napalm were called down on to known enemy positions. Simultaneously all available artillery in range, including that situated in neighbouring fire bases, was brought to bear on the enemy in the hopes of catching him in the open. Squadrons of B-52 Stratofortresses, each carrying 54,000 pounds of high explosives, were also brought to bear against the enemy's known or presumed supply routes and staging posts. When the monsoon reduced the cloud-base making accurate bombing impossible, ground-positioned radars situated in Khe Sanh were employed to guide the aircraft on to their targets. In all over 2,700 B-52 airstrikes and 24,000 tactical sorties were flown between 21 January and 31 March. Over 100,000 tons of bombs and 150,000 tons of artillery rounds were delivered on to known or assumed enemy positions.

Operation *Niagara* undoubtedly broke the enemy's will to fight. The precise number of casualties sustained by him as a direct result of the aerial bombardment is unknown but it must have been in the tens of thousands. As the monsoon subsided and the weather improved it became increasingly clear to both adversaries that the siege was doomed to failure. The North Vietnamese began to melt away across the Laotian border leaving the defenders able for the first time in weeks to enjoy the occasional uninterrupted nights's sleep.

Khe Sanh was formally relieved at 11.50 p.m. on 6 April when elements of the 3rd ARVN Airborne Taskforce were airlifted to Khe Sanh and linked up with the 37th Rangers. Two days later 2/7 Cavalry which had been leading the sweep along Highway 9 linked up with the 26th Marines. On 14 April, Easter Sunday, 3/26th Marines rounded off the battle by retaking Hill 881 North from which their Company I had been forced to withdraw some eleven weeks earlier.

Khe Sanh was undoubtedly a major victory for the U.S. Marine Corps and its allies. Heavily outnumbered they had held out for nearly three months and in their opinion could have done so for a further three years if so ordered. Although it had cost the lives of 205 Americans and South Vietnamese, the seige had proved that the North Vietnamese Army simply did not have the logistics to prosecute conventional hostilities against the might of the United States war machine. If she could only draw the enemy into the open the United States would be assured of victory.

Ironically this was not to be. The Tet Offensive which had taken place during the early stages of the siege had precipitated the war into the theatre of politics. Individual battles no longer counted. The American public ignored the lessons of Khe Sanh and began to agitate for withdrawal from Vietnam. In June 1968, less than three months after the lifting of the siege, Khe Sanh was quietly evacuated.

Royal Australian Regiment, Diggers in Vietnam, 1970

Australia sent its first advisers to Vietnam in August 1962. Initially the Australian Army Training Team Vietnam (AATTV) consisted of no more than 30 officers and NCOs and worked exclusively with the South Vietnamese Army. By 1964, however, it had been increased to 80 personnel, many of them members of the Special Air Service Regiment (SASR), and had begun to work closely with the U.S. Special Forces who held its expertise in great esteem.

In April 1965, in response to a request from President Johnson for international support on the ground, Australia deployed the 1st Battalion, Royal Australian Regiment (1RAR) to Bien Hoa outside of Saigon. In July of that year the battalion was augmented by a 105mm battery of New Zealand artillery and two months later by a further battery of Australian gunners.

In March 1966, spurred on by the success of the existing force, Canberra agreed to increase its presence to full Task Force status. The Task Force usually consisted of two infantry battalions with dedicated armour and artillery, a squadron of SASR, logistics, signals and other support. The Royal Australian Air Force's contribution to the war consisted of a squadron of Canberra bombers which flew 11,963 sorties for the loss of only two aircraft. Later that year the 1st Australian Task Force as it was now designated was redeployed to Phuoc Tuy, a coastal province to the north-east of Saigon, within which it was granted full autonomy. Geographically the area was ideally suited to the Australian concept of counter-intelligence warfare, which was alien to the United States regular army. About 3,900 sq kms (1,500 square miles) in size, it consisted basically of scrubland with a few low hills and the occasional patch of virgin jungle. The population of 100,000, many of whom were well indoctrinated Communist sympathizers, was largely concentrated along the coastline where movements would be easy to monitor. The 5th Vietcong Division was known to be hiding in the May Tao Hills to the north-east, supported by the locally raised D445 Battalion which operated covertly from the local villages.

Australian Army Minister Lynch flanked by Generals Hay and Tam review the Australian Expeditionary Force at Tan Son Nhut.

Until the arrival of the Australians, the area had been largely ignored by the United States and South Vietnamese forces. Brigadier Jackson, in command of the ATF, decided however to make his presence felt at once. Having set up his Force headquarters at Vung Tau, on the coast, he established a small hill base at Nui Dat, some twenty miles to the north. Having placed his artillery in Nui Dat he ordered his infantry to begin a policy of 'aggressive patrolling' under the protection of the guns with the aim of clearing the Vietcong from the local villages, so driving a wedge between them and the main population centres.

Nui Dat was not an ideal location. It had few facilities, the gun pits soon became waterlogged and the troops were forced to live under canvas. Nonetheless, the Australian volunteers soon acclimatized. Unlike their American counterparts they had received jungle training before being posted to Vietnam and so were able to begin a purposeful routine of patrolling, the success of which soon made them the envy of their allies. SASR teams would push deep into Phuoc Tuy to spring ambushes on the unsuspecting, and until then relatively safe, Vietcong, leaving the line infantry to create a fire zone around the base to secure it from sniper and mortar fire. A combination of 5.56mm M-16s and heavier 7.62mm FN automatic rifles were carried by each patrol to give it a unique blend of firepower and versatility. In the process the villages of Long Phuoc to the south and Long Tan to the east were evacuated, their somewhat unwilling occupants being moved to less vulnerable areas.

Australian intelligence, however, was not always accurate, allowing the Vietcong the occasional luxury of a success. On17 August 1966 a Communist patrol managed to pierce the outer defences at Nui Dat and mortar the sleeping Australians, killing one and wounding 23. Brigadier Jackson was facing a dilemma. At the time the ATF consisted of two line battalions, 5 and 6RAR and was fully committed. Jackson had been left with only three infantry companies with which to guard the base and pursue the enemy for all of 5RAR and one company of 6RAR were out on patrol. He immediately ordered the recall of the outlying patrols to counter the possibility of a large-scale attack and dispatched B Company, 6RAR on a sweep of the area to the east of the base.

Having found nothing that day, the Company was ordered to return to base next day, when the search would be continued by the 108 officers and men of D Company under command of Major Harry Smith. Unknown to the Australians,

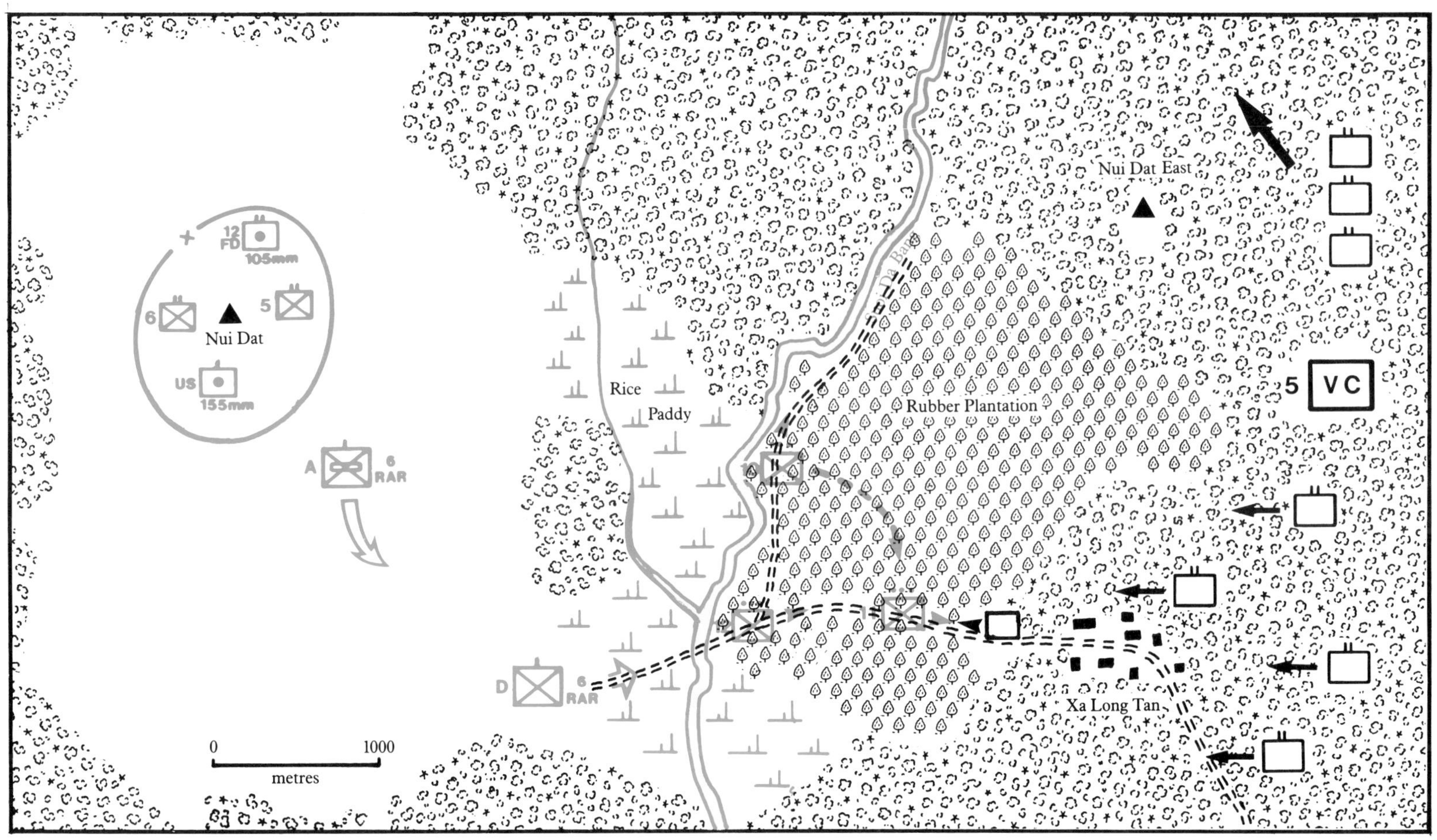

Above: Women comprising a minority of the troops engaged against the Australians at Long Tan.

The battle for Long Tan epitomized the sheer professionalism of the Australian forces in Vietnam. On the morning of 18 August 1966, D Company 6RAR was ordered to patrol the rubber plantation to the east of Long Tan village in search of Communist infiltrators. As it entered the plantation, 11 Platoon continued east along the main track while 10 Platoon moved north along an alternative axis. Almost at once 11 Platoon came under fire from the leading elements of four regular Vietcong battalions. The Australians immediately formed a defensive position and called down support from the New Zealand and U.S. artillery batteries positioned in Nui Dat. 10 and 12 Platoons attempted to come to the assistance of 11 Platoon throughout the afternoon but were initially beaten back by the ferocity of the enemy fire. Relief came at about 6.00 p.m. when A Company 6RAR supported by the 1st APC Squadron fought its way through to the 12 Platoon position. A Company defensive position was formed into which 10 and 11 Platoons were able to retire. The Vietcong attack continued throughout most of the night. By dawn, however, the enemy had melted away, leaving the Australians in firm control of the area.

the Vietcong had decided to destroy Nui Dat completely and were at that precise moment converging on it with seven battalions comprising over 4,000 men. Three of the battalions were swinging north away from the area of immediate Australian interest. Four battalions however, were approaching their objective through the Long Tan rubber plantation to the east, the same area through which D Company was destined to patrol.

At 11.00 a.m. on 18 August, D Company left Nui Dat with 12 Platoon, commanded by Second Lieutenant David Sabben in the lead. Two hours later they safely liaised with B Company who showed them evidence of Communist activity near the Long Tan Plantation some 2,000m (2,168 yds) east of the Nui Dat perimeter. Having completed his reconnaissance of the area, Smith ordered his company forward along a clearly defined track into the plantation. After about 300m (327 yds) the track split into two, the left hand fork going north and skirting the edge of the plantation, the right hand fork continuing forward directly into the rubber trees. Second Lieutenant Geoff Kendall in command of 10 Platoon was ordered to probe north, while Second Lieutenant Gordon Sharp's 11 Platoon, supported by 12 Platoon and the Company Headquarters element, continued east into the plantation.

Above: A squadron of M-113 APCs such as this broke the back of the Vietnamese atack on Long Tan.

Left: ADF troops board a U.S. Chinook to return to their base at Nui Dat having taken part in a 'recce' operation.

At approximately 3.45 p.m., after 40 minutes of painstakingly slow progress, Private Allen May, the forward scout of 11 Platoon, spotted a squad of six Vietcong. The Australians opened fire without warning, taking the young Vietcong completely by surprise. The survivors fled further east deeper into the plantation, pursued by the leading elements of the Australian platoon. At 4.08 p.m., as 11 Platoon entered a small clearing which marked the eastern boundary of the plantation and the beginning of jungle, it came under sustained fire. Two Australians died immediately as the rest of the platoon dived for cover. Fortunately the highly trained infantrymen did not panic but instead remembered their basic training and formed an area of all round defence,

Left: A Royal Australian Artillery crew near a 105mm M101 A1 gun in Vietnam.

frustrating Vietcong attempts to overrun their position. Company headquarters, with 12 Platoon to its rear, attempted to advance in support but were brought under heavy mortar fire and stalled leaving Sharp's men alone and perilously exposed.

The situation might have resulted in total disaster had Captain Morrie Stanley, the Royal New Zealand Artillery forward observation officer attached to D Company, not been able to bring down accurate and sustained 105mm artillery fire from the guns at Nui Dat directly on to the enemy's position. Supported by a battery of American 155mm field guns co-located at Nui Dat the 24 M101 guns available continued firing ceaselessly for two and a half hours, ranging to and fro across the enemy's forming up points making it impossible for him to execute a concerted assault on the exposed Australian lines.

Hearing the firefight, 10 Platoon located to the north, immediately attempted to relieve the pressure. Under the cover of a cloudburst and assisted by the noise and confusion of the battle, the platoon managed to infiltrate the enemy's position unseen before opening fire. The enemy quickly recovered however, and at once shifted some of his available reserves to threaten Kendall who was then forced to draw his own men into a hastily improvised defensive position.

Lieutenant Colonel Colin Townsend, the commanding officer of 6RAR, had not been idle while his men had been under attack. He had immediately begun to assemble a relief force from the few personnel available to him in headquarters. A Company, recently returned from patrol, was ordered to replenish its ammunition stocks and enbus on a section of ten elderly M-113s attached to the 1st APC Squadron.

At 5.45 p.m. A Company left its position at Nui Dat and headed for a crossing point on the Suoi Da Ban River. By this time the much battered D Company was running dangerously short of ammunition. An attempt by two sections of 12 Platoon to fight through to their colleagues in 11 Platoon had failed, leaving the latter in desperate straits. At 5.00 p.m. Smith had ordered the survivors of 10 and 12 Platoons to reform on his headquarters now positioned in a small hollow some way to the west but 11 Platoon, unable to extradite itself and completely surrounded, had to be left to its own devices.

At approximately 6.00 p.m. in an act of particular heroism, two Australian-crewed UH-1 helicopters took off from Nui Dat and overflew D Company's new defensive position. Guided by coloured flares and taking advantage of a deliberate halt in the barrage they hovered low over the headquarters to enable desperately needed ammunition boxes to be dropped to the men below. Almost simultaneously the Vietcong mounted a suicidally brave human-wave assault which the Australians were only able to counter with extreme difficulty. Grasping his opportunity admirably, Sergeant Bob Buick, in command of 11 Platoon since the death of its officer, used the ensuing pandemonium to lead the remnants of his men through the enemy positions to the new company lines. For the first time in three hours of bitter and vicious fighting the survivors of D Company were reunited.

Royal Australian Artillery gunners man a battery of U.S. made M101 A1 field guns.

Despite their heavy losses, the Vietcong continued their relentless attempt to annihilate the remnants of Smith's command. D445 Battalion was ordered to sweep west behind the Australians to complete the encirclement. In so doing they ran directly into A Company's advancing APCs. Both sides were taken completely by surprise but training came to the fore and the Australians recovered quicker. Remaining on the move they brought their vehicle mounted 50-cal machine guns into devastating effect, cutting swathes through the confused and terrified Communists. One vehicle was forced to withdraw when its commander was badly injured but the other nine continued their advance and, at 6.40 p.m., entered the D Company perimeter.

B Company, which had fought its way to the scene on foot, took advantage of the occasion, organized its own breakthrough, and joined its colleagues in the now rapidly strengthening defensive lines. Disorientated and confused, the Vietcong broke off the action and retired to the comparative safety of the jungle. Townsend, who had arrived with A Company, now assumed command and at once set about regrouping on a small clearing to the west. The dead and wounded were evacuated by helicopter, leaving the survivors to spend a restless night listening to the sounds of the jungle. The Vietcong made no further attempt to attack but instead busied themselves scouring the area for their own casualties.

Supplies were brought forward, both to Nui Dat (where the artillery had expended 2,639 rounds of 105mm and 155 rounds of 155mm ammunition) and to the 6RAR perimeter itself.

At daybreak, D Company was ordered to reconnoitre and if possible secure the battlefield. They found the area devastated but deserted. Two wounded Australians were discovered and evacuated but otherwise the area was empty save for the bodies of the fallen whom the Vietcong had not managed to drag away in the night.

The battle for Long Tan gave the Australians the initiative in Phuoc Tuy and enhanced their rapidly growing reputation as fighters. They had lost 17 dead in the battle but Vietcong fatalities had been enormous.

A total 0f 245 bodies were located and buried but everywhere there were signs of others having been removed. The influence of the Vietcong 5th Division was eroded. In the next few months it would be destroyed completely.

Throughout the engagement at Long Tan the initiative had rested with the Vietcong yet they had been soundly defeated. The Australian Task Force had demonstrated that firepower alone is no substitute for excellent leadership, a cool head and experience. Nowhere in Vietnam was the truth of the maxim 'train hard, fight easy' more ably demonstrated than at Long Tan.

Mirbat, The SAS in the Radfan, July 1972

In 1970 Britain was drawn with some trepidation into what was to be her last major colonial war. Since 1962 Sa'id bin Taimur, the aged and despotic Sultan of Oman, had been engaged in a losing battle with Marxist inspired guerrillas in the southern province of Dhofar. Using the People's Democratic Republic of Yemen (P.D.R.Y.) as a base they had mounted an increasingly successful campaign against the small government presence in the area and were by 1970 threatening to destabilize the entire region. That year the unpopular and by now totally out of touch Sultan fell victim to a British inspired, bloodless palace coup and was replaced by his only son, the Sandhurst trained Anglophile Sultan Qaboos bin Said.

Qaboos requested and was immediately granted British military assistance to crush the insurrection. SAS teams were introduced within days (there is some suggestion that elements were already in position) and at once began to implement Operation *Storm*, the regaining of the initiative in the south.

The Dhofari terrain was uncompromising and totally alien to the SAS troopers sent to Qaboos' aid, many of whom had until recently been serving in the jungle. It consisted of three distinct regions: a narrow coastal plain some 60 km (37.5 miles) long and 10 km (6.25 miles) wide centering on the capital of Salalah, the mountainous Jebel Qarra with its deep wadis and numerous caves running south of Marmul and Thumrait and west to the Yemeni border, and the Negd, a generally flat desert between the mountains and the Empty Quarter.

The Dhofari people were, and still are, very different to the Omanis of the more affluent north. The town tribes of the coastal plain were basically of Kathiri origin, industrious and comparatively sophisticated. The Jebalis of the mountains, however, were hot tempered, highly intelligent and fiercely independent. Drawn from the Qarra peoples they were unswervingly loyal to self, livestock, family and tribe in that order. As the SAS were to discover they made loyal friends but bitter enemies. The Bedu of the Negd were drawn from the Mahra and Bait Kathir tribes originating from the Yemen. They had their own languages and were equally independent. Nomads, they derived their wealth almost exclusively from the camels and goats.

Above: SAS troopers unload fuel from an R.A.F. Blackburn Beverley in the Radfan.

Above: Officers of A Sqn 22SAS take part in a debriefing after a routine patrol.

Lieutenant-Colonel Johnny Watts, the commanding officer of 22 SAS and a veteran of earlier Omani campaigns, realized that his greatest battle was for the hearts and minds of the indignant and much abused indigenous population. If he could successfully convince them that their future lay with the regime of the young Sultan Qaboos and not with the Adoo, or Marxist rebels, he could starve the rebellion of manpower making the task of the conventional Jordanian and Iranian infantry also operating in support of the Sultan far easier.

To this end he introduced an intelligence cell to monitor the activities and test the reaction of the enemy. He created an information team to counter Marxist propaganda and to advise the locals of the very real material benefits of participation in the embryonic civil community development schemes. He brought doctors and special forces paramedics to the villages to inoculate the tribesmen and their families against preventable but to them previously lethal diseases and introduced veterinary teams to tend to their livestock.

Most importantly, he gave the Dhofaris the opportunity to take up arms and protect themselves against the increasingly brutal Adoo. Initially many Dhofaris had offered at least tacit support to the rebels in their prosecution of a war in which the mountain tribes had no real interest. Most however had since become alienated by the Marxist's inalienable hatred of family and religion, both crucial tenets in Dhofari culture. The newly formed groups of fighters were trained, armed and paid but not directly commanded by the SAS. Known as *firqat* they were allowed to elect their own leaders after which they were given almost total autonomy.

After several months of painstaking effort during which small teams of SAS lived with the *firqat*, gaining their trust and in many cases their admiration, Watts felt strong enough to carry the war to the enemy. In March 1971, a force of about 60 *firqat* and 40 SAS climbed an untried route into the mountains and began the aggressive patrolling of an area previously ignored by the Sultan's regular army. They fought a twelve day battle killing at least nine enemy before withdrawing.

Watts appreciated that a single victory would not be enough to turn the tide of local opinion in favour of the Sultan. To

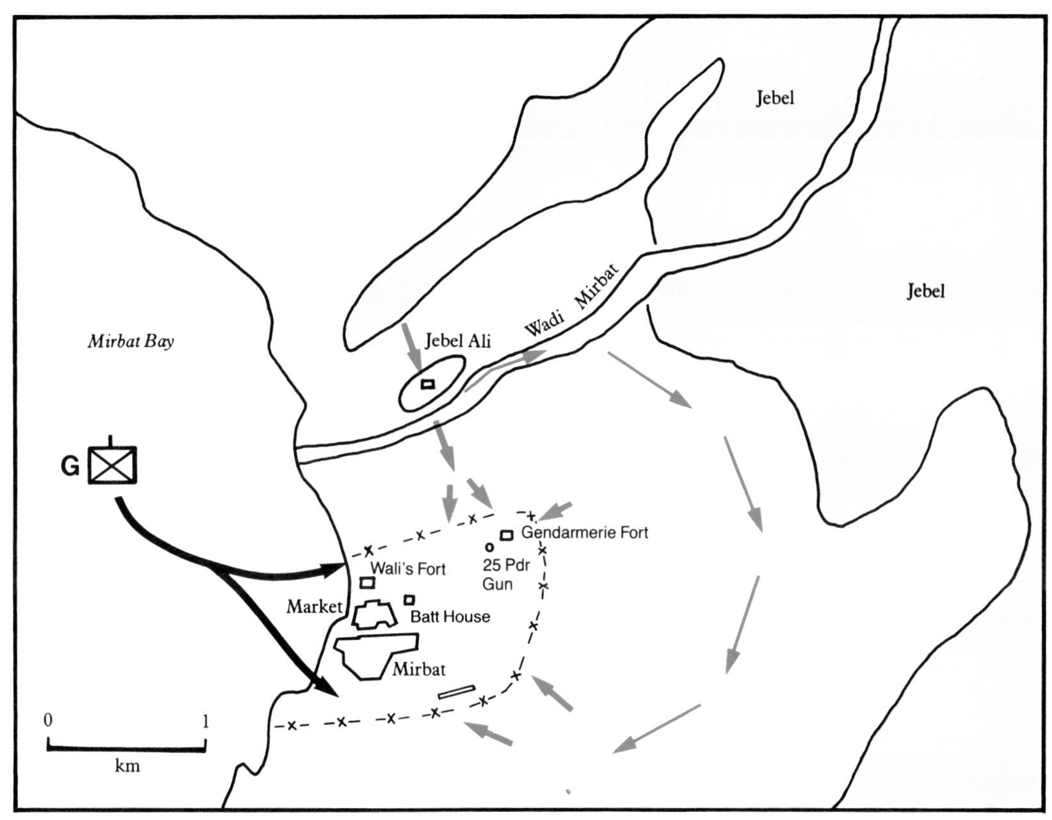

At the time of the attack Mirbat was defended by 30 Askari tribesman from Northern Oman, a small number of local firqat, 25 Dhofar Gendarmerie stationed in the old fort and a team of nine SAS living in the BATT House at the far side of the compound. The only heavy weaponry consisted of a single 25 pdr artillery piece dug in close to the fort, a .5in Browning machine-gun and a 7.62mm GPMG on the roof of the BATT House. The initial attack, mounted by an extended line of some 40 Adoo, was mown down by accurate machine gun fire from the BATT House. Now aware of the SAS position the Adoo began to strafe the BATT House as well as the fort. Unperturbed, Captain Kealy and Corporal Tobin left the comparative safety of the BATT House to dash, under concentrated fire, to the gun pit some 200m (215 ft) away to render assistance to the hard-pressed crew. With their help the 25 pdr was maintained in action throughout the brief but ferocious engagement. Disillusioned and confused by the unexpected high level of resistance the Adoo began to withdraw in disorder, straight into the arms of the advancing SAS rescuers.

Left: Firqat irregulars, themselves 'turned' guerrillas, rest during a patrol into the Radfan.

Below: The Radfan mountains behind Mirbat were inhospitable and virtually uninhabited, yet the SAS made them their second home in their fight against the Adoo.

succeed he would have to establish permanent bases on the Jebel itself. In October 1971, immediately after the monsoon, he launched Operation Jaguar with precisely this in mind. While a feint was made by one SAS team under Captain Branson, who with two *firqats* climbed the Jebel to the east, the main force under Watts, with a squadron of SAS, a number of Baluchis and two other *firqats*, A'aasifat

and Salahadin, climbed up to seize the deserted airfield at Lympne. Having secured the airstrip Watts seized the village of Jibjat and began to patrol along the sides of the Wadi Darbat dislodging the unsuspecting Adoo from the plateau. On 9 October a secure base was established at White City from which the 350 strong force was able to control the entire plateau above the coastal plain.

In response to local pressure for the resumption of normal trading Watts now implemented his most audacious plan. On 27 November he organized what was later described as 'a Texas-style cattle drive supported by jet fighter cover and 5.5 inch artillery'. Over 1,400 head of goats and several hundred cattle were either airlifted or driven from the plateau to the coastal market in Taqa. Most of the animals belonged to *firqat* families, but many of them belonged to men serving in the Adoo and were confiscated by the *firqat* during the drive. In only a few months Watts' very personalized blend of psychological warfare had virtually destroyed the authority of the Adoo in the Jebel. Over 700 Dhofaris had joined the *firquat*, there were established bases on the Jebel and the coastal plain was firmly in government hands.

The Marxists knew that they would have to strike a single devastating blow against the authority of the Sultan if they were to stand any chance of winning the battle for the hearts and minds of the people. They decided to annihilate a major military base and chose as their target the coastal town of Mirbat.

The town was defended by 30 Askaris from Northern Oman armed with bolt-action .303 in Lee-Enfield rifles, a number of *firqat*, 25 Dhofar Gendarmerie positioned in an old fort and armed with British 7.62mm S.L.R. semi-automatic rifles, and an SAS training team. The latter consisted of nine men under command of Captain Mike Kealy (later to die under tragic circumstances in the Brecon Mountains) who were stationed in the BATT (British Army Training Team) House. Their heavy weaponry consisted of a single 25 pdr artillery piece dug in close to the fort, a .5 in Browning machine-gun and a 7.62mm general purpose machine-gun (GPMG) both on the roof of the BATT House.

The attack, executed by an estimated 250 well-armed Adoo supported by at least one battery of mortars firing from the Jebel Ali, began at 5.30 a.m. Unusually the enemy mounted an initial infantry assault directed against the Gendarmerie in the fort. Most of the SAS team were in the BATT House some 400m (430 yds) away. However when Trooper Savesaki received a report that his fellow Fijian, Trooper Labalaba who was himself in the fort, was injured, he sought and was granted permission to run to his friend to offer medical assistance.

The initial attack was mounted by an extended line of some 40 Adoo. Using a shallow wadi between the perimeter wire and Jebel Ali for protection they skirted in front of the BATT House, turned towards the fort and broke into a run. As soon as they broke cover they were mown down by Corporal Chapman manning the .5 in Browning on the roof of the BATT House. Now aware of the SAS dispositions the Adoo began to strafe the BATT House as well as the fort with machine gun and mortar rounds. Having radioed Salalah for assistance Kealy at once took stock of the situation. Failing to get a reply from the gun pit near the fort on his short wave radio Kealy decided to go there himself. Leaving Corporal Bradshaw in command at the BATT House he and Tommy Tobin, the SAS medical specialist, began their hazardous dash for the gun pit one man sprinting, the other giving him cover. Miraculously the pair made it some 200m (215 yds) before the enemy fully realized their intentions and brought down concentrated fire to bear on them. Even so both made it uninjured to the gun pit. Once there the carnage which greeted them was indescribable. Several gendarmes were dead, one was alive but quite mad. The Omani gunner was seriously injured as were both of the Fijians. The 25 pdr, although momentarily silent, was still able to fire. As the elated Adoo closed in for the kill Labalaba, who had now received basic first aid from Tobin, brought the 25 pdr into action once again. As he fell his place was taken by Tobin, covered as far as was possible by Kealy, and by now supported by concentrated fire from the BATT House. What happened next is confusing. The at times suicidally brave Adoo continued to press their attack, on occasion coming within feet of the SAS survivors, but were constantly beaten off by the courageous Kealy and his seriously injured team.

Above: A Sqn prepare for another day's patrolling into the Radfan.

Above: Wessex helicopters of 815 Sqn ready for action at Thumeir

Grenades and bullets continued to feed the carnage until suddenly two Cessna Skymasters of the Sultan's Air Force appeared overhead and began to strafe the bunching Adoo. Disillusioned and confused by the unexpectedly high level of resistance, the Marxists began to withdraw in disorder. As they did they were met by the concentrated fire of ten GPMGs. Fortunately elements of G Squadron had been in the area at the time of the attack prior to their taking over responsibility for the sector. They had at once boarded three helicopters and had made all speed to the assistance of their comrades. As the hapless Adoo withdrew across open ground they were met by the 23 members of G Squadron advancing unseen from the south-east.

The battle for Mirbat, one of the shortest but most savage in the history of the SAS, broke the Marxists' will to fight and convinced the still non-aligned in the area of the invincibility of the Sultan and his allies. Kealy's own bravery and leadership were acknowledged by the award of the Distinguished Service Order. Several other names appeared in the dispatches but, in the time-honoured traditions of the SAS, these were never openly published.

If there was ever an occasion when the Special Air Services truly lived up to its world-renowned motto *Who Dares Wins* it was on 19 July 1972 at the battle of Mirbat.

The Yom Kippur War, October 1973

By October 1973 the Israeli generals had become dangerously complacent. They had defeated their Arab neighbours in war on every occasion. They had destroyed their enemy on the ground and in the air in 1956 and 1967 and were confident of repeating victories.

They had however reckoned without Nasser's determination and the renaissance of the Egyptian Army. Since October 1967 Egypt had spearheaded a so-called *War of Attrition* against Israel. She had constantly probed the Israeli defensive positions along the *Bar-Lev Line* and had instigated numerous small-scale Special Forces raids into the occupied territories.

More importantly unknown to Israeli intelligence, Egypt had rearmed with the latest generation of Soviet anti-tank and anti-aircraft missiles.

Initial plans for the recrossing of the Suez Canal, initially codenamed Operation *Granite Two* but subsequently renamed Operation *Badr*, demanded the complete rebuilding of the Egyptian Army. Officers studied Hebrew and Israeli topics at university while the educational and technical skills level of the average soldier was markedly improved. The man-portable RPG-7 anti-tank and SA-7 anti-aircraft missiles were introduced into front line service in great numbers while selected troops were taught the intricacies of the revolutionary wire guided AT-3 Saggar missile.

Under the command of Chief of Staff General Sa'ad Es-Din Sha'azli, the Egyptians were honed to a level of fitness and confidence never before seen in an Arab Army. Final planning was as meticulous as it was impressive until, by October 1973, the entire war machine was ready to go on to the offensive. Aided somewhat by alarming gaps in Israeli military intelligence, the Egyptians succeeded in keeping their intentions secret. Having completed their final training exercises against facsimiles far to the west, troops were moved into their battle positions out of sight of Israeli border watchers. Canal guards continued to swim, play games and sunbathe in their time-honoured lethargic fashion while behind them the assault engineers, tasked with the breaching of the canal defences silently formed up.

Above: Egyptian T-55 tanks take part in a post-war victory parade.

The Syrian preparations for war along the Golan Heights were less well concealed. For weeks Israeli reconnaissance aircraft reported a steady buildup of armour and artillery in the area but this was discounted as empty sabre-rattling. Minister of Defence, Moshe Dayan, moved an additional armoured brigade to the area and placed the army on general alert, but otherwise did nothing. When the cabinet met a few days before Yom Kippur the possibility of war was not even discussed.

On 4 October the thousands of Russian advisers in Egypt and Syria began to evacuate their families. Syrian armour and artillery began to advance to the border

Below: An Israeli tank crewman, relaxed but alert, rests during a lull in the battle.

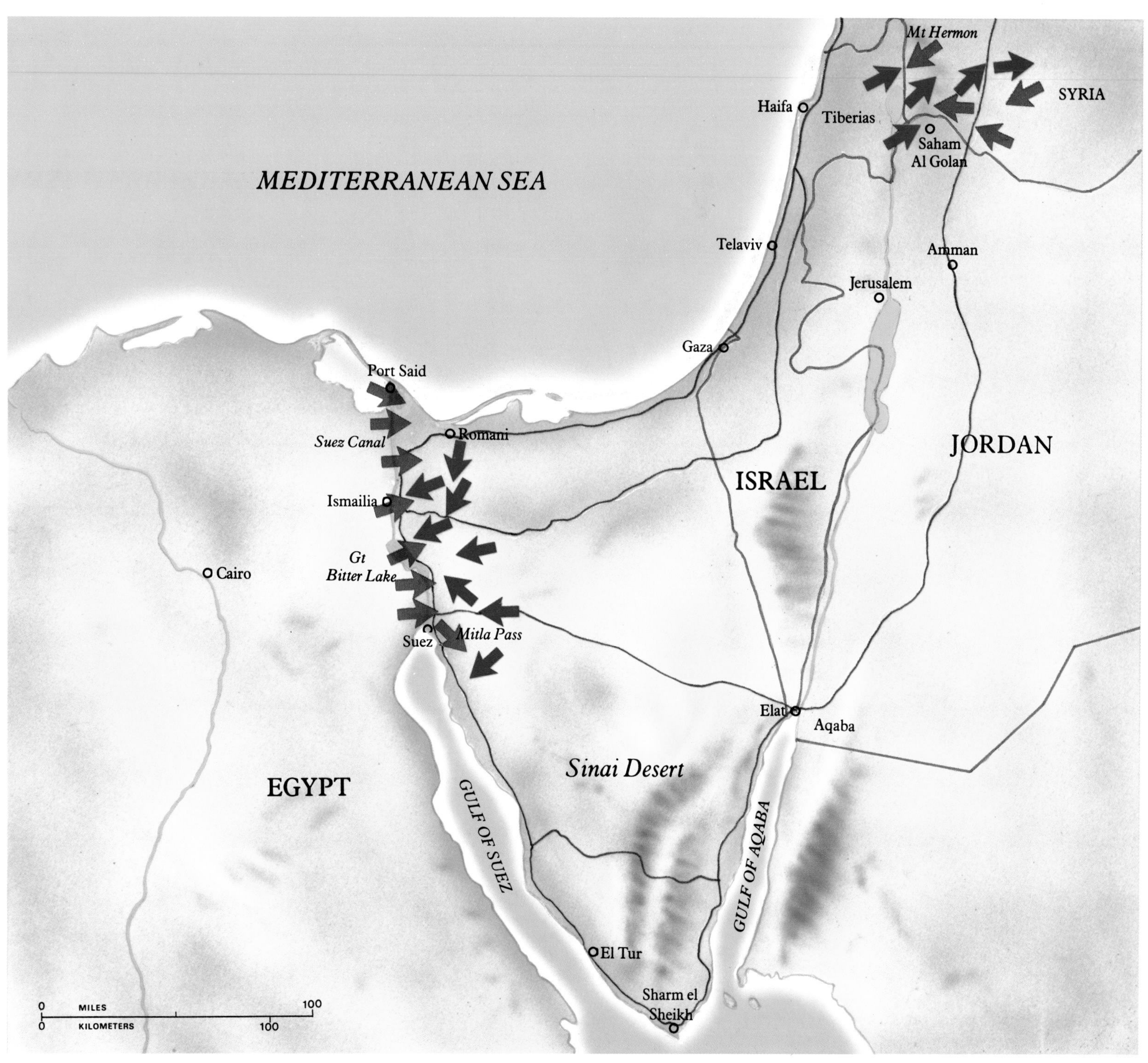

and the Israelis, by now thoroughly alarmed, ordered the armed forces to the highest state of readiness. On the eve of one of the most solemn occasions in the Jewish calendar, military leave was cancelled. Men on leave were recalled and preparations were made for general mobilization.

The Arab attack was launched at precisely 2 .00 p.m. on the afternoon of 6 October. Syrian armour rolled across the Golan Heights in the north and Egyptian commandos and engineers crossed the Suez Canal in small boats in the south.

The Yom Kippur War was fought on two fronts. At 2.00 p.m. on 6 October Syrian armour rolled across the Golan Heights in the north while Egyptian commandos and engineers crossed the Suez Canal in small boats in the south. Despite early heavy losses the Syrians came close to attaining their objectives. The Israeli front line was broken and Mount Sinai captured by special forces. However Israeli armoured reinforcements gradually regained the initiative throwing the Syrians back behind their own borders. In the south the Egyptians made excellent headway across the Suez Canal until they too, were stopped in a series of bloody firefights by Israeli reinforcements. On 14 October the Israelis in the south took the initiative forcing their own crossing of the Canal to cut off the Egyptian fighting troops from their bases. Panic ensued within the Arab camp as they began to realize their predicament and withdraw, pursued by the Israelis. The fighting ended in stalemate when the superpowers intervened to enforce a ceasefire.

Despite early heavy losses, the Syrians in the Golan came close to attaining their objectives. The 30,000 troops and 1,000 tanks which followed the mine clearing tanks and MTU-55 armoured bridgelayers across the border defences were decimated by the Israeli 7th Armoured Brigade artillery. Notwithstanding, they pressed on regardless of casualties, demonstrating a new found bravery and resilience which took the defenders completely by surprise.

As the Syrian armour broke free of the Israeli forward defences, it deployed into a straight line and, with the mechanized infantry following, began to threaten the main Israeli positions. The Israeli Centurions and Patterns began cutting great swathes into the Syrian lines with their superior 105mm guns but were too few to halt the advance alone. When the Chel Ha'Avir (the Israeli Air Force) was summoned to redress the balance, its pilots found themselves flying into an intense and wholly unexpected missile barrage, losing 34 aircraft in the first few hours of fighting. Only after they discovered and destroyed the missile radar installations were the Israeli pilots able to grab the initiative and go on to the offensive. By then, however, they had lost a staggering and irreplaceable 80 aircraft.

During the afternoon's fighting, Syrian Special Forces launched a series of ambushes in the Israeli rear, destroying a number of tanks and killing the second-in-command of the *Barak* Armoured Brigade. Twenty-five Frog-7 surface-to-surface missiles were launched ineffectively against Israeli strategic ground targets including airfields. Mount Hermon, sacred to all Israelis, was captured by helicopter-borne paratroops.

By nightfall the position on the Golan looked bleak. However the Air Force had managed to gain air superiority and armoured reserves, having driven through the night, and were about to enter the battle. Throughout the next day the Syrians were held, their position weakened considerably by the death of Brigadier General Omar Abrash, the inspirational commander of their 7th Infantry Division. By Monday morning the Israelis, now fully up to strength, were ready to take the initiative.

The initial Arab attack across the Suez Canal came even closer to success. As 1.45 p.m. on 6 October, Sha'azli launched his attack. Fifteen minutes later the first of 30,000 Egyptian troops, spearheaded by paratroops and *As-Sai'qa* 'lightning' or special forces began crossing the Canal. Commandos, many of them veterans of earlier action in the Yemen, swam across the Canal under cover of the initial artillery barrage to set up anti-tank mines and defences against armoured counter-attack. Explosives were ferried across to knock holes in the huge sand walls on the far bank to allow access to the swarms of amphibious PT-76 light tanks which followed. Specially trained commando groups then attacked the 30 static fortifications along the *Bar-Lev Line*, destroying any vehicle which moved with their seemingly endless supplies of RPG-7s and AT-3 Saggars.

Above: An Egyptian half-track shows signs of battle fatigue.

Simultaneously, the 130th Amphibious Brigade forced a crossing of the Little Bitter Lake. Relying totally on untried Soviet doctrine and tactics the brigade ferried 37 PT-76 light tanks, 74 BTR-50 PK and PU APCs and command vehicles and 18 PTRK *Malyutkas* to the east bank where they formed up and began to head immediately for the Giddi Pass.

Fortunately for the Israelis, in so doing they ran straight into Colonel Dan Shomron's 401st Armoured Brigade. Overwhelmed and outgunned, the Egyptians were forced to withdraw with heavy losses after an hour-long battle. Elsewhere, Egyptian commando raids also experienced severe reverses. Attempts to transport a battalion sized group by helicopter into the Ras-Sudr area of the Sinai, well behind Israeli lines, failed when the slow-moving Mi-8 Hip helicopters were intercepted by the Israeli Air Force. Fourteen were shot down and more than 250 men killed, wounded or captured.

Although the battle for the peripheries of the Sinai went well for Israel, the crucial battle for the Canal itself did not and within a few hours had become critical. Having secured the east bank, the Egyptians moved high pressure hoses into the area to smash down the remnants of the sand ramparts. PMP mobile bridging was then brought forward and a total of ten pontoons constructed by nightfall. Under cover of darkness, five Egyptian divisions and 500 tanks crossed into Sinai while battered and confused, the Israelis withdrew their armour inland to the protection of the passes.

Shortly after sunrise on the morning of 7 October, the Israeli Air Force went on to the offensive against the Egyptian forward positions only to receive a severe rebuff. Sixty percent of the attacking aircraft were destroyed by batteries of SA-6 surface-to-

Below:Egyption engineers threw a number of bridges across the Suez Canal taking the Israelis completely by surprise.

air and SA-7 shoulder-fired missiles which had been brought forward during the course of the night.

The sheer success of the Egyptian offensive took both sides by surprise. Sha'azli had anticipated 30 percent casualties on the first day but in fact suffered no more than 300 dead. Had he been more positive, he could almost certainly have stormed the passes on 7 October, breaking the back of the Israeli Army in the process. Instead he delayed, preferring to consolidate under the protective umbrella of his missiles and in so doing the Israelis provided a vital breathing space.

During the days of stalemate that followed, first the Soviet Union and then the United States began to flood the area with new munitions. Egypt received new tanks and artillery, and Israel was supplied with much needed replacement aircraft, TOW anti-tank and anti-radar missiles.

By 14 October the Israeli Army under the command of Sharon and Dayan recalled to active service and now replenished and up to strength, was ready to take the initiative. A force of three mechanized brigades, their armoured strength reduced to 200 tanks, a mechanized parachute brigade and a team of assault pioneers was secretly brought together with orders to smash west across the Canal, deep into the Egyptian rear. Once there they were able to cut off the Egyptian fighting troops from their bases, starving them of resupply and logistical support. The plan bore the simplicity of despair. One brigade was to make a feint against the Egyptians while a second seized a critical road permitting the third brigade and the rest of the force to reach the canal. A bridge would then be constructed over which the entire force would cross.

Initially the plan went badly wrong. The diversionary brigade drew the enemy fire so well that a full-scale tank battle ensued in which the Israeli armour was annihilated. Nonetheless its sacrifice enabled the rest of the force to succeed in its objective of reaching the canal, albeit well behind schedule. The initial crossing was made at 1.00 a.m. on the morning of Tuesday 16 October against little opposition. However the defenders soon recovered and began to bring down heavy fire on the Israelis, causing the destruction of several tank-laden ferries. Notwithstanding their heavy losses, by 9.00 a.m. the Israelis had established an unassailable bridgehead upon which they continued to build strong enough to take the offensive.

Although Egyptian command in the area was adequate, it soon became clear that her control and communications were not. Sharon was left alone to reinforce his position, hampered only by the occasional localized counter-attack. He was able to send his armour with virtual impunity on raiding excursions into the enemy lines destroying installations wherever they were able to find them. Four missile command centres were located and destroyed, granting the Israeli Air Force a window through the previously impenetrable Egyptian air defensive umbrella.

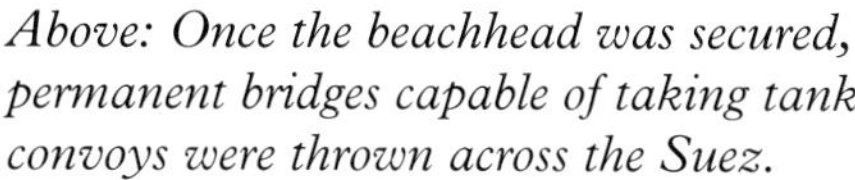

Above: Once the beachhead was secured, permanent bridges capable of taking tank convoys were thrown across the Suez.

Below: An Egyptian half-track advances into the Sinai.

Below: Two destroyed Egyptian T-55 tanks offer testimony to the ferocity of the Israeli defences.

During the next 24 hours, three fresh armoured brigades, under the command of General 'Bren' Adam, crossed the canal into Egypt until the force became strong enough to repel even the most concerted of counter-attacks. On the Wednesday night the Egyptians attacked in strength, the 140th Parachute Brigade engaging the 247th Parachute Brigade in fierce close quarter combat, but to no avail. The next morning 8,000 men and 200 tanks broke out north and south from the Israeli bridgehead and went on an orgy of destruction annihilating every military installation in sight.

By now the Israelis had seized the initiative along the Golan Heights and had begun to force the Syrians back. Iraq and Jordan both joined the battle with mixed results. While the Iraqis were ill-trained and of poor quality, the Jordanian armoured brigade was excellent if dogged by ill luck and the incompetence of its allies. On 16 October it spearheaded an armoured thrust through the Israeli positions. This would almost certainly have succeeded had it not been shelled by Iraqi artillery and strafed by Syrian fighters which mistook its Centurion tanks for the Israelis.

Slowly but perceptibly, panic began to overtake the Arab camp as they began to realize that early success was quickly turning to failure with the very real possibility of defeat. Simultaneously the major powers began to sense the danger of escalation. As if to compound the West's problem, Saudi Arabia threatened to cut off oil supplies until the restoration of peace in the Middle East. On 22 October a hurried cease-fire was agreed, to the relief of both the Arabs and the Israelis, although fighting continued in the Sinai for a further three days.

The Yom Kippur War provided a salutary lesson for the Israelis. It taught them that the Arabs, particularly the Egyptians, were no longer a soft military option. Ultimately it led to a negotiated if not tenuous peace between Israel and Egypt.

Right: The ruins of a small town on the banks of the Suez Canal.

Below Right: An Israeli gunner on the Golan Heights looks out over Syria.

Below: A burnt-out Arab jeep. The Israeli civilian buses in the background would suggest that peace has returned.

Kabul,
The Soviet Airborne in Afghanistan, 1979

The invasion of Afghanistan in 1979 represented the Soviet Union's first incursion into the non-Communist bloc since 1945. It brought with it international condemnation and an extensive boycott of the 1980 Moscow Olympic Games. It also caused the Soviet Army to become embroiled in a bitter and uncompromising guerrilla war in an alien environment against some of the finest irregulars in the world.

The Soviet decision to invade was not taken lightly nor with territorial gain in mind. Afghanistan was becoming increasingly vocal in its support of Islamic fundamentalism and was creating considerable instability in the three neighbouring border states of Khazakstan, Uzbekhistan and Turkestan. Moscow felt it had to act if only to preserve its own integrity.

Afghanistan had been the recipient of considerable Soviet aid since 1953 when Mohammed Daoud Khan, a cousin of the king, had seized power. In 1978 two left-wing parties, the Khalq and Parcham, named after their rival newspapers, had wrested control and moved the country even closer to the Soviet sphere of influence. The new president, Mohammed Takriti, had introduced a series of sweeping reforms, including the emancipation of women, which had upset the majority of the fiercely traditional and religious population. When the programme had been accelerated by Prime Minister Hafizullah Amin in 1979 discontent had turned to open rebellion which prompted a reply from the government by way of wide-scale repression. Ignoring warnings from the Soviets to temper the speed of his reforms, Amin had engineered Takriti's death in September 1979 and assumed total control. It was then that Moscow decided to intervene and began to formulate a top secret plan for invasion.

Uniquely, the majority of the Soviet troops engaged in the overthrow of the Afghan government were in situ prior to the event. They had been invited into the country by the unsuspecting Amin in response to an offer from Moscow to assist him in the maintenance of Communist order. Between 8 and 10 December 1979, some 14 days before the invasion, an airborne regiment with more than 1,500 men with tanks and artillery was deployed to Begram, a key town to the north of Kabul, to secure the Salang Highway with its critical tunnel. Between 10 and 24 December a battalion from the regiment was moved to Kabul International Airport only 3 km (1.86 miles) from the city centre. Simultaneously large quantities of Afghan armoured and transport vehicles were recalled to workshops by Soviet 'advisors', ostensibly for servicing before a big push against the rebels. President Amin was persuaded by the Soviet military command to retreat to his palace complex at Darulaman, some 11.25 km (7 miles) south-west of Kabul, which was deemed to be more secure.

Above: Soviet-built T-55 tanks of the Afghan Army patrol ahead of a convoy.

Below: An Afghan soldier of the15th Armoured Regiment stands guard over his regimental headquarters.

Between 24 and 27 December, troops from the Soviet 105th Guards Airborne Division, supported by Spetsnaz, landed at the secured Kabul Airport together with the air force bases at Bagram, Shindand and Kandahar. Once the bases were secured the two regiments of the division not yet

Above: Ahmadshah Massound typified the Mujahideen resistance: brave, resourceful, but totally lacking in strategic foresight.

Above: Mujahideen guerrillas file through a market garden on the outskirts of Mazar-i-Sharif.

Below: Mujahideen in a captured jeep near Aliabad. Maintenance was non-existent; when vehicles broke down they were abandoned.

Above: Mujahideen fighters scaling a mountain face in Badakhshan Province, in North East Afghanistan.

Left: Mujahideen fighters armed with Soviet-made RPG-7 rocket launchers. These weapons created havoc against Soviet convoys.

committed landed at Kabul and Bagram and began to prepare for offensive action. On the next night, the still unsuspecting Afghan government gathered en masse at the Kabul Intercontinental Hotel for an evening's entertainment to be hosted by the Soviet Embassy. They were arrested. At approximately 7.00 p.m. the same evening, Spetsnaz teams demolished the central military communications centre, captured the still functioning Ministry of the Interior, the Kabul radio station and several other key points. By dawn the next morning the city was firmly in Soviet hands.

The crux of the attack was the assault on Darulaman where Amin remained under the protection of a loyal armoured regiment supported by eight T-55 tanks. The attack was led by Spetsnaz forces with K.G.B. assistance, supported by two or three airborne battalions equipped with BMD armoured personnel carriers. Amin was killed as was his family, security force and entourage. For their part, the Soviets sustained a reported 25 dead, including the K.G.B. Colonel Balashika killed in crossfire by his own troops. There were 225 wounded.

By the time that Moscow Radio broadcast a report stating that Soviet troops had moved into Afghanistan at the request of the government to assist it in the restoration of order, the leaders of the government were dead, killed by their very protectors. The path to initial Soviet victory was paved by the painstaking use of *maskarovka* backed up where necessary by the brutal but devastatingly effective use of local force. Spetsnaz had been in evidence in all the major key areas and had been instrumental in the elimination of Amin and his entire faction.

The takeover continued smoothly into January with little obvious employment for Spetsnaz. Four motor rifle divisions, followed shortly afterwards by two more, crossed the frontier one column moving through Herat in the west, the other coming down from Termez. Babrak Kamal, the new puppet Afghan leader, attempted to restore order by releasing large numbers of political prisoners, most of whom would later join the Mujahideen, and revoking the most unpopular areas of agricultural reform.

Above: Panjshiri resistance fighters stop to eat en route to a new ambush.

Few Afghans felt comfortable with the new atheistic Marxist regime. In February 1980 a general strike in Kabul was suppressed with violence. As matters deteriorated, guerrilla activity in the mountains began to increase, forcing the invaders to stick to the main highways. The provinces of Paktia, Nangahar and Nuristan in the east, Hazarajat in the centre and Herat in the west fell almost totally under the control of rival and often warring Mujahideen factions.

By late 1981 the Soviets had become

Above: Afghan guerrilla with captured AGS-17 automatic grenade launcher capable of firing 30mm projectiles over 1,000 metres.

Above right: Freedom fighter with RPG-7 during an attack on a Afghan Army post in Badakhshan Province.

Right: A Soviet-built recoilless rifle brought to bear against an Afghan Army position in Nahrin in Eastern Afghanistan.

reconciled to the fact that they could no longer prosecute the war as though it were being fought in the plains of Northern Germany. Their over-reliance on roads was making them vulnerable to ambush and was doing nothing to defeat the guerrillas who remained secure, immune from attack in their mountain bases.

In response the Soviets began to introduce new, far more effective tactics. While continuing to stage large all-arms operations and sweeps in conjunction with the rapidly disintegrating Afghan Army, they introduced helicopter-borne troops to the mountains. Spetsnaz and paratroop forces who until then had been confined to defensive security operations were released to go on to the offensive. As the months progressed the number of special forces in Afghanistan doubled to two independent brigades, one stationed at Khandahar, the other at Shindand. Mujahideen fighters lured into the open to attack 'conventional' convoys were suddenly themselves set upon by surprise squads of airborne soldiers working closely with the ground forces.

In 1983 the Soviets went on the offensive, using their considerable fixed wing and helicopter air power to carry the war into the mountains. Groups of between 500 and 1,500 helicopter-borne troops were used independently or in conjunction with ground troops in major search and destroy operations against isolated towns and villages. 'Turned' ex-guerrillas and Khad (Afghan secret police) agents were infiltrated into the Mujahideen camps to report on their strengths and intentions. Nocturnal commando raids were mounted by specially trained Spetsnaz units against previously impregnable Mujahideen strongholds and hideouts. Guerrilla lines of communication were ambushed and villages suspected of harbouring or in any way assisting the Mujahideen were razed to the ground in a scorched earth policy reminiscent of the Americans in Vietnam.

In spring 1985, divisional Spetsnaz troops began to work in close conjunction with conventional ground troops in an attempt to rid the major valleys of large-scale enemy activity. During two sorties along the Kunar Valley and subsequently during the Paktia offensive, helicopter-borne troops were inserted on high ground ahead of the advancing tanks and APCs in an attempt to catch the enemy in the open. Casualties on both sides were ferocious but, in Soviet military eyes, acceptable.

While the valleys were being cleared with the aid of divisional Spetsnaz forces, small independent Spetsnaz units were deployed to the borders with Pakistan and Iran to operate in a counter-infiltration role. Fighters returning to the war after a period of rest with their families were ambushed in once friendly territory close to, or even across, the border until nowhere could be deemed safe.

In July 1985 General Mikhail Mitrofanovich Zaitsev assumed command of the Soviet troops in Afghanistan and began to emphasize the role of highly mobile rapid intervention special forces. For the first time in Soviet military history, battalion and company commanders were allowed – even expected – to use their initiative.

While divisional Spetsnaz troops, most of whom were conscripts inducted into the special forces for their fitness and political reliability rather than their experience, continued to operate in close support of the ground forces, independent Spetsnaz units were given almost complete autonomy. Comprising regular soldiers, the majority of whom were in their thirties, battle-hardened and totally acclimatized to mountain warfare, the independent units quickly began to register successes.

Maskarovka, the art of military deceit in which the Soviets excel, was frequently employed to mask Spetsnaz intentions.

Above: Mujahideen cleaning a home made machine gun. The stock and magazine are British, the barrel Soviet.

Below: A Mujahideen light mortar engages an Afghan fort. Positions like this were vulnerable to Spetsnaz counter-attack.

Below: As the war progressed, Spetsnaz infiltrated into the Panjshir Valley made open movement like this dangerous.

Small groups would often dress as peasants, in one instance actually driving a flock of sheep ahead of them, to enable them to move unnoticed about the mountains. Other groups would be dropped by helicopter many kilometres from their objective and would then use vehicles to move silently by night to their ambush points. Still more would disguise themselves as Mujahideen and move openly through friendly areas desecrating holy places, stealing and raping as they went in an attempt to discredit the guerrillas in the eyes of their supporters.

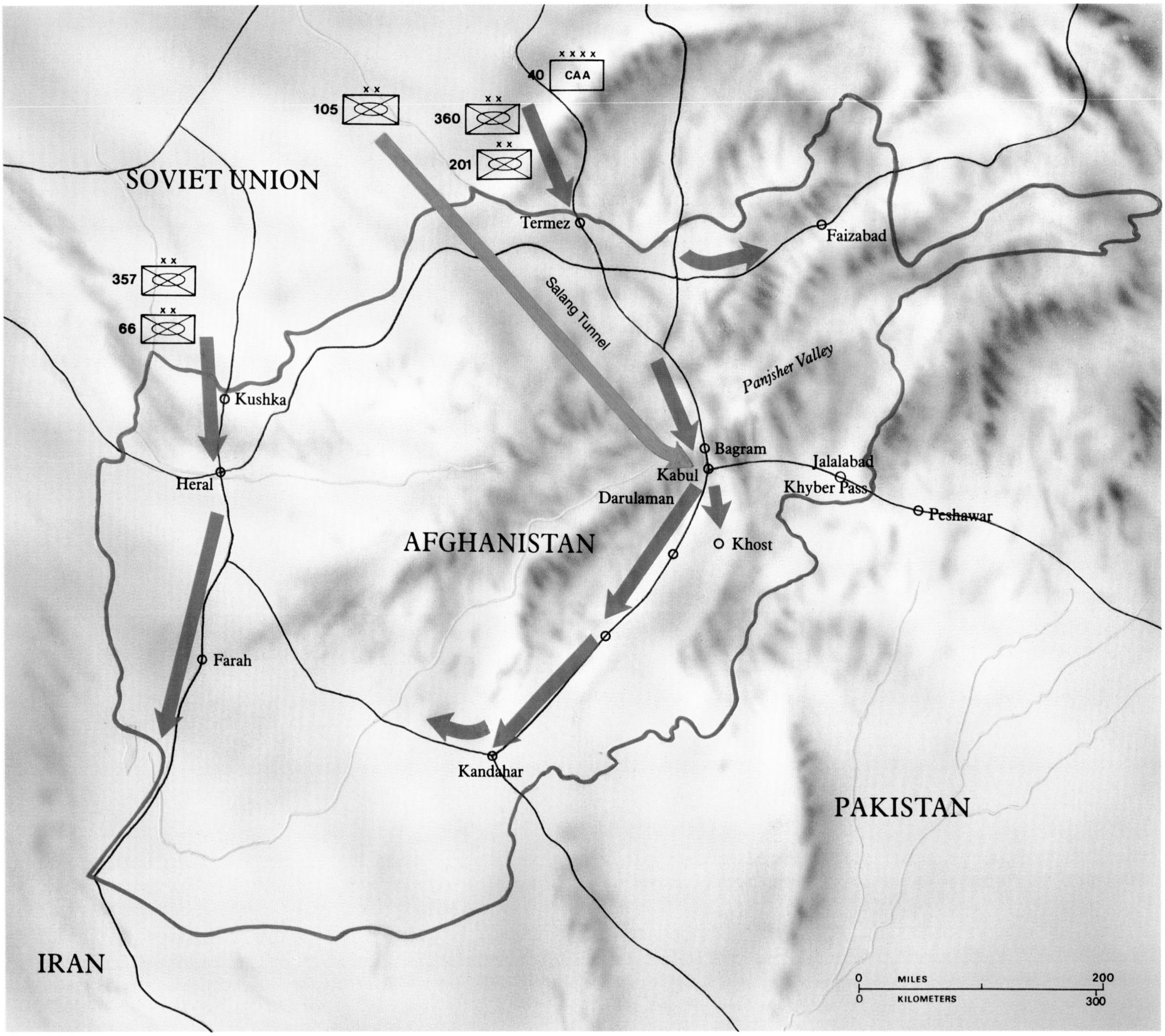

Between 8 and 10 December, a regiment of the 105th Guards Airborne Division with more than 1,500 men deployed to Begram. Between 24 and 27 December other Airborne units, supported by Spetsnaz, landed at and secured Kabul Airport, together with the air force bases at Begram, Shindland and Kandahar. The remaining elements of the 105th Airborne were then airlifted to Begram where eventually they were joined by mechanized troops from the 360th and 201st Motor Rifle Divisions proceeding by road through Ternez and the Salang Tunnel. Simultaneously the 357th and 66th Motor Rifle Divisions advanced south through Kushka, Heral and Farah to Kandahar.

Few Western reporters in Afghanistan fully appreciated the true diversity of Spetsnaz and frequently misreported their activities confusing them with airborne and commando operations. Hardly any seemed to realize their role in *razvedka*, the gathering of reconnaissance. Throughout the latter part of the war, Spetsnaz troops were involved in short and long-range helicopter-borne insertions, patrols and

Most Mujahideen were deeply religious, a factor which in itself turned them against Marxism.

the manning of reinforced, though covert, observation posts on high ground overlooking the valleys and main trade routes. In the words of Abdul Haq, the finest and most successful of the Mujahideen leaders, troops involved in *razvedka* were, 'very good at camouflage, map reading, at finding food from nowhere; they are physically strong and good at reconnaissance'. They were also invariably regular Spetsnaz troops who reported not the local regimental commander but direct to their own integral high level authority in the Soviet Union.

Had the large-scale introduction of U.S. Stinger hand-held surface-to-air missiles into the Mujahideen arsenal in 1988 not completely changed the course of the war (from which the Soviets were ultimately to withdraw ignominiously), it is wholly possible that the introduction by Zaitsev of localized tactics supported by large-scale Spetsnaz intervention would have led ultimately to victory.

Right: Zabihullah, depicted here in a death notice, was one of an increasing number of Mujahideen leaders to fall victim to Spetsnaz.

Below: Ahmadshah Massoud, commander of the Mujahideen forces in the Panjshir Valley, talks to his guerrilla forces.

Tumbledown,
The Scots Guards in the Falklands, 1982

At about 4.30 a.m. on Friday 2 April 1982, 140 Argentine Special Forces landed at Mullet Creek on the British Falkland Islands. They immediately launched an attack on the Royal Marines barracks at Moody Brook just outside of the capital of Stanley and surrounded Government House. Simultaneously, larger forces landed near Stanley airport, which is situated on a small isthmus to the east of the town. The 61 Marines of Naval Party 8901, the Island's only effective defensive force, now completely outnumbered, were ordered by the Governor to surrender some four hours later at 9.25 a.m. Following the surrender, pictures of British POWs spreadeagled on the ground were distributed to the world's press by the gloating Argentine government.

Suffering a great embarrassment, the British Government ordered the creation of a task force to retake the Islands by force of arms if neccessary. The carriers *Invincible* and *Hermes*, suppported by the assault ship *Fearless*, sailed for the Falklands on 5 April to be joined four days later by the cruise liner *Canberra* which was by then carrying the nucleus of 3 Commando Brigade.

On 12 May, 5 Infantry Brigade, having completed a series of exhausting exercises in the Welsh Mountains, sailed from Southampton in support. Although its

An abandoned Argentine mortar position. Most ordnance pointed south, away from the British line of advance.

Right: Tumbledown from the outskirts of Stanley.

headquarters had been left intact, 5 Brigade itself, had been stripped of two of its three battalions when 2nd and 3rd Battalions Parachute Regiment had been detached to 3 Commando Brigade. The authorities decided to ignore the obvious course of action, which would have been to replace these top class battalions with battle trained line infantry units. The Green Howards, a highly trained Yorkshire regiment, then on 14 hours' standby to go anywhere in the world, were not even considered. Instead social pressure prevailed and it was decided to fill the void with two Guards battalions, 2nd Battalion Scots Guards and 1st Battalion Welsh Guards, both then on public duties.

By the time 5 Brigade landed at the San Carlos bridgehead, elements of 3 Commando had already advanced on foot well into the north of East Falkland and 2 PARA had won a remarkable victory at Goose Green. Immediately, 5 Brigade, with 2 PARA now under command, were brought forward along a southern axis to link in with the Commando brigade for a final assault on the Argentine static defensive positions guarding the approaches to Stanley. Only then was it realized that neither Guards battalion was fit enough to undertake a lengthy *tab* across the barren and uncompromising terrain of the Falklands. Reluctantly it was accepted that both battalions would have to be transported forward either by air or sea. The Scots Guards were embarked on *Intrepid* and ordered to sail to Bluff Cove, then under 2 PARA control and within striking distance of the capital. Fearful of air attack however, *Intrepid* declined to sail beyond Lively Island, which was some way from her objective, leaving the guardsmen to complete the last seven hours of their voyage in open-topped LCUs, battling against heavy seas and driving rain. The fact that the young guardsmen not only disembarked in good order but were able immediately to take over 2 PARA's defensive positions despite their obvious discomfort and fatigue testifies to the extremely high standard of junior leadership within the battalion. Even so there were a few exposure cases one of whom only recovered after emergency resuscitation by his platoon commander, the now famous Lt. R. A. Lawrence.

On 9 June the battalion received its first operational casualties. As soon as the battalion had settled into its new position, the reconnaissance platoon, under command of Captain R. A. Scott, was ordered forward some 12 km (7.5 miles) to establish a covert advanced patrol base within the enemy's area of operations. When the commanding officer, Lt. Col. M. I. Scott, received orders to prepare for an advance on Stanley he was forced to compromise the existence of the patrol position by sending a helicopter forward to extract the reconnaissance commander who was now required urgently for detailed briefing. Suddenly aware of the close proximity of the enemy the Argentinians brought down heavy mortar fire on the reconnaissance platoon's position forcing

Above: A Royal Marine stands vigil in Stanley. Note the SUIT sight fitted to his SLR.

Below: A Royal Marines gun group. The GPMG in the foreground is accurate in expert hands to ranges in excess of 1,800 metres.

it to retire. In the ensuing withdrawal Sergeant Allum, the acting commander, and two of his guardsmen were injured. All three were evacuated by helicopter to the field hospital at Ajax Bax and subsequently made a full recovery.

The original plan for the assault on Stanley required 45 Commando to attack Two Sisters, 42 Commando to attack Mount Harriott and 3PARA to put in an attack on Mount Longdon. Simultaneously, 1st/7th Duke of Edinburgh's Own Gurkha Rifles were to patrol Mounts Tumbledown and William with the Scots Guards advancing to their right to control 3 Commando Brigade's southern flank. Should the Gurkhas meet stronger than anticipated resistance which they were unable to overcome, it was planned that the Scots would assault the remaining enemy positions at first light on either 12 or 13 June. After consultation with his senior officers Lt. Col. Scott reported that the plan as it stood would necessitate his men making a frontal assault uphill in daylight across difficult and open ground. Fortunately the colonel's objections prevailed (it was subsequently discovered that the intended approach was dominated by ten Argentine machine guns) and 5 Brigade's original plan was abandoned. Instead the Scots Guards were ordered to assault Tumbledown at night using as forming up points positions to the west recently captured by the Commandos. 1st/7th Gurkhas were ordered to attack Mount William should it prove necessary while the demoralized Welsh Guards were kept in reserve.

The battle for Mount Tumbledown, which took place on the night of 13/14 June 1982, epitomizes the war for the Falklands (Malvinas). A series of small interlocking and interdependent engagements, it was won by a combination of excellent training, thorough reconnaissance, and painstaking planning both at brigade and battalion level.

The troops facing 2nd Battalion Scots Guards were no dispirited amateurs. Rather, they were drawn from the 5th Marine Infantry Battalion commanded by Carlos Robacio, one of the most experienced and efficient of the Argentine field officers. The Marines were well armed and had been equipped with cold weather clothing far superior to that available to the British. They had had since April to dig in and familiarize themselves with the area and were fully up to strength. At the time of the battle they had even been reinforced by elements of the 4th, 6th and 12th Regiments which had managed to extricate themselves from the fighting around Two Sisters and Mount Harriott two nights earlier.

Above: San Carlos Water. The entire British force was landed here, often under fire.

Left: Tumbledown from the south-west. The Stanley - Mount Pleasant Road in the foreground was built after the war.

Below: Wessex V and Sea King helicopters played a crucial role in the maintenance of British mobility.

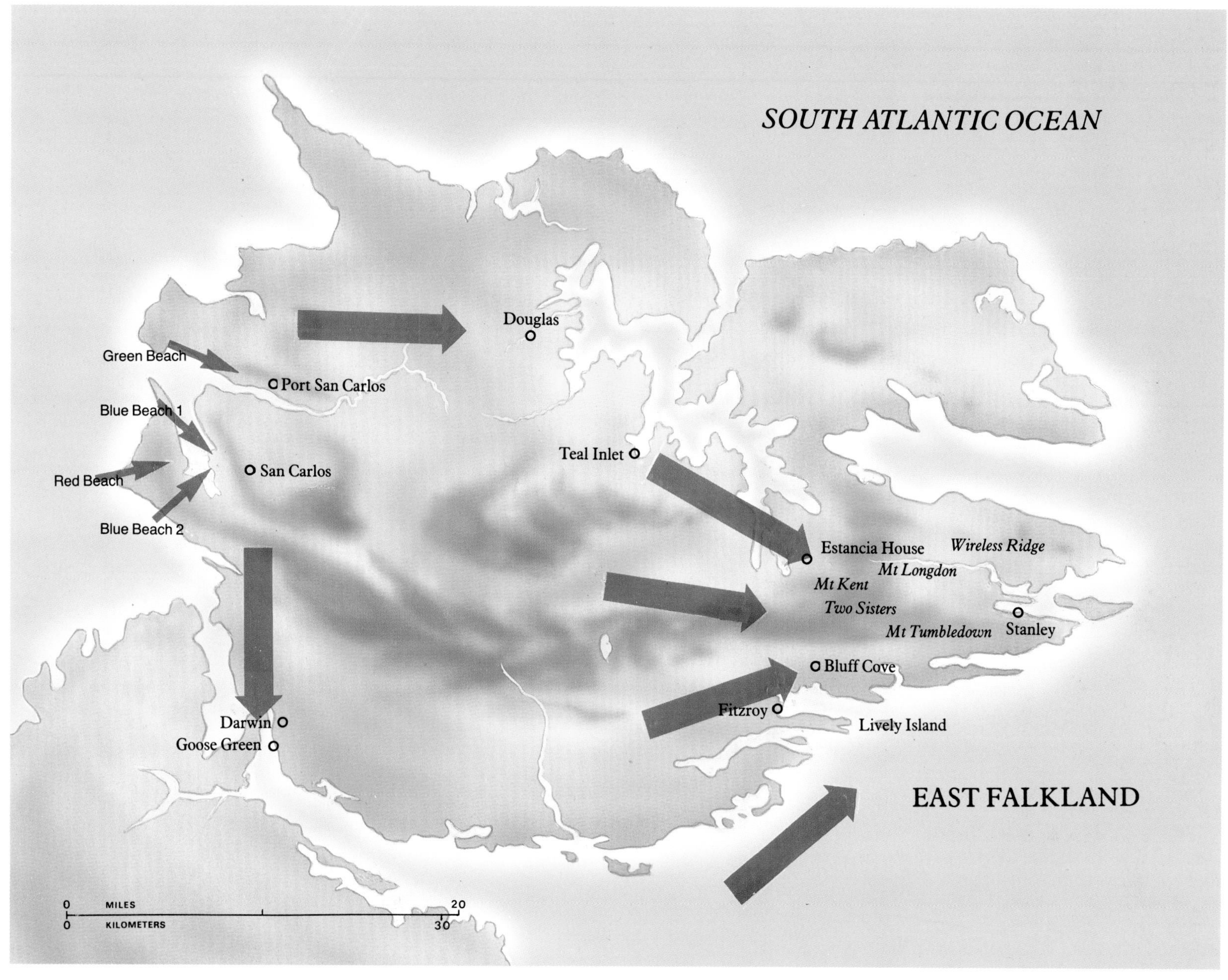

Immediately before the battle, in anticipation of a British thrust east along the main track to Stanley, Robacio had redeployed O Company, the weakest of his fighting units, forward to fresh positions close to Mount William. He had reinforced N Company, dug into sangars on Tumbledown itself, and had formed a series of counter-attack groups situated in the area of battalion headquarters some two km (1.2 miles) to the rear.

Unaware of the enemy's precise strength, and ignorant of the recent redeployment forward of O Company, Colonel Scott ordered a three phased attack on Tumbledown to be proceeded by a small diversionary attack from the south. It was planned that carrier based Harrier jets would provide fighter ground support while five batteries of 105mm light guns together with the main guns of *HMS Yarmouth* and *HMS Active* would attempt to neutralize Argentinian strong points. The battalion mortars of 42 Commando and 1st/7th Gurkha Rifles would be made available to supplement the Scot's own support weapons which would bring close support fire against individual enemy sangars.

It was envisaged that each phase of the attack would be mounted at company strength. Immediately after the diversionary attack G Company, under the command of Major Dalzel-Job, would assault the western approaches to the mountain. Once these had been secured, Left Flank Company under command of Major Kiszely, would pass through G Company's position to secure the mountain top itself. Finally, Right Flank Company, under Major Price, would mop up enemy resistance to the east. It was anticipated that Tumbledown would be in British

The 3 Commando Brigade landed on the beaches surrounding San Carlos Water. The Commandos and 3 PARA moved out east on their epic yomp through Douglas, Teal Inlet and on towards Stanley while 2 PARA cut south towards Darwin and Goose Green. By the time that 5 Brigade landed at the San Carlos bridgehead 2 PARA had already won a remarkable victory at Goose Green. It was decided to move 5 Brigade, with 2 PARA now under command, forward along a southern axis to link in with the Commando Brigade for a final assault on Stanley. However it was soon realized that the two Guards battalions were simply not fit enough for the task and alternative arrangements were made for their transportation by sea. The Scots Guards landed safely and, on the night of 13/14 June, successfully assaulted an enemy Marine position on Mount Tumbledown.

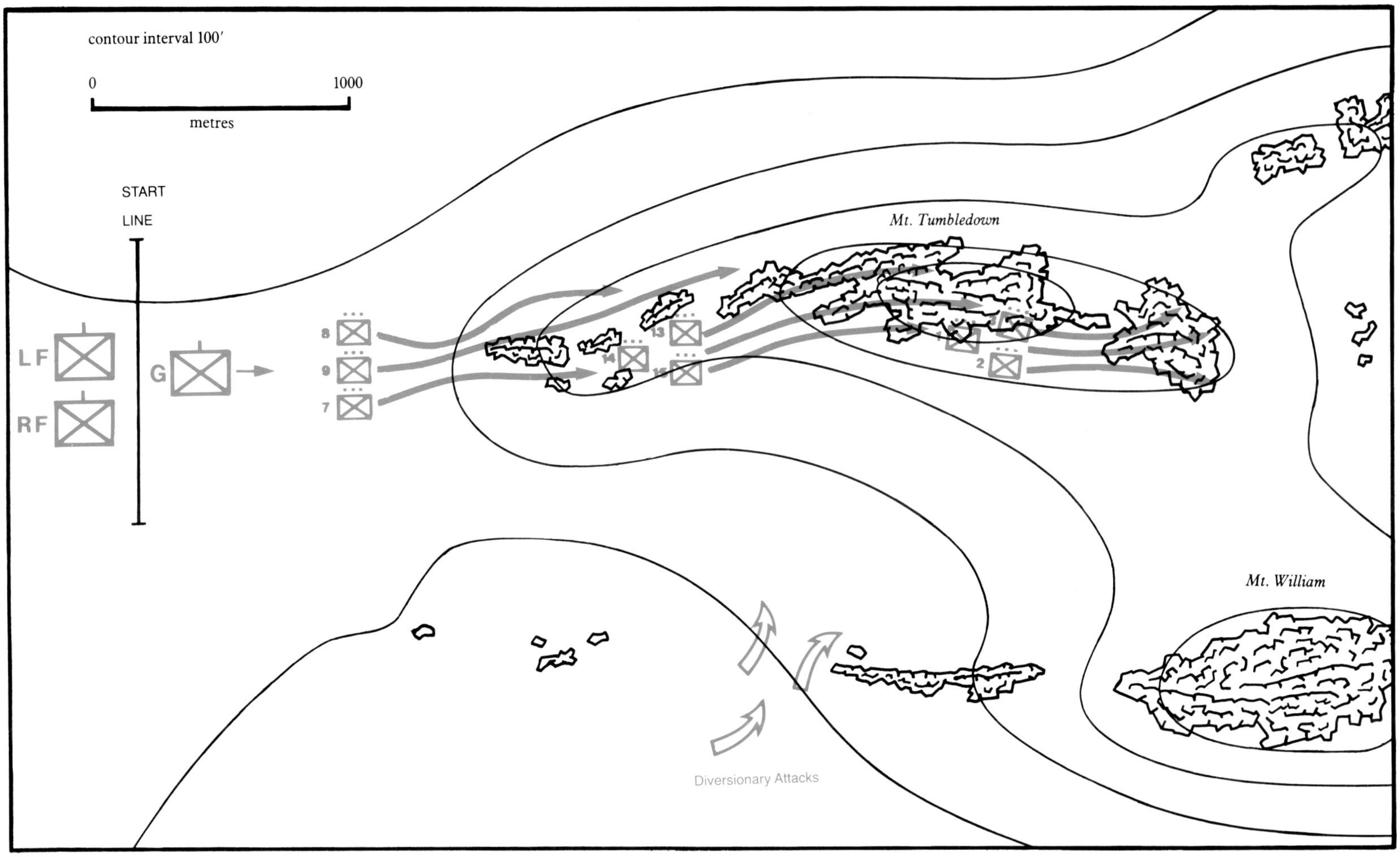

contour interval 100′

0 1000

metres

START LINE

LF

RF

G

8

9

7

14

13

15

2

Mt. Tumbledown

Mt. William

Diversionary Attacks

hands before first light.

The attack was postponed for twenty-four hours to 13 June when it was discovered that there were insufficient helicopters available to transport the battalion forward to its forming up points. However the day was not wasted. Reconnaissance patrols were sent forward to observe the enemy positions closely and to establish as far as possible his new strong points. Finally it was decided to abandon the conventional NATO password system in favour of the less formal but more practical *Hey Jimmy!* Although superficially a flippant point this simple expediency enabled the Scots to identify each other easily during the heat and confusion of battle considerably reducing the possibility of injury from friendly fire.

The initial diversionary attack consisted of three four-man assault sections supported by two Royal Engineers acting as scouts, artillery and mortar fire controllers, and a troop of the Blues and Royals mounted in Scimitar armoured cars. Amazingly, although the Argentinians were clearly anticipating an attack, the troops occupying the forward sangars were asleep and the Scots were therefore able to infiltrate deep into the enemy positions before opening fire. Once alerted however,

Tumbledown was in every respect a soldier's battle, fought as it was at close quarters between two excellent adversaries. The Scots Guards' assault was in three phases, preceded by a diversionary attack from the south. The diversionary attack consisted of three four-man assault sections supported by two Sappers acting as scouts, a team of artillery and mortar fire controllers and a troop of the Blues and Royals mounted in Scimitar armoured cars. The main attack from the west was led by G Company which began its advance at 9.00 p.m. unseen by the enemy. The Company quickly attained its objective securing the western extreme of the ridge. Left Flank Company, advancing through the G Company positions, thereafter coming under concentrated enemy fire. Advancing with 13 and 15 Platoons forward and 14 Platoon in reserve, the Scots were forced to resort to the use of anti-tank weapons to clear the well placed enemy sangars. After 7 hours of vicious fighting, much of it at the point of a bayonet, Left Flank Company secured Tumbledown Peak allowing Right Flank Company to move against the remaining Argentinian positions which were dug into the east of the mountain.

A Sapper of 59 Commando Squadron, Royal Engineers, carefully examines an abandoned mine.

the Marines answered with heavy and accurate fire from several directions causing the Scots to take severe casualties during their withdrawal. Drill Sergeant Wright and Lance Corporal Pashley of the Royal Engineers were killed, and six Guardsmen, including Major Bethell in command of the attack, were injured. Nonetheless the assault served its purpose admirably. Robacio, assuming that the main attack would come from the south, made no attempt to reinforce his positions to the west from which direction G Company was about to mount its assault. The Scots were therefore able to leave their forming up point as planned at 9.00 p.m. and advance unnoticed, their movement shrouded by the noise and confusion of the diversionary attack to the south. By 10.30 p.m. they had obtained their objective without spilling blood. The western approaches of the mountain were in British hands and Left Flank Company was able to continue the advance as planned.

Almost immediately it began its ascent of the main feature of the mountain, Left Flank Company came under concentrated fire. Advancing with 13 and 15 Platoons forward and with 14 Platoon in reserve, the Company was soon forced to resort to the use of 66mm and 84mm anti-tank rocket launchers and M79 grenade launchers to clear the well-placed enemy sangars. Argentinian resistance was brave, at times even suicidal. During the final stages of the battle, with little concern for themselves, the defenders called down mortar and artillery fire on their own positions in an attempt to stem the advance but to no avail. After seven hours of bitter fighting, much of it at the point of a bayonet, the Scots secured Tumbledown peak. Over 30 Argentine bodies were subsequently removed from the area. There were 20 prisoners taken and an unknown number of enemy put to flight. The cost to the British was seven Guardsmen killed and 21 wounded of whom 18 were evacuated to hospital.

The sheer length of the main assault created difficulties for Right Flank Company which had yet to move against the remaining enemy positions to the east of the mountain. Their move had to be delayed to 6.00 a.m., less than 30 minutes before daylight. Denied artillery and mortar fire (the former was unavailable and the latter out of action) the Company was forced to advance with two platoons forward using its own anti-tank weaponry to bludgeon its way through the enemy's sangars. In two hours of bitter hand-to-hand fighting, during which the Argentinians lost seven dead and fourteen captured and the Scots sustained five wounded, the Company secured the finalhighpoints on Tumbledown. At 8.15 a.m., some twelve hours after the diversionary unit had engaged its first enemy and with Tumbledown now firmly in their hands, the 2nd Battalion Scots Guards were ordered to cease fire. Less than a day later the Argentinians surrendered.

Above: Major General Jeremy Moore holding the Declaration of Surrender signed by General Galtieri.

The battle for Mount Tumbledown proved that whatever the advantages of modern technology there is no substitute for physical fitness, team spirit and the will to win. Final victory had been gained through a combination of superior reconnaissance, clear and precise leadership, iron discipline and unremitting training.

Above: A Royal Marines patrol sets off on its epic 'yomp' across East Falklands.

Below: Exhausted but victorious, a Royal Marines platoon poses with a Falklands' flag on the outskirts of Stanley.

Fort Frederick,
SEAL Involvement in Grenada, 1983

Above: U.S. Marine Corps M-60A tanks of the 22nd MAU wade ashore.

The island of Grenada was first discovered by Columbus in 1498. Thereafter it passed from Spanish to French control, finally coming under British sovereignty during the 18th century. Britain governed Grenada directly as part of its Windward Islands administration until the 1950s. Having failed to form her Caribbean colonies into a single federation, Britain began to offer them autonomy within the Commonwealth system. Grenada was the first to receive her independence in 1974.

Grenada's early flirtations with democracy were not always happy. Her first Prime Minister, the eccentric Sir Eric Gairy, headed an administration combining a bizarre foreign policy with domestic repression and corruption. In March 1979 he was overthrown in a coup by Maurice Bishop, a respected politician and long-time opponent of Gairy.

Bishop's *New Jewel* government quickly came under the influence of Cuba as its economic problems increased. Over the next four years, Bishop invited increasing assistance from Castro, even asking him to construct the island's proposed international airport at Point Salines. Work began on the airfield in late 1979 with completion schedules for early 1984. The proposed runway was 2,750m (9,022 ft) long, far in excess of that required by local civilian aircraft but ideal for the military transports staging between the Soviet Union and Nicaragua. The United States watched with growing concern.

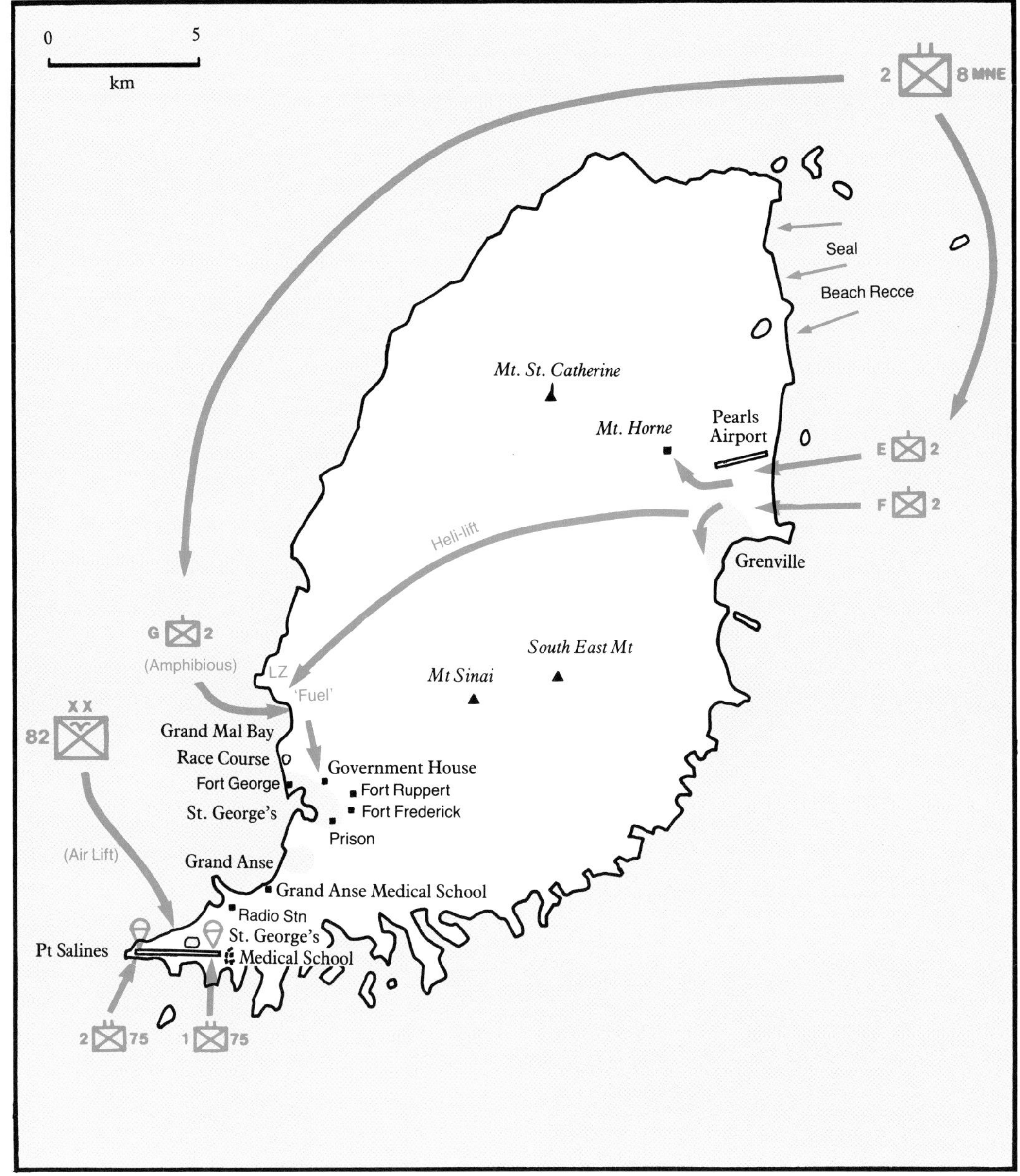

Urgent Fury, the United States attack on the Marxist Government of Grenada, began as a rescue mission. However when this proved impossible it soon turned into a full-blown invasion spearheaded by some of the finest troops available to the American armed forces. Although the landings by the Marines and the 82nd Airborne were relatively successful, both sustained problems and none of the special operations went to plan. Both the Delta Force attack against the prison and the SEAL's rescue of the Governor General were ill-conceived, relying far too heavily on technology to the detriment of resourcefulness. Had the SEALs in particular not been able to rely upon massive air support when subjected to unexpected fierce attack from unexpected reinforcements, their fate at the hands of their Grenadian adversaries might have been very different. Fortunately the Pentagon learned a number of valuable lessons which its forces were able to put into effect eight years later in the Gulf.

By 1983 it was becoming clear that the island's flirtation with Communism had not been wholly successful. The economy was stagnant and the Cuban interference in domestic matters oppressive. Notwithstanding, a faction of *New Jewel* now demanded closer links with Marxism. The Party split, and in October 1983 Deputy Prime Minister Bernard Coard, with the support of the military under General Bernard Austin, ordered Bishop to stand down from office.

When Bishop failed to cooperate, he and several of his ministers were placed under house arrest. Coard had, however, failed to take account of public reaction. A general strike was called and massed demonstrations held. A crowd forced the release of Bishop and then marched to Fort Ruppert where it was rumoured that several ministers were being held. Without warning, the pro-Coard military opened fire on the crowd killing over 100 Grenadians. Bishop and several of his ministers were rearrested and summarily executed.

Austin, with the assistance of Coard, seized power and immediately imposed a curfew. During the next few days, prominent pro-Bishop citizens were arrested and, in several instances, shot. The normally placid Eastern Caribbean was shocked. Representatives of the larger islands, (Dominica, St Lucia, St Vincent, Montserrat, St Kitts-Nevis and Antigua), met to discuss intervention but realized that alone they were too weak.

Fearful for the safety of its 1,000 citizens on the island, the United States had been closely monitoring the situation since Bishop's death a week before. When the Caribbean states requested United States assistance, President Reagan reacted.

At the time the United States had two Navy Task Forces at sea and in the area. The first, Task Force 124, comprised the helicopter carrier *Guam* and four landing ships of Amphibious Squadron Four. Embarked were 1,700 combat-ready Marines of 22nd MAU (Marine Amphibious Unit) together with landing craft, tanks and amphibious tractors. *Guam* also carried the aircraft of Marine Medium Helicopter Squadron 261 (Reinforced). The second group, the *Independence* Carrier Battle Group comprised the *Independence*, her escort of cruisers and destroyers, and the aircraft of Carrier Air Wing 6.

Initially, it was intended that the Marines would simply conduct a routine non-combat evacuation of American citizens from the island. However by 20 October the possibility of carrying out such an operation bloodlessly had been discounted due to the state of near civil war then prevailing on the island. In its stead Reagan agreed a military solution. Warning orders were issued to selected units of the Army and Air Force on the evening of 21 October. Both Ranger battalions (one at Fort Stewart the other at Fort Lewis), the Ready Brigade of the 82nd Airborne at Fort Bragg and elements of the 1st Special Operations Command were put on stand-by.

Austin anticipated a military reaction from his Caribbean neighbours and even the possible intervention of the Marines. He did not, however, expect the full scale United States response then being planned. The original United States response, code-named *Urgent Fury* was based on an exercise successfully held in the area two years earlier. After preliminary reconnaissance the Marines would go ashore on the morning of 25 October to secure Pearls Airport. At the same time Rangers would seize Point Salines Airport, one company landing by parachute, the rest by C-130 transport aircraft. Several hours later more

C-130s would bring in a battalion of the 82nd Airborne to reinforce the Rangers. More paratroopers would deploy to Barbados, from where, in conjunction with the local Caribbean forces, they would deploy to Grenada. Simultaneously teams from the élite SEAL Team Four would secure Government House, ensuring the safety of the Governor-General, and destroy the Radio Free Grenada transmitter. A counter-terrorist *Delta Force* unit would attack Richmond Hill Prison, releasing the political prisoners before the guards had the opportunity to massacre them.

During the course of 23/24 October, members of the SEAL and Delta teams were parachuted on to the island using HALO (High Altitude, Low Opening) techniques. Tragically due to equipment failure one of the aircraft missed its drop zone, depositing its jumpers into the sea. Four of the SEALs drowned when they became entangled in their parachutes. Throughout that night bad news was followed by worse. SEAL reconnaissance teams landed on the north-east coast reported that the surf was running high making the next morning's intended amphibious landing highly dangerous. To compound problems the airfield at Point Salines was found to be blocked, making a C-130 landing impossible, and the surrounding area heavily defended.

Hurriedly the plan was revised. The entire Ranger force, already en route, was now ordered to parachute on to Point Salines, part of the amphibious landing was cancelled and two of the three intended helicopter landing zones moved to less well defended areas.

Initially the landings went well. The Marines secured the main airfield and Grenville, the island's second largest town, and the Rangers the airstrip at Point Salines by 6.30 a.m. Although the defenders, supported by their Cuban allies, fought bravely, they were no match for the vastly better armed and trained Americans. Using a curious mixture of requisitioned trucks and bulldozers, the Rangers succeeded in opening their airstrip by mid-morning, allowing the C-130 transports to land with their jeeps and heavy equipment.

Above: Elements of 82nd Airborne deploy from C-130 Hercules.

Left: USMC LVTP-7 amphibian wades ashore on Grenada.

Below left: Once ashore, its sheer size and lack of armour makes the LVTP-7 highly vulnerable to enemy fire.

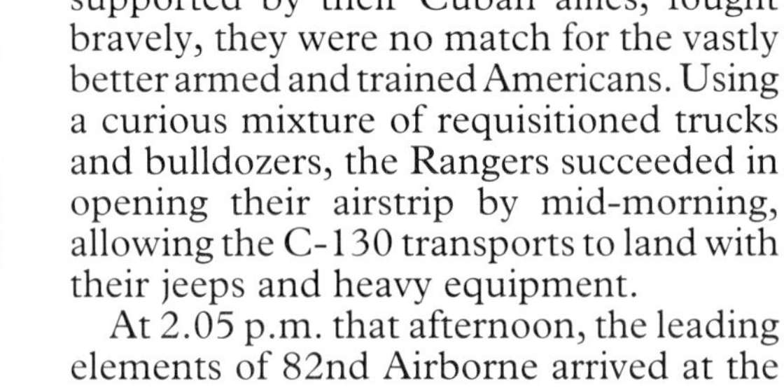

At 2.05 p.m. that afternoon, the leading elements of 82nd Airborne arrived at the airstrip and set up a forward command post. Throughout the next four hours, transports continued to land carrying the rest of the Marines, together with contingents of the Caribbean Peacekeeping Force. The local medical school was captured, the injured evacuated, and a perimeter built to hold the hundreds of prisoners now surrendering.

Unfortunately none of the special operations went to plan. Raid 2, the SEAL attack on the radio transmitter, was

Left: Marines aboard a helicopter assault ship prepare for embarkation.

relatively successful. Although Austin succeeded in broadcasting a few early morning exhortations to arms, the transmitter was seized without too much difficulty and went off the air at 6.15 a.m.

Raid 3, the Delta Force attack on the prison, failed completely. The attack was delayed by 45 minutes to coincide with the Ranger's rescheduled battalion jump on to Point Salines by which time the enemy were fully alerted. The ground component of the raid, due to be supplied by helicopters of the 101st Airborne, was aborted when two of the lead helicopters were hit by accurate anti-aircraft fire.

Raid 1, the rescue of the Governor-General by a force of 22 Navy SEALs, also began badly. The Americans were slowed when they came under fire as they assaulted

Below: Caribbean troops rest during the final stages of Operation Urgent Fury.

the grounds of Government House. When the Grenadians brought up reinforcements, including three armoured personnel carriers, the SEALs found themselves trapped.

Attempts to provide the SEALs with air cover met with catastrophe. Two Marine AH-1T Cobra helicopter gunships sent in support were forced down by heavy fire from anti-aircraft batteries positioned in Forts Frederick and Ruppert.

A subsequent attack launched by a Grenadian company supported by the three APCs failed when the SEALS called in an AC-130 gunship which immediately destroyed one vehicle and immobilized the rest. An uneasy stand-off followed, broken by a telephone call from the island's chief of police to the Governor-General. He asked how many Americans there were and if they were well armed. Having been advised by the skillful, if less than truthful, diplomat that the Americans were both numerous and well armed the attackers decided to surround the building but take no other action. Throughout the next few hours A-7 Intruders from *Independence* pounded the surrounding anti-aircraft batteries severely damaging an adjacent mental hospital in the process.

Above: Paratroopers of the 82nd Airborne Division deploy inland. Their training and firepower would prove decisive.

Top right: A Soviet-made SU-23-2 anti-aircraft gun lies silent and abandoned.

Above right: An American 105mm battery opens fire to suppress enemy activity.

The company of Marines whose earlier amphibious landing had been aborted now came into play. They were to sail around the island and effect a landing at Grand Mal Bay, a few hundred metres north of the capital, and from there to proceed with all speed to Government House. The landing met little resistance, an enemy BRDM reconnaissance vehicle being destroyed by an M60A1 tank, and was able to proceed without incident to Government House. The exhausted SEALs were relieved at 7.00 a.m. and, in the company of the Governor-General and his staff, removed to the safety and comparative comfort of *Guam*.

Afterwards the Marines, now at battalion strength, attacked south to occupy the Queen's Park Race Course and establish a helicopter landing zone. Fort Frederick was taken by the Marines at 5.00 p.m. and Fort George later that afternoon. By nightfall it was clear that the American operation was succeeding, if not always entirely to plan.

During the course of the Wednesday over 200 students were evacuated from the Grand Anse university campus by a joint Rangers/Marine operation and flown to safety in Barbados. The 82nd Airborne, by now with two battalions on the ground, continued its advance east from Point Salines mopping up the diminishing pockets of Cuban resistance as it went.

On the 3rd day the Marines, by now at full brigade strength, liberated the capital of St. Georges, reopening its airfield to military transport. By now the fight was over. Hundreds of Grenadian soldiers, and the few remaining Cubans, meekly surrendered to the Americans who quickly found themselves protecting their prisoners from the vengeance of the local population.

Operation *Urgent Fury* cost the lives of 19 American servicemen - 12 soldiers, three Marines and four Navy SEALS. Cuban casualties numbered 25 dead and 59 wounded. The Grenadians, both military and civilian, lost 45 killed and 350 wounded. The operation marked an important change in American policy within the Caribbean and culminated in the eclipse of Cuban influence within the area. Militarily it demonstrated the readiness and capability of the American forces. It also, however, showed up a number of weaknesses hitherto unrecognized within the special forces. Had the SEALs not been able to rely upon massive air support their fate at the hands of the troops attacking GovernmentHouse might have been very different. In the opinion of many they relied, and, still do rely, far too heavily on technology to the detriment of resourcefulness, a fact which was to become apparent yet again in the Gulf War eight years later.

Above: Even when resting this G.I. keeps his M-16A2 rifle firmly under his control.

Left: An 82nd Airborne trooper takes a few minutes to win the hearts and minds of a Grenadian family.

Operation Just Cause, Panama, 1989

Operation *Just Cause,* the invasion of Panama, has proved the most significant in a recent series of United States military interventions abroad. President Reagan sent the Marines to the Lebanon, invaded Grenada, sent a massive fleet to the Persian Gulf and bombed Tripoli. As if to emphasize a continuity in policy since his inauguration, President Bush has stationed the U.S. 6th Fleet provocatively close to the Libyan and Lebanese shores and has invaded Panama.

The Panama crisis began on 12 December 1989 when Manuel Noriega, the President of Panama and one time ally of the United States but now her mortal enemy, ordered his parliamentary assembly to proclaim him *Maximum Leader.* Three days later, in an act of extreme provocation, he declared the existence of a state of war between Panama and the United States. Initially White House spokesman Marlin Fitzwater was content to dismiss this act of sabre rattling bravado as 'all words, no action'. However the situation deteriorated within hours when Marine Lieutenant Robert Paz was killed at a Panamanian road block and a U.S. Navy officer and his wife who witnessed the event were arrested and humiliated. On the next day, 17 December, President Bush secretly order the invasion of Panama, the arrest of Noriega, and the establishment of a democratic government.

Bush was subsequently to defend his actions to a not entirely unsympathetic world in a number of ways. First, the United States had treaty obligations to defend the Panama Canal; second, it was her duty to restore democracy and assist the rightful government of Guillermo Endara cheated from office by the patently fraudulent May 1989 elections, and third, it was her right to bring Noriega to trial to face charges of international drug trafficking. Above all, under the terms of Article 51 of the United Nations Charter, the United States had the right to defend herself against the aggression of a neighbouring country which had unilaterally declared war on her.

Tension mounted over the next two days. On 18 December a nervous U.S. Army lieutenant shot and wounded a Panamanian corporal who was allegedly reaching for his gun and on the following afternoon C-130 Hercules transports began arriving at Howard Air Force Base in the U.S. controlled Canal Zone, at the rate of one every ten minutes. An over keen and somewhat naive television company reported on the open press that the majority had departed from Fort Bragg, the home of the élite 82nd Airborne Division.

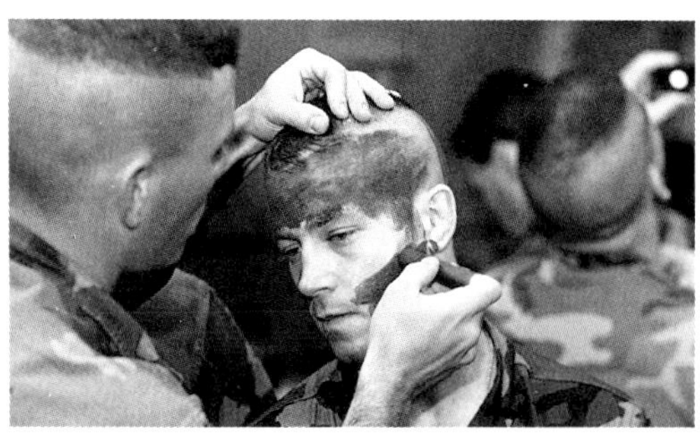

Above: Men of the First Ranger Battalion flying to Panama on board C-141 transports from Hunter Army Airfield, Georgia. Their deployment was widely reported in the press.

Although Noriega realized that a massive buildup was taking place — the airlift had been overseen by local workers and he received regular and excellent intelligence from his network of agents within the United States itself — he had utterly failed to appreciate its size and potential.

According to a subsequent report issued by General Colin Powell immediately prior to the buildup, the United States had over 13,000 troops based in and around the Canal Zone. These included the 193rd Infantry Brigade enhanced by unspecified elements of the U.S. Marine Corps, a battalion from the 7th Infantry Division based at Ford Ord, California and a mechanized battalion from the 5th Division based at Fort Polk, Louisiana. Less openly but perhaps more importantly, the 3rd Battalion, 7th Special Forces Group and a full Psychological Operations Group (POG) were also in situ to render specialist support. During the buildup they were joined by a brigade from the 82nd Airborne Division, two Army Ranger battalions and an unspecified group of 'selected special operational units'. By midnight on 20 December General Maxwell Thurman, who had recently assumed command of the operation, had no less than 24,000 troops — many of them low-intensity warfare specialists — available for action. Even this massive force would eventually have to be supplemented by further elements of the 7th Infantry Division and by the 16th Military Police Brigade within hours of the opening action to bring the ultimate total of troops on the ground to 27,500.

To counter this, Panama had a total

force of no more than 7,300 men and women of whom the vast majority, 6,000, were in the army. The soldiers' personal weapons were of a high standard but they had no tanks and only 29 lightly armoured American-built Cadillac Gauge V-150 and V-300 Commando reconnaissance vehicles. They had no artillery, their heaviest ordnance comprising 60mm mortars and a few 3.5 in rocket launchers. The Navy was no more than 900 strong and commanded nothing stronger than a flotilla of six inshore patrol boats supported by four landing craft. The air force, with 400 personnel, had neither combat aircraft nor armed helicopters available. Noriega did however have a police and National Guard force of some 12,300 officers and men which included a series of so called *Dignity Battalions* — with an estimated 2,000 members — who were known to be proven street fighters and fiercely loyal to their President.

Immediately prior to the execution of *Just Cause* which began on 21 December, Senior Guillermo Endara was sworn in as the new President of Panama in a ceremony presided over by a judge and conducted in an American Air Force Base. Strangely, when questioned, few of those reported to have attended the ceremony could remember either its format or the name of the presiding judge.

As an inducement to the Panamanian civilians, whom it was thought had no love for Noriega and would rapidly turn against him, a reward of $1 million was offered for his capture. The sum of $150.00 was also offered to any Panamanian, military or civilian, handing in a firearm to the American authorities.

The American invaders were divided into five Task Forces each vastly superior in numbers and firepower to the enemy whom they were ordered to overcome.

A Ranger battalion attached to Task Force Red parachuted on to Rio Hato, some 60 miles to the south-west of the Panama Canal, to neutralize the 6th and 7th Panamanian Defence Force Company. A second Ranger battalion attached to the same Task Force parachuted on to the Torrijos International Airport and, having secured this, fanned out across the Pacora River to the east. Once it was safe to do so,

Below: A vessel from Special Boat Unit 26 at Redman Naval Station Panama ties up at Fort Sherman.

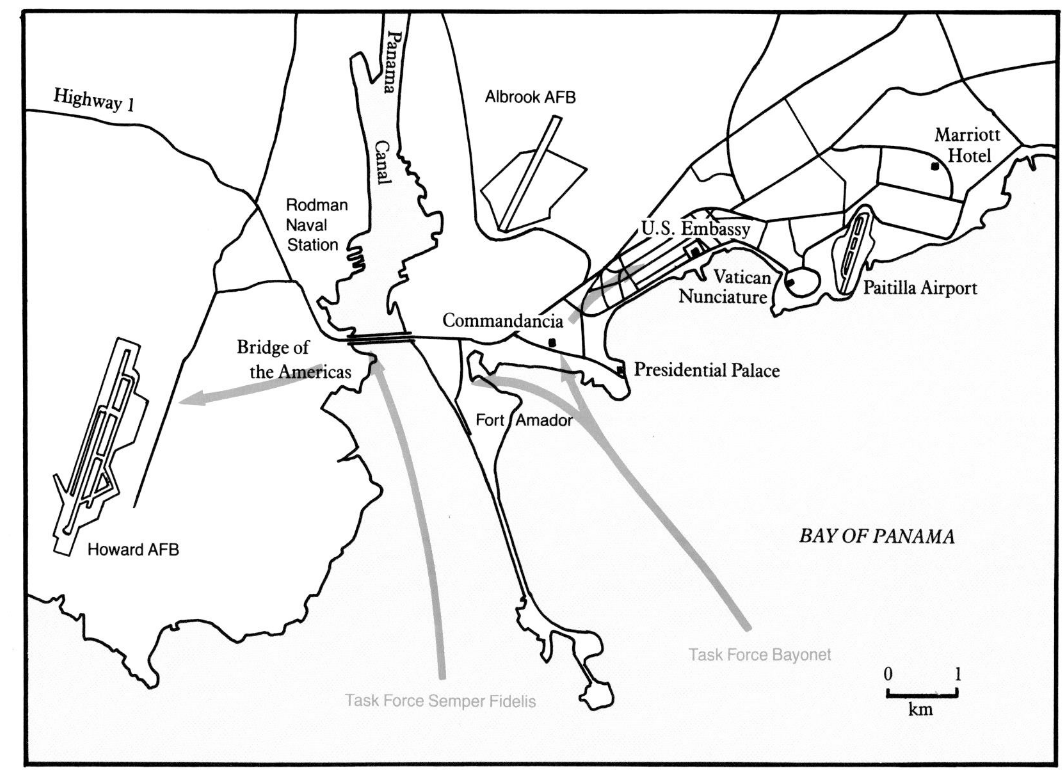

Operation Just Cause *was undertaken on an awesome scale. The American invaders were divided into five Task Forces each vastly superior in numbers and firepower to those of the enemy. Ranger battalions attached to Task Force Red were ordered to parachute on to Torrijos International Airport and the military base at Rio Hato some 97km (60 miles) southwest of Panama City. A brigade of the 82nd Airborne, designated Task Force Pacific, was then to parachute on to the airfield and deploy westward towards the city centre. Task Force Atlantic, comprising infantry and airborne troops already in situ, was to overwhelm the Panamanian army and marine units in the area of the Madden Dam north of the Canal while Task Force Semper Fidelis, with its armoured cars, was to secure the Bridge of the Americas across the Canal itself. Finally, and most crucially, Task Force Bayonet was to secure the* Commandancia, *block a potential counter-attack from Fort Amador and fan out into the city's commercial centre to prevent a breakdown in law and order.*

a brigade of 82nd Airborne Division, designated Task Force Pacific, parachuted on to the airfield and began to deploy westward towards the city centre.

Task Force Atlantic, made up of infantry and airborne troops, overwhelmed Panamanian infantry and naval infantry units to secure the Madden Dam at the northern end of the canal.

Task Force Semper Fidelis, comprising a U.S. Marine Corps company supported by light armoured fighting vehicles, secured both the Bridge of the Americas across the Panama Canal and the Howard Air Force Base situated strategically to the south of its western approaches.

The most demanding, complex and important mission fell to Task Force Bayonet made up of the 5th Bn, 87th Regiment with artillery, helicopter gunships and a platoon of light tanks in support.

Dividing into three small teams they secured the *Commandancia* which acted as Noriega's headquarters, blocked a potential counter-attack by the 5th Panamanian Defense Force Company based in Fort Amador across the canal from the Howard Air Force Base and fanned out into the commercial centre of the city where they encountered and successfully neutralized the 1st, 2nd and elements of the 6th and 7th Defense Force companies. Without exception the primary objectives were secured within an hour. Noriega, however, evaded capture.

Despite often indiscriminate American firepower, which reduced parts of Panama City to smoking ruins and caused many casualties among the civilian population, Panamanian resistance was not quickly overcome. Noreiga's *Dignity Battalions* were particularly stubborn. A week after the invasion General Thurman was forced to concede that hostilities were far from over. Indeed it was estimated that 1,800 troops still remained combat effective and were in many instances fighting under centralized control.

Ominously Noriega's crack *Battalion des Hombres de la Montana,* his special forces group, were discovered to have deserted their barracks in the City and to have redeployed in the surrounding mountains.

Noriega's Lear jet and fast patrol boats, kept in constant readiness at Paitilla Airport, had been destroyed at the outset of the invasion by a team of Navy SEALs two of whom were killed in the action. It was therefore rightly assumed that Noriega had not managed to flee the country but wrongly assumed that he had fled to the mountains at the head of his troops.

Frustrated and embarrassed by their lack of immediate success in capturing Noriega, on 22 December the bulk of the United States troops fanned out into the hills in pursuit of their illusive quarry, leaving Panama City itself dangerously underpoliced. Thereafter followed several days of rioting and looting, in which much of the commercial centre of the City, including many of its banks, was destroyed. Astonishingly, and in the eyes of many unforgivably, the United States planners had failed to appreciate the close relationship between the paramilitary police and the Noriega regime. Within hours of the invasion the police had simply disintegrated as a potent force leaving the city and its environs without any form of cohesive civilian protection. Anarchy reigned in the void during which the poor, and occasionally not so poor, citizenry helped itself to the contents of the local shops whilst the helpless owners looked on.

Above: Sergeant Kaylif Wilder of the 24th Security Police Squadron stands guard at Howard Air Force Base.

The 16th Military Police Brigade was eventually summoned from Fort Bragg to restore order but not until immense damage had been done to the fabric of the city. On 28 December elements of the newly created 1,000 strong Panamanian Public Forces — drawn from the less criminal elements of the old military — began to appear on the streets to release the 16th Brigade for its more traditional role.

Ironically Noriega was not in the mountains at all. He was in fact staying in the opulent villa of his mistress, less than a mile from the Marriott Hotel and close to the Airborne Brigade headquarters. Realizing that his capture was inevitable and that the Nicaraguan and Cuban embassies which would otherwise have offered him protection were barred, he surrendered himself on Christmas Day to the unsuspecting and highly embarrassed Vatican Diplomatic Mission.

Below: The ruins of a hangar at Altbrook AFB, after a U.S. counter-attack against enemy firing from Quarry Heights.

After a day of unsuccessful conventional negotiations, General Thurman ordered the Mission to be enveloped in a sea of noise. Massive loudspeakers were brought to the site and at once Noriega, together with his unfortunate (and innocent) hosts, began to be blasted with non-stop pop music. At the same time reporters were invited to inspect his headquarters where they were shown portraits of Hitler, pornographic material and treatises on devil worship as if to emphasize the ex-President's instability.

Thurman's handling of the Vatican Nunciature siege was subsequently to bring into doubt his suitability as a leader. It was to be described by Admiral LaRocque, the Director for Defense Information in Washington, as 'the most atrocious, barbaric and unsophisticated act I have ever seen from a U.S. military commander'. Certainly it was eccentric. It drew on none of the established lessons of previously successful psychological operations yet it seems to have worked. Denied access to a telephone, unable to sleep because of the noise and surrounded by enemies Noriega became rattled. Seeing no other way out he surrendered to the United States authorities early in the New Year and was transferred immediately to Florida to stand trial on a series of narcotics charges.

During the brief war, 23 U.S. soldiers and 293 Panamanian troops were killed. Civilian deaths were estimated at 700. The Americans took several thousand prisoners and seized 44,000 weapons.

Even so, the war had not been a complete success. The United States had long foreseen the need to invade Panama and had given the Pentagon ample time to prepare for one. Over 13,000 troops were already on station in Panama before the invasion and the ground was well known to the commanders. Nonetheless the initial attack, having begun well, faltered at the first sign of real resistance. Although the enlisted soldiers fought admirably the junior officers often proved excitable and indecisive under fire. Artillery was used, often indiscriminately, and without justification. Civilian deaths numbered 400, with a further 2,000 wounded and 15,000 made homeless.

However superficially successful it may have appeared, *Just Cause* proved that the United States military still lacks low-intensity warfare potential. Whether or not the lessons learned from *Desert Storm* will prove useful in helping to overcome this deficiency, still remains to be seen.

Below: U.S. troops undertake house-to-house clearing after the invasion.

Above: Blackhawk helicopters refuel at the 193 Support Battalion Hotpit Refuelling Point during Operation Just Cause.

The French Thrust to Al Samawah, Iraq, 1991

France has often been accused of a degree of amorality when dealing with arms sales to the Third World. She has traditionally followed a course of self-interest, regardless of regional consequences, to the occasional extent of arming both sides in a conflict. Few in Britain have yet forgotten that the Exocets which wrought such havoc to the Royal Navy during the 1983 Falklands War were of French manufacture.

France, therefore, found herself in something of a dilemma when Saddam Hussein invaded Kuwait in August 1990. She was on good commercial terms with Iraq yet could not afford to upset her other trading partners by seemingly condoning so flagrant an act of aggression.

To compound her problem, Britain, then still under the premiership of Margaret Thatcher, reacted immediately, joining the United States in outright condemnation of Saddam. President Bush began to gather together a massive military force in the area and it quickly became apparent that only a complete capitulation by the Iraqis would prevent an eventual war. Britain, Egypt, and a host of other countries prepared to offer material assistance in the form of men, ships and money. It began to look as though France would be left on the sidelines as seemingly impotent as Germany and as unwilling as Japan to involve herself. While the generals called for action the pacifist Defence Minister Jean-Pierre Chevenement refused to act. It began to look as if the Force d'Action Rapide, France's much vaunted 50,000 strong élite out-of-area force, would not be called upon to play its role in the international events then unfolding.

Eventually President François Mitterand reacted to growing internal demand for action, forced Chevenement to resign, and committed a flotilla of the French fleet to the Gulf. Jubilation turned to embarrassment however, when the venerable aircraft carrier *Clemenceau,* which had set sail amid considerable pomp and circumstance, was forced to limp back to harbour with unspecified mechanical problems. Many suggested that the ship was, in fact, quite serviceable but that the

Above: Gunners attached to the 11th Naval Infantry man their 155mm TFF-1 artillery pieces.

Left: French-crewed Mirage 2000 jet fighters refuel over the Saudi desert.

Super-Etendard jets on board were so old that they would have stood no chance against the French manufactured Mirages of the Iraqi Air Force in a dog-fight.

When Britain sent an armoured brigade to the Gulf, French sensibilities could stand no more and a small military force was dispatched to join the French Air force Mirages and Jaguars already in the area. The French force settled in at once, liaising well with the sometimes volatile Arab units with which it was co-located. To the pride of the French military it was stationed far

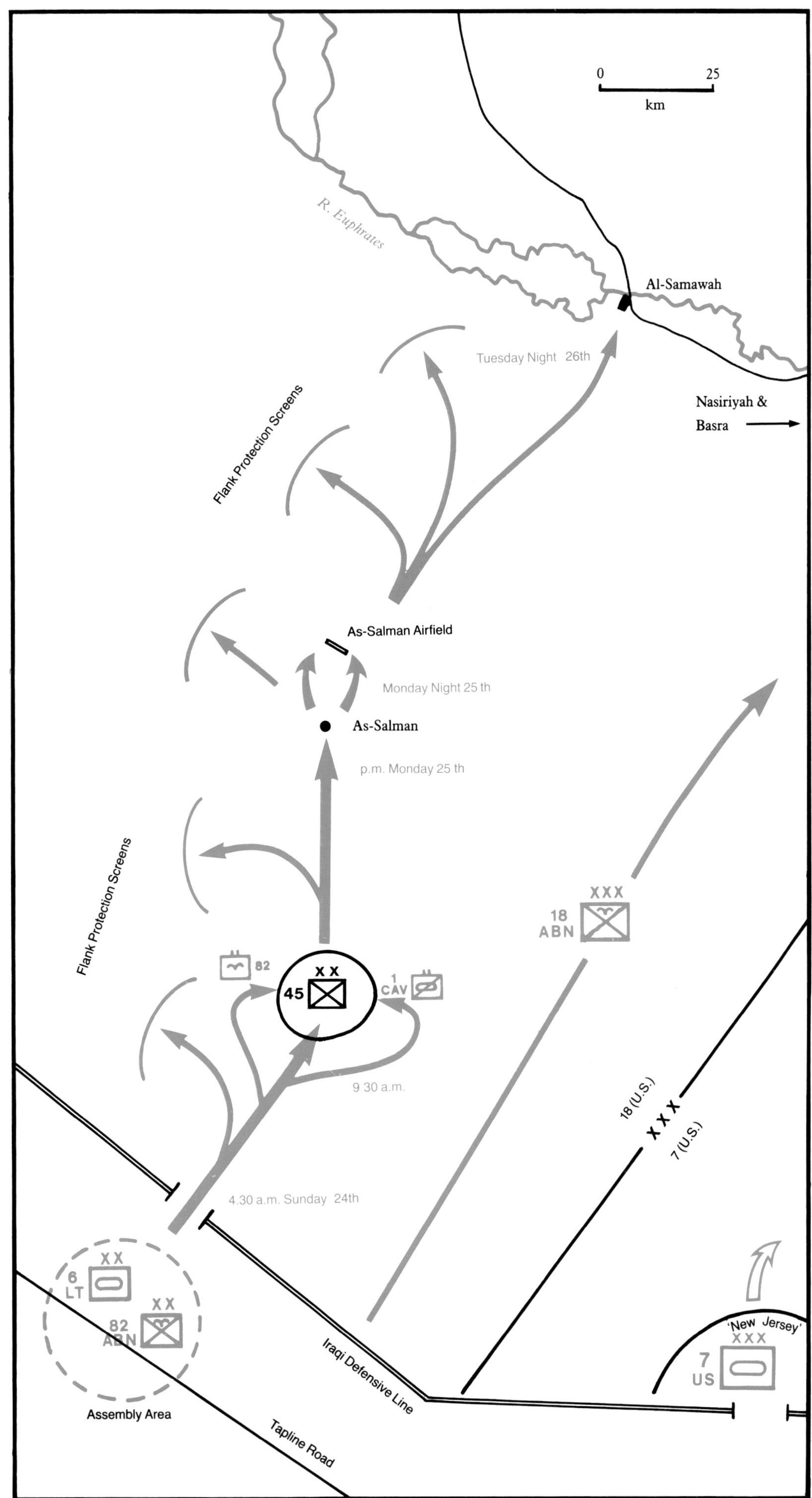

The French 6th Light Armoured Division was drawn exclusively from the Rapid Action Force. It was lightly equipped, highly manoeuvrable and thoroughly professional. As such it was ideally suited to operations on the open left flank of the Coalition forces. The French formed part of the 18th U.S. Airborne Corps but took under command elements of the U.S. 82nd Airborne Division. During the first day's fighting the French completely destroyed the Iraqi 45th Infantry Division moving on to secure the air base at Al-Salman. By Tuesday night elements of the Division had reached Al-Samawah and were poised to cross the Euphrates if ordered. During the 100 hours of combat the French advanced further and faster than any other Allied unit, reinforcing the role of the light division in modern warfare.

forward, well ahead of the leading United States Army and British units.

Under the codename *Daguet* the French contingent was steadily enhanced until, by January 1991, it comprised a small division with 10,000 men and 40 tanks. Designated 6th Light Armoured Division and commanded by Brigadier Jean-Charles Roquejeoffre, (and later by General Bernard Janvier), it contained the cream of the Rapid Action Force. Armoured support was provided by the 40 fast but lightly armoured AMX-30B2 tanks of the 4th Dragoons. Mobility came in the form of the 1st Spahis and the Foreign Legion's 1st Cavalry Regiment, each equipped with 36 AMX-10RC heavy armoured cars. This was further enhanced by a jeep-mounted Milan anti-tank reconnaissance company founded from the 1st Parachute Hussars. The infantry were drawn from the Legion's 1st Infantry Regiment and from a composite battalion of the Marine Infantry. Artillery support was provided by the 24 AU-F-1 155mm self-propelled guns of the 11th Marine Artillery Regiment.

It soon became apparent that the French division's potential lay in its speed and versatility. It was much too lightly armoured to take on the regiments of Soviet-built Iraqi T-72 tanks massed across the border, yet it was ideally suited to flank protection duty. Therefore, amid great secrecy, the French division was moved to the west flank of the Coalition forces where it began to train in earnest with the United States 82nd and 101st Airborne Divisions.

With uncharacteristic humility, General Maurice Schmitt, in command of the French Army, consented to Roquejeoffre's division being placed under General Norman Schwarzkopf's overall command. In return, elements of the 82nd Airborne Division were subordinated to the French. The Americans soon became captivated by the Frenchmen's cool professionalism. Any reservations which may have existed soon evaporated as the two very different cultures and styles merged into a single potent fighting force.

During the days immediately before the ground war French Gazelle light helicopters equipped with HOT anti-tank wire-guided missiles joined with the AH-1 Cobra attack helicopters of the 82nd Airborne to attack Iraqi positions to their front. In so doing they not only caused the already battered enemy severe damage, but forced him to withdraw his reconnaissance shield leaving him totally ignorant of the Coalition dispositions.

Above: An AMX-30 B2 tank of the 4th Dragoons moves towards its final forming up point prior to the land battle.

Below: A French Air Force commando mans a Mistral SAM system at Trahsa Air Base.

At 4.30 a.m. on the morning of Sunday 24 February, within minutes of Schwarzkopf implementing Operation *Desert Storm* the French crossed the Iraqi border unopposed. With parade ground precision they raced forward, their armoured bulldozers, mobile bridges and tanks to the fore. The entire effort was protected by the attack helicopters flying hither and thither, often within feet of the ground, in search of enemy armour.

By 9.30 a.m., the French had advanced 50 km (31 miles) into Iraq and had reached their first objective, the 8,000 strong 45th Infantry Division codenamed *Rochambeau* and backed by Soviet-made T-55 tanks. For the first time they met resistance. Rejecting a frontal assault as potentially too costly, Janvier ordered the implementation of a complex triple manoeuvre. While an American battalion was transported by helicopter to the west, French Foreign Legion tanks circled to the east. After a short but intense artillery and helicopter bombardment, the Americans supported by the tanks of the 4th Dragoons assaulted. The sight of the tanks brought terror to the ill-trained Iraqis who began to flee or surrender in their thousands. With a loss of nine American lives, and an unknown number of Iraqi, the position was taken. The 45th Infantry Division, which had had weeks to dig in and which was larger and better armed than its opponent, simply disintegrated in the face of the Franco-American onslaught.

Having pre-empted a counter-attack from the north, the French paused briefly to regroup and consolidate. They had suffered no tank losses and only two soldiers were injured – one the result of an exploding mine, the other in an accident. Janvier now found himself slowed by an unexpected logistical phenomenon. Although 5,000 Iraqis had fled into the desert, many hundreds had chosen to stay. Janvier's troops found themselves having to deal with in excess of six times the number of prisoners anticipated. Fortunately, however, most seemed relieved and delighted to meet their captors, whom they had been warned would maltreat them, and were easily disarmed.

Fearful of repeating this problem, the French overcompensated the next day.

Left: Tanks of the 4th Dragoons rest during one of the final training exercises.

They arrived at their final objective, the fort at As Salman (later dubbed 'Rushdie' by the troops), with two lorry-loads of provisions, to find only fifteen remaining Iraqi soldiers who were almost embarrassingly eager to surrender. By that night the French had captured the nearby airfield and were able to report the area under their complete control. By Tuesday night their advance elements had reached the strategically important town of Al Samawah astride the Euphrates.

Ironically, the French, who had advanced 160km (100 miles) without serious loss, now suffered their first fatalities. Two Marines were killed and 24 injured while

Below: Legionnaires man an anti-aircraft gun position. In the event the threat from Iraqi aircraft was non-existent.

clearing a minefield. Working in close conjunction with the men and helicopters of the 82nd Airborne the French had succeeded in advancing further than any other coalition force into enemy territory.

They had guarded the flanks of the more ponderous United States and British heavy armoured divisions operating to their right and had caused chaos among the Iraqi supply routes. They had brought a strong, highly professional division to the banks of the Euphrates and had given Bush and Schwarzkopf the very real option of taking Baghdad. They had taken on elements of the Iraqi regular army annihilating them, and in so doing had proved beyond doubt the effectiveness of the light division as a concept of warfare. They had demonstrated that, if resupplied from the air, tanks supported by tracked reconnaissance and mechanized infantry could pursue their own battle independent of the main force, behind enemy lines if necessary.

The 6th Light Armoured Division would not have been able to operate with such speed and élan without the logistical support provided by the lift helicopters of the 82nd Airborne but this was quickly forgotten in the euphoria of victory. In less than three days, *Daguet* had begun a French military renaissance. The ignominies of the World War II collapse, the capitulation at Dien Bien Phu, even the nightmare of Algeria were erased as Paris toasted the new French Army. France was the first nation to announce that its troops would be awarded campaign medals and granted a victory parade. Mitterand, who in deference to the sensibilities – and votes – of his 3.7 million Arab immigrants had earlier tried to confine the war to Kuwait, now demanded France's rightful place on the coalition victory table. France offered a peace-keeping force to Kuwait and began, as one of the five permanent members, to extol the virtues of a strong United Nations security council involvement.

Only the most optimistic (or politically naive) expect France's flirtation with her Anglo-Saxon neighbours to last forever. What is certain is that her armed forces need never again feel subconsciously inferior to the vastly better armed and equipped United States, Germany and, to a lesser extent, Britain. As a direct result it is wholly possible that France will now begin to come in out of the military cold and start to play her rightful part in the defence of Europe.

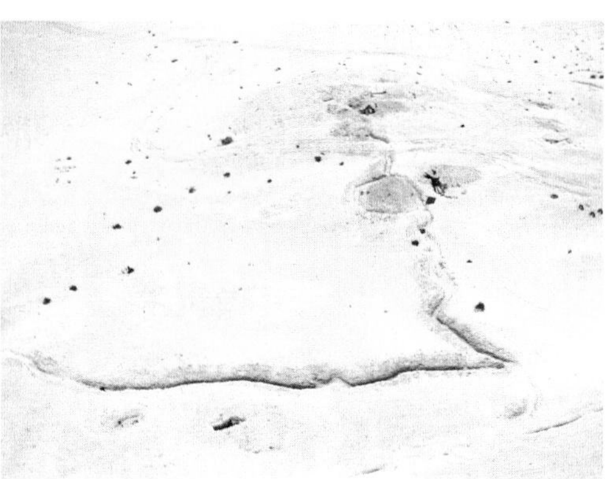

Right: Iraqi defensive positions dug in along the Saudi border offered little resistance.

Below: French officers inspect the remains of a destroyed Iraqi T-55 tank deep inside enemy territory.

Operation Desert Storm, The U.S. Army in Iraq, 1991

On 2 August 1990 Saddam Hussein committed one of the most patent acts of political piracy of the twentieth century. Without just cause or provocation he ordered his massive army to advance into neighbouring Kuwait, annexing the tiny Sheikdom as the 19th province of Iraq.

World condemnation was instantaneous and profound. The United Nations Security Council demanded the immediate and unconditional withdrawal of all Iraqi forces. The United States declared an economic embargo against Iraq and in conjunction with France, Britain and Italy froze all Kuwaiti and Iraqi assets. Iraq retaliated by ceasing the repayment of debts to Washington, London and Paris.

Saddam undertook publicly to withdraw his forces within 48 hours but this was discounted as worthless rhetoric when U.S. satellite intelligence revealed that he was, in fact, reinforcing his troops in Kuwait and had moved armoured units into the neutral zone between Kuwait and Saudi Arabia.

On 6 August, in an act of pure provocation, the Iraqis began the round up of American and European nationals in Kuwait with a view to moving them north to Baghdad. On 7 August King Fahd of Saudi Arabia issued an invitation to friendly nations to help defend his kingdom. President Bush immediately ordered an F-15 squadron and the 82nd Airborne Division to Saudi Arabia and announced the redeployment of three aircraft carrier groups to the Gulf and the Eastern Mediterranean. Britain and France sent reinforcements to their naval patrols in the area and Prime Minister Margaret Thatcher announced the dispatch of two fighter squadrons. Oman, Qatar and the

Top: An American F16 fighter jet flies low over a Turkish mosque as it returns from a mission over Iraq.

Right: A U.S. soldier stands beside a destroyed Iraqi Mirage F1 at Nasiriyah Air Base only 300 km south of Baghdad.

other G.C.C. members mobilized and troops from Egypt and Morocco began to deploy to the region.

During the course of the next few weeks over twenty nations sent troops, ships and logistical support to the growing Coalition forces. By mid-January their numbers were only marginally less than their Iraqi adversary, meanwhile enjoying a vast superiority in the air. Coalition forces totalled 475,000 ground troops, supported by 3,100 tanks and 2,200 aircraft. They faced 540,000 Iraqis with 4,200 tanks and 500 aircraft.

Although, for political expediency, command of the Coalition forces was given to the Saudis, control in reality passed to General H. Norman Schwarzkopf, a bear of an American four-star general with a reported I.Q. of 170. The vastly experienced Schwarzkopf had masterminded the United States' incursion into Grenada and was ideally suited to the diplomatic as well as military task ahead. Although Britain, France, Egypt and Syria each had divisional-sized forces in the area, the overwhelming majority of troops within the Coalition, some 350,000 by the commencement of ground hostilities, were American. Comprising the 1st and 2nd Marine Expeditionary Forces, under command of Lieutenant-General Walter Boomer, and the III U.S. Army, commanded by Lieutenant-General John Yeosoch they represented the most powerful United States task force in history to be deployed outside of the European theatre.

Schwarzkopf was tasked publicly with the implementation of a series of U.N. Security Council Resolutions demanding Iraq's removal from Kuwait. Less overtly he was tasked with the destruction of her military superstructure, primarily Saddam's N.B.C. (Nuclear, Biological and Chemical) capabilities.

By good fortune he was able to formulate his plans on a proven strategy which he had

Above: After the invasion many Kuwaitis volunteered for military service. Kuwaitis were the first troops into the capital.

Left: A U.S. B-52 bomber lands at Fairford Air Base, England, having returned safely from a sortie over Iraq.

Above: General Norman Schwarzkopf, Commander-in-Chief U.S. Forces, addresses the press.

In 1990 Iraq was truly an armed camp. From the Turkish border to Kuwait over 1 million armed men, with 4,200 tanks and 500 aircraft, stood ready to repel the United States-led Coalition forces. Many of the Iraqi airfields were situated in the far west of the country close to the Jordanian border and ready to threaten Israel. Others, the product of an earlier bloody war, were to be found on the Iranian border. Air defence centres were positioned at Rutba in the west, Kirkuk in the north and Baghdad and Nasiriya in the south. Known nuclear sites were located at Arbil and near Quyyarah in the Kurdish north. Despite the obvious might of the Iraqi war machine it proved no match for Coalition air power. Within days of the commencement of the air war the majority of the airfields were closed and the nuclear and missile sites destroyed.

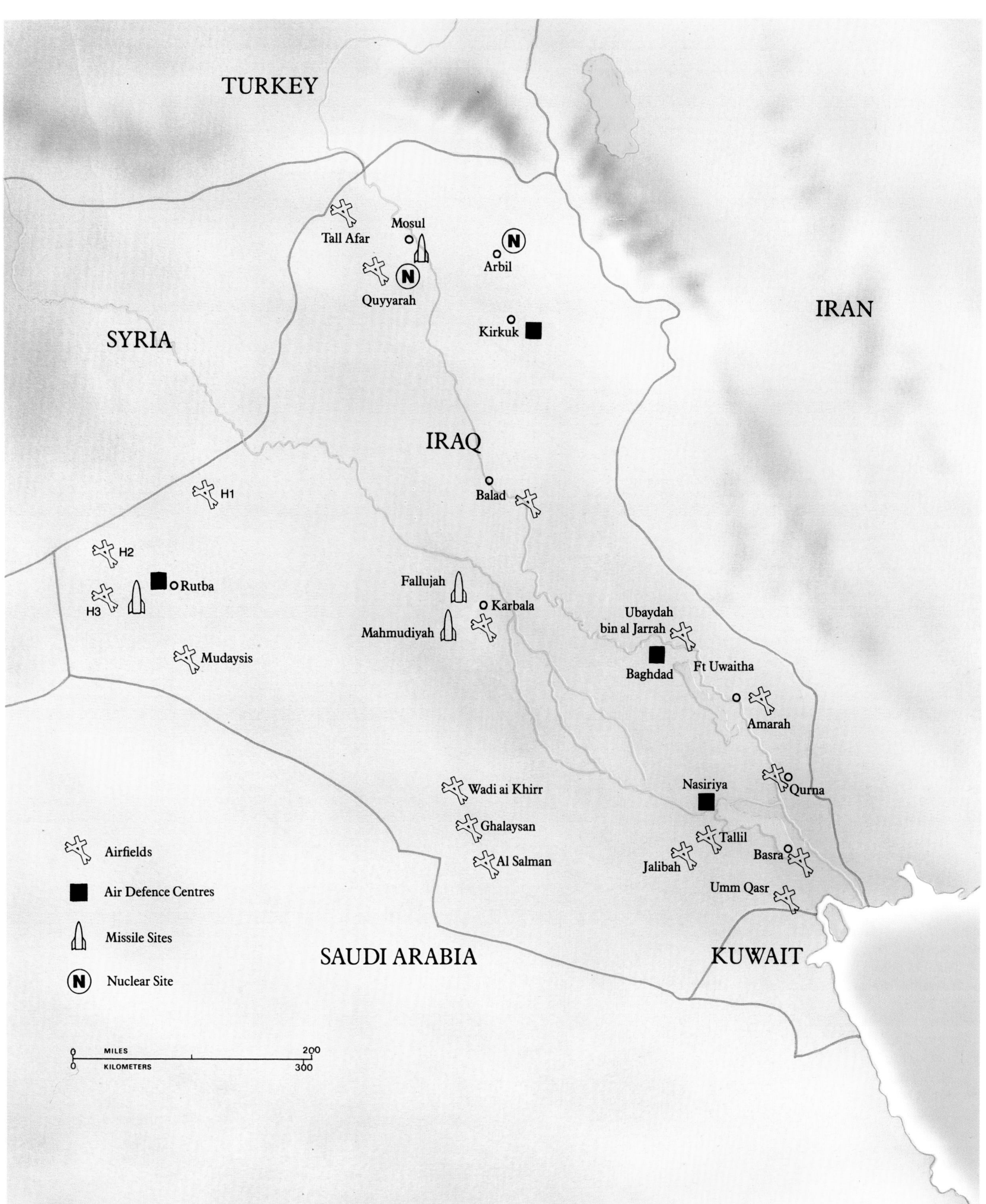

TURKEY
SYRIA
IRAN
IRAQ
SAUDI ARABIA
KUWAIT
Tall Afar
Mosul
Arbil
Quyyarah
Kirkuk
Balad
H1
H2
Rutba
H3
Mudaysis
Fallujah
Karbala
Mahmudiyah
Ubaydah
bin al Jarrah
Baghdad
Ft Uwaitha
Amarah
Wadi ai Khirr
Ghalaysan
Al Salman
Nasiriya
Qurna
Tallil
Jalibah
Basra
Umm Qasr
Airfields
Air Defence Centres
Missile Sites
Nuclear Site
0 MILES 200
0 KILOMETERS 300

Left: A-10 Thunderbolts operating closely with the ground forces, accounted for the destruction of numbers of enemy tanks.

put into effect on an exercise only five days before the Iraqi invasion. The plan called for an initial period of reconnaissance, analysis and intelligence gathering during which the size and disposition of the Iraqi forces would be studied in detail. Thereafter, an air assault would be launched against previously identified military and economic targets to be followed if need be by a ground advance into Kuwait.

A masterpiece of deception caused Saddam to believe that the land-attack, when it came, would be launched along the coast. A Marine Amphibious Unit (M.A.U.) was left at sea causing the Iraqis and press analysts alike to assume that the invasion would include a beach landing near Kuwait City. Simultaneously, state of the art electronic jamming of radar and communications 'blinded' the Iraqis to the Coalition's genuine intentions.

Top secret Electronic Warfare (E.W.) techniques were used in conjunction with satellite and aircraft imagery to identify Saddam's nuclear and chemical factories. His C^3I. (Command, Control, Communications and Intelligence) centres were pinpointed and his major troop concentrations and arms dumps located. Agents within Iraq (*Humint*) watched and reported the movement of senior Government officials and, where possible, of Saddam himself.

The second stage of Schwarzkopf's plan, the air war, began at approximately 2.00 a.m. local time on the morning of Thursday 17 January 1991. Although it was widely expected, its ferocity astounded the Iraqis. During the first 24 hours of the air war U.S., R.A.F. , Saudi, Kuwaiti and later French aircraft launched a total of 2,000

Below: An Iraqi deserter surrenders to U.S. troops. He was returned to face an uncertain fate.

Bottom: Smoke rises in downtown Baghdad after a successful Allied air raid.

Left: An F-15 fighter of the Royal Saudi Air Force takes off on a night sortie into Iraq.

Below: Although comparatively unsophisticated, Iraqi Scud missiles wrought havoc when they fell into densely populated areas.

Bottom: Jan 18, 1991, Israeli officials inspect the ruins of a Tel Aviv property hit by a Scud missile.

sorties from bases throughout the Arabian Peninsula and from aircraft carriers in the Gulf. One hundred Tomahawk cruise missiles, capable of map-reading their designated route, were launched at Iraqi targets from the battleships *Wisconsin* and *Missouri*. U.S. Marine helicopters attacked Iraqi artillery installations near the border town of Khafji while B-52 bombers attacked Republican Guard troop concentrations south-west of Basra. Four-fifths of the Iraqi air force was either destroyed or marooned in hardened shelters.

During the next three weeks Baghdad was pounded with bombs and laser-guided 'smart' weapons which struck with uncanny accuracy. Cruise missiles and smart bombs gutted Saddam's palace and many other government buildings. Airfield denial bombs closed enemy airfields, albeit briefly while block-busters blasted their way through metres of reinforced concrete into the heart of military and Baathist Party command bunkers. Furious, Saddam ordered the officers in charge of Baghdad's air defences to be court-martialled and shot.

By the end of January, Saddam's political and economic infrastructure had been all but obliterated. His chemical and biological centres had been bombed, reducing considerably his potential for escalating the war. The majority, although not all of his static and mobile Scud launchers had been destroyed. All but a few bridges across the Tigris and Euphrates had been made impassable, while his main highways had become extremely dangerous even at night. Less obviously but equally importantly his military land lines had been severed irreparably, forcing him to transmit his orders to the front line by radio. This enabled Coalition E.W. intercept units to listen in.

By that time also the Coalition had flown over 22,000 sorties. They had destroyed 49 Iraqi aircraft in the air and an unknown number on the ground for a loss of 24 allied aircraft. More crucially they had shattered the confidence of the Iraqi aircrew. Over the next few days an increasing number of Iraqi warplanes, among them Saddam's latest fighters, began to fly to Iran. Within ten days an estimated 120 aircraft, a quarter of the entire fleet, were in Iranian hands where they were destined to remain throughout the rest of the conflict.

Early in February the air war emphasis shifted from the shattered cities and industrial centres to the front line. Squadrons of B-52 bombers flying from Guam, Spain and Britain saturation-bombed known armoured and artillery concentrations behind the front lines. Psychological Operations (Psy. Ops) teams dropped leaflets on the ill-trained, exhausted and hungry Iraqi conscripts in the front line, advising them of the time of the next bombing raid and inviting them to surrender. Although few were able to do so, many of the conscripts had no real idea of where they were and were terrified of reprisals by Republican Guard execution squads - those who did brought reports of crumbling morale everywhere.

By the time that Schwarzkopf was ready to put the third and final stage of his plan — the ground offensive — into operation, victory was virtually assured. Weeks of bombing had shattered the Iraqi front line both physically and psychologically.

During the early course of the air war, Schwarzkopf moved his ground troops forward towards their assumed start lines for the land battle ahead. Unknown to the Iraqis however, they did not stay long in their anticipated positions but instead entered into a massive plan of deception.

Left: U.S. Marines practise mine-clearing operations before the commencement of the ground war.

Left: Iraqi prisoners being led to captivity and safety inside Saudi Arabia.

U.S. and British Special Forces probed the Kuwaiti coast while an amphibious unit lay offshore, tying down five crack Iraqi divisions in the area of Kuwait City. The 1st and 2nd U.S. Marine Divisions moved into the edge of the disputed Neutral Zone and began slowly to probe Saddam's most vaunted defences. Saudi, Egyptian, Kuwaiti and Qatari forces operated with them. The British, who had earlier provided their armoured and engineering support, now moved westward with the bulk of the United States heavy armour. U.S. VII Corps, comprising the 1st British Armoured Division, 1st and 3rd U.S. Armored Divisions and the 1st U.S. Infantry Division, deployed west of the Wadi al Batin ready to strike directly into Iraq before turning eastward into Kuwait. To its left, the U.S. 24th Mechanized Infantry Division stood ready, impatient to strike deep into the Tigris and Euphrates valleys. Further to the west sat the helicopters of the 101st Airborne, tasked

Above: U.S. troops arm an F-15 fighter with AIM-9L Sidewinder air-to-air missiles.

Right: Iraqi prisoners guarded by U.S. troops. The sheer number of POWs overwhelmed the Coalition forces.

with cutting a swathe through the enemy defences before setting up their forward base (aptly codenamed *Cobra*) at Talil, less than 20km (12.4 miles) from Nasiriyah. Finally, on the extreme left, the French Daguet Division stood poised with the 82nd Airborne to set up a flanking guard.

The Coalition ground offensive burst on the Iraqis with explosive speed and power in the early hours of the morning of Sunday 24 February. Arab Coalition forces and U.S. Marines broke through the berms and oil-filled ditches along the south-eastern Kuwaiti border and began to head directly for the capital. Saudis and Egyptians broke through east of the Wadi al Batin directly into the area where the Iraqis had anticiptated the main American thrust. The U.S. 101st Airborne and 24th Mechanized Divisions made such good

Hundreds of vehicles, both military and civilian, pressed into service by the Iraqis in their attempt to escape from Kuwait City were caught in the open and destroyed by the combined might of the U.S. V11 Corps and the Coalition air forces.

Above: Vietnam forgotten: U.S. civilians join in open support of their Armed Forces in the Gulf.

time that they covered in one day, the ground which their analysts reckoned would take them five. Meanwhile the French destroyed the entire Iraqi 45th Division at Salman. More importantly, the U.S. VII Corps broke through in the centre and began to sweep right, attacking the main Iraq forward defences and reserves from the flank.

Opposition was scant. Ten thousand Iraqi front-line troops surrendered at the first opportunity to be funnelled back to the waiting, and already overwhelmed, prisoner-of-war camps in Saudi Arabia. The only counter-attack, by 80 tanks of the Republican Guard, was repelled with massive loss, by artillery and air strikes.

Right: U.S. Navy SEALS in their converted dune buggy secure the American Embassy in Kuwait City.

Right: Psychological Operations played a major role in the Allied victory. Leaflets were prepared for an air-drop.

By the third day the French and 82nd Airborne had reached their objective at Samawah and were poised to move on Baghdad if required. The 101st had established *Cobra,* the U.S. Marines with their Arab allies were nearing the outskirts of Kuwait City, and the U.S. VII Corps, its objectives taken, was resting before moving forward into Kuwait.

Within hours the war was over. Iraqi troops, terrified of encirclement, began to flee north. Thousands of those attempting to leave Kuwait City were slaughtered by U.S. forces at the Mutlah Gap. Elements of the Republican Guard trying to flee north were caught by the combined might of U.S. 101st Division's helicopters and U.S. VIIth Corps' armour and forced to surrender.

President Bush ordered a cease fire at 5.00 a.m. G.M.T. (midnight Washington

Below: An oil refinery south of Kuwait City torched by the fleeing Iraquis spreads a pall of smoke across the Gulf skies.

time), after a land offensive which had lasted 100 hours. Coalition victory was absolute. Over 3,000 Iraqi tanks were destroyed or captured on the battlefield as were 2,140 artillery pieces and 1,860 armoured personnel carriers. Over 50,000 prisoners were taken and an unknown number of Iraqis killed.

It is easy to say that the victory was born of overall superior technology. Of course this played a major part but so, it must be remembered, did the sheer professionalism of the participating troops and air crew. The United States Army has now finally left Vietnam behind. It showed itself capable of rapid deployment in Grenada and Panama and has demonstrated its ability to prosecute large-scale 'conventional' warfare. Many mistakes

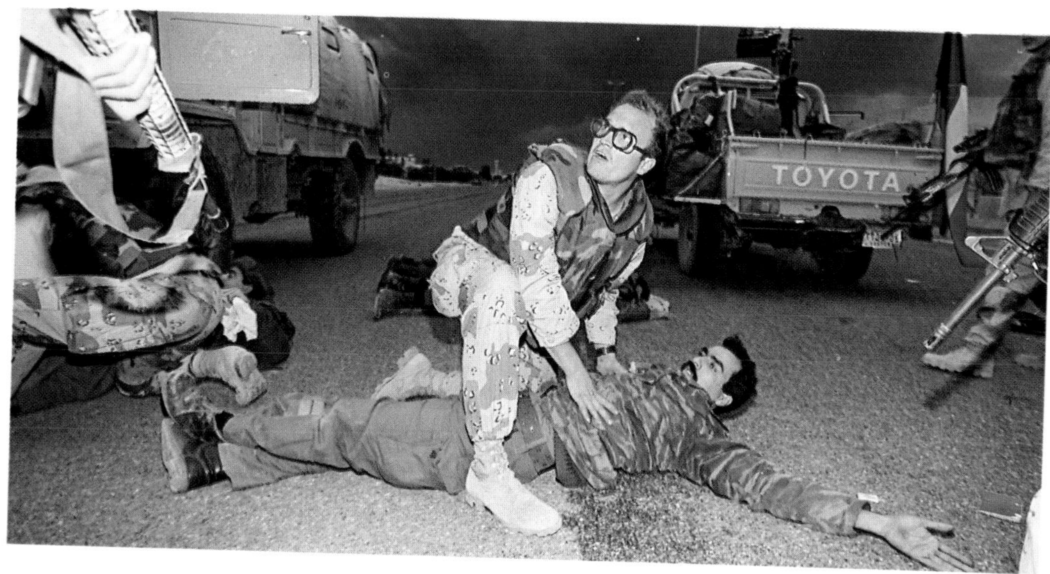

Left: Saudi troops guard captured Iraqi soldiers on their way to a prisoner-of-war camp.

Above: U.S. Marines search an Iraqi prisoner while sweepng a small town for snipers.

Below: U.S. Marine Corps special forces halt to watch smoke billowing from an oil refinery.

were made in Saudi Arabia but hopefully lessons have been learned and those mistakes will not happen again. The U.S. III Army, the U.S. Marine Corps, the U.S. Air Force and — above all — General Norman Schwarzkopf, for the major parts they played in the liberation of Kuwait and the defeat of Iraq, justly deserve the true acclaim of the American people.

Right: Saudi 155mm tracked artillery opens fire on Iraqi positions during the first morning of the ground attack.

Below: Area of downtown Baghdad destroyed by Allied bombing.

Left: Israeli rescuers search the ruins of a Tel Aviv building destroyed by a Scud missile.

Below: Burning oil-fields on the Kuwait-Iraq border.

Operation Granby, British 1st (Armoured) Division in Iraq, 1991

Britain's contribution to the Gulf War was greater than that of the rest of Europe combined. Under the codename *Granby* she committed first one armoured brigade, then a second and finally a divisional headquarters. By the start of the ground war, 1st Armoured Division constituted the largest and most powerful task force in British post-war history. All volunteer, though heavily enhanced in certain quarters by Reservists, it was perhaps the most professional force in the Gulf. Equipped with late generation Challenger 2 tanks specially adapted for the desert, its firepower was, to use the idiom of the day, 'truly awesome'.

The 7th Armoured Brigade, descendants of the 7th Division – the original Desert Rats of World War II – were the first to be sent to the Gulf. The brigade comprised some of the oldest regiments in the British Army. The Royal Scots Dragoon Guards and the Queens Royal Irish Hussars with their 117 tanks and the infantry of the 1st Battalion the Staffordshire Regiment in their Warrior M.I.C.V.s (Mechanized Infantry Combat Vehicles) supplied the frontline teeth. Support was provided by the 24 M-109 155mm self-propelled howitzers of 40 Field Regiment, Royal Artillery and a squadron of sappers from 21 Field Regiment, Royal Engineers. The brigade was enhanced to wartime strength by a squadron of the 17/21st Lancers and a company of the Grenadier Guards, the latter quickly making it abundantly apparent that they had no intention of compromising their standards of smartness. To make the brigade truly independent, integral medium reconnaissance was provided by A Squadron, The Queens Dragoon Guards.

Initially, the Saudis objected to the stencilling of the Desert Rat symbol on the side of the brigade's vehicles, arguing that the rat was an unclean animal and for this reason its depiction was offensive. Arab sensibilities were placated however, when it was pointed out that the 'rat' was in fact a jerbil and therefore offensive to no one.

Initially, it was intended that 7 Armoured Brigade should serve as the heavy armour of the U.S. Marine Corps expeditionary force, its own M-60 A3s and Sheridan light tanks being considered under-gunned for the task. Training commenced with the two allied forces working well together under unified command. However, when Schwarzkopf called for a doubling of manpower and Britain responded by deploying a second Brigade and a divisional command, it was considered a more useful exercise to transfer the new division west to join the far superior Abrams tanks of the U.S. VII Armored Corps. To make matters easier, Major General Rupert Smith of the Parachute Regiment, in command of the 1st British Armoured Division, had worked closely with VII U.S. Corps on NATO exercises in Germany and already knew, and was highly respected by, its senior officers.

Above: Lieutenant-General (now General) Sir Peter de la Billière, commander British Forces in the Gulf.

Below: Despite earlier misgivings the Challenger tank rendered excellent service to the British armoured forces.

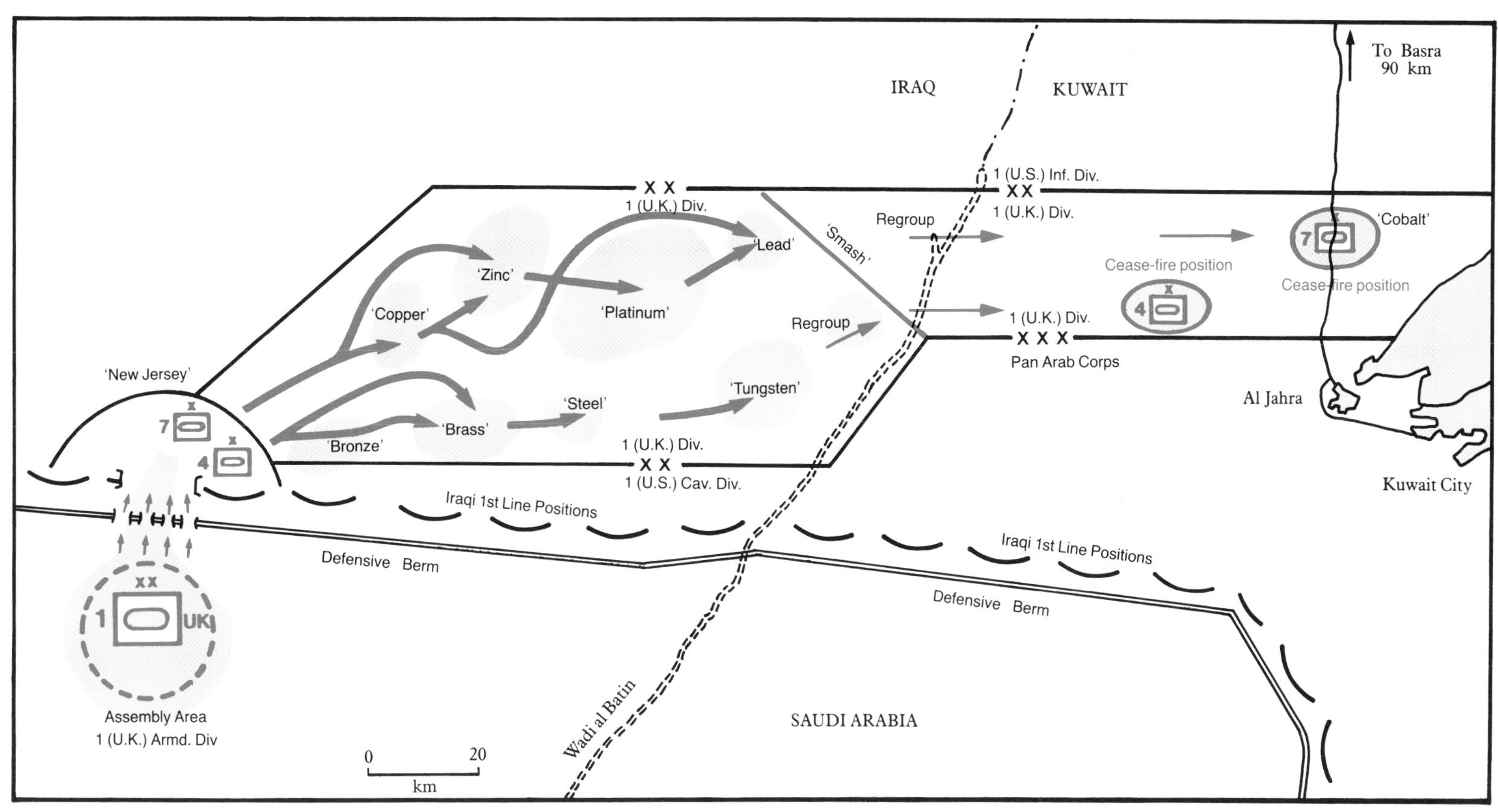

Above: Food (but not alcohol) from home provided a welcome relief to standard compo rations.

When Britain sent 7 Armoured Brigade to the Gulf it was initially intended that they should act as the heavy armour of the U.S. Marine Corps' expeditionary force. However when Britain responded to Schwarzkopf's request for a doubling of manpower by deploying a second brigade and divisional command structure, it was felt better to transfer the new division west to form the right flank of the far stronger U.S. VII Armored Corps. The 1st Armoured Division began its advance at 2.00 a.m. on Sunday 24 February. The perceived aim of the British was to protect the flank of the U.S. 1st and 3rd Armored Divisions and the 2nd Armored Cavalry Regiment as they advanced into Iraq. In pursuance of this aim they were to seize a series of Iraqi battalion and regimental defensive positions, each codenamed with the name of a metal and previously identified by aerial and satellite reconnaissance. In less than 100 hours of fighting, the Division neutralized several regular army tactical reserve divisions before receiving orders to halt northwest of Kuwait city.

Above: C-130 Hercules transport aircraft provided much-needed logistic support to the British forces.

Above: Multi-barrelled rocket launchers.

The new brigade was the 4th Armoured, also based in Germany. Its offensive capability consisted of the 59 Challenger tanks of 14/20th King's Hussars augmented by a squadron from the Life Guards and two infantry battalions. These were made up of the 1st Battalion, the Royal Scots and 3rd Battalion, the Royal Regiment of fusiliers, supplemented by Queen's Company and II Company, 1st Battalion the Grenadier Guards. Support was again provided by 24 M-109 howitzers, on this occasion drawn from 2 Field Regiment, RA as well as by a squadron of sappers.

Divisional support was provided by the Scorpion reconnaissance vehicles of 16/5 Queen's Royal Lancers and by the heavy guns and missiles of 26 Field Regiment, 32 Heavy Regiment and 39 Heavy Regiment RA. All engineer armoured bridging and mine clearing assets available were also sent to provide each brigade with a full Engineer Regiment as were 10 regimental bands to act as stretcher bearers and several (mainly Scottish) infantry battalions to act as battlefield casualty replacements and prisoner of war guards. To their intense disappointment few of these additional units were destined to see action.

Royal Navy Lynx anti-submarine helicopters were used in several attacks on Iraqi shipping in the Northern Gulf.

The 1st Armoured Division began its advance from its staging point at 2.00 a.m. on Sunday 24 February, but was not ordered to cross the Iraqi border for several hours. Much of the division's pre-battle training had been taken up practising for the initial assault on the complex of sand ramparts or berms, oil-filled ditches and minefields constituting the Iraqi front line. In the event these proved far less effective than anticipated and were easily neutralized by the U.S. Engineers leading the VII Corps advance. They did, however, serve to create a traffic jam which prevented the British from reaching their forming up point on phase line New Jersey until the middle of the next afternoon.

Once committed to 'the mother of Battles' the perceived aim of the British was to protect the right flank of the U.S. 1st and 3rd Armored Divisions and the 2nd Armoured Cavalry Regiment as they advanced into Iraq. They were to neutralize the regular army tactical reserve divisions behind the front line. Thereafter, they were to seek out and destroy the élite Hamarabi and Medina Divisions of the much vaunted Republican Guard. In pursuance of this aim they were to seize a series of Iraqi battalion and regimental defensive positions, each codenamed with the name of a metal, previously identified by aerial and satellite reconnaissance.

Both brigades were ordered to attack Iraqi mechanized infantry positions dug into a large complex codenamed *Copper*. Thereafter, 7 Brigade was to proceed forward to *Zinc* and onwards to *Platinum* while the battle-groups of 4 Brigade swung south to engage *Brass* and *Steel*.

At 3.00 p.m. 7 Brigade began its move forward over three hours ahead of 4 Brigade to its right. Almost immediately it ran into trouble. The TOGS thermal-imaging night

sights which gave the tanks their nocturnal capability failed to function in the driving rain while the revolutionary new satellite receivers, capable of pin-pointing a tank's position, malfunctioned. At 5.30 p.m., 7 Brigade came to a complete standstill for over an hour while the electricians worked feverishly to rectify the problems. Luck did not smile upon 4 Brigade either. Enemy positions turned out to be far stronger and more numerous than it was originally thought, causing them to encounter a massive and unanticipated defensive complex to the south-west of *Copper.*

Unperturbed and waiting only for confirmation that the unidentified Iraqis were not in fact an off course friendly force, the commander of the brigade, Brigadier Hammerbeck, called down fire from the 203mm M-110 howitzers and multi-barrel rocket launchers of the divisional artillery group on to the enemy position. The effects were devastating. In less than an hour the position was annihilated, causing the majority of the

Above left: A Gazelle helicopter retrofitted with an observer's stabilized sight and exhaust deflector to minimize I.R. signature.

Left: A Chinook helicopter in desert livery.

Below: An Army Air Corps headquarters position somewhere in Saudi Arabia.

Above: LAW 80 light anti-tank weapons were first used in the Gulf and proved highly successful.

Above: Improvised flags abound as a 7th Armoured Brigade Striker anti-tank vehicle leads a Centurion AVRC deep into Iraqi territory.

Right: An Army Air Corps Lynx helicopter with TOW mountings. The missiles have yet to be fitted.

defenders, who were already shaken by weeks of bombing, to flee. Those brave few who remained to man their ancient T-55 tanks were either killed by the advancing 14/20th Hussars or taken prisoner by the screening infantry.

As the Hussars began to push the fleeing Iraqis north into *Copper*, it became clear that the enemy had neither the stomach nor the training for modern night warfare. Although they had had weeks to prepare their defensive positions most of them

Above: A spindle-mounted GPMG mounted on a Lynx helicopter.

Right: A Chinook lands but keeps its rotors turning while the loadmaster calls forth the next batch of troops.

were badly dug. The artillery pits were too deep, preventing the guns from traversing more than a few degrees, while most positions lacked all-round defensive capability. Provided Saddam did not resort to chemical warfare, the outcome of the battle was already a certainty.

At 10.50 p.m. the leading tanks of the 14/20th Hussars began to fire on the southernmost defensive positions of *Copper*, catching four enemy tanks unawares. Suddenly an almost unbelievable phenomenon occurred. Hundreds of Iraqis began to leave their defensive shelters and walk slowly towards the British. Initially it was difficult to judge whether it was their intention to fight, withdraw or rally for a counter-attack. However, white flags soon began to appear in profusion as it became clear that the Iraqis were throwing in the towel. Weeks of bombing had weakened their resolve and the artillery barrage which had preceded the armoured attack had proved too much to bear. Silently but obediently they abandoned their weapons, formed up and awaited their fate. The Grenadier Guards acting as infantry support to the Hussars were ordered forward to marshal the dispirited Iraqis and conduct them back to the cages at the rear. Thereafter the far from happy Grenadiers found themselves providing a P.O.W. 'mechanized taxi service' until overwhelmed by the sheer numbers surrendering.

As dawn broke on the Tuesday morning, G+2, 7 Brigade continued its advance to *Zinc* while 4 Brigade turned south towards *Brass* and *Steel*. By now the attacks were assuming a familiar pattern with many more tanks, trucks and bunkers in the way

Above: An L2A2 anti-personnel grenade primed and ready for action.

Below: An R.A.F. C-130 Hercules during refuelling. The in-flight fuelling probe allowed for direct flights from Britain where necessary.

than had been suggested by Intelligence. Each individual assault was carried out with set-piece precision borne of years of painstaking training on the plains of North-west Germany. The target was first subjected to massive artillery and rocket fire on a scale and intensity which the Iraqis had not believed possible. Batteries of rocket launchers, each firing 12 x 220mm missiles, combined with 203mm (8 in) howitzers to obliterate individual grid squares destroying virtually everything in the area. Battle groups combining armoured squadrons with mechanized infantry then moved forward to neutralize any remaining pockets of resistance.

During the course of the Tuesday afternoon, as 7 Brigade attacked the massive divisional position on *Platinum* and 4 Brigade the lesser position on *Steel*, tragedy struck. The British, who until then had suffered no deaths and only a few minor injuries, sustained their first fatalities. Two of the Fusilier's Warriors suddenly exploded, killing nine of their young passengers. Originally it was thought that the vehicles had wandered into an uncharted minefield. However it soon became apparent that they had been hit by so called 'friendly' Hellfire missiles fired at maximum range by an American A-10 Thunderbolt anti-tank aircraft which had wandered from its target areas to the north.

Lieutenant-General Charles Horner, in overall command of the allied air forces during the conflict, later claimed that the

Above: A Sea King helicopter fitted with sand filters to enable it to fly low over the desert.

Below: Royal Navy Lynx and Sea King helicopters aboard the Royal Fleet Auxilliary Argos.

pilot had been given clearance to fire his missiles by a British air-traffic controller who had not realized that 4 Brigade was so far forward. Relatives of the dead countered that the vehicles were stopped at the time with the crews resting beside them and should have been easily identifiable to the pilot. Whatever the truth, the tragic incident accounted for the single biggest loss to any British unit throughout the entire war.

That evening, 7 Brigade, led by the Scots Dragoon Guards, and 4 Brigade, led unusually by a Fusilier battle group, attacked *Lead* and *Tungsten* respectively. The latter was of particular importance. Guarding the Wadi Al Batin, the area where the Iraqis had anticipated the Allied attack, it contained the majority of the enemy's newest and most powerful guns. After the battle several of the much vaunted South African G-5s – designed by Gerard Bull, the architect of the Big Gun – were recovered in virtually mint condition. Had the Iraqis chosen to fight for *Tungsten* they had had available the resources to prosecute a long delaying action. By now, however, they were to all intents and purposes a defeated army, without order or direction, intent only on getting north to safety.

That night the leading elements of 1st Armored Division reached Line Smash, the final objective set it by VII Corps. It had reached in two days a line which it had been optimistically expected to attain in ten yet it was not allowed more than a few hours rest. The Iraqis were now in full retreat and the division was ordered forward to the Kuwait border to give chase. Sadly, the infamous fog of war now set in threatening to mar victory with farce. Its formal battle plan now completed, VII Corps began to issue conflicting orders to its divisions which, if not countered, would have put the British Armored Division and the 1st and 3rd U.S. Armoured Divisions on a collision course. Discretion being the better part of valour, the British were ordered to halt while the Americans sorted out their priorities.

Above: A Naval leading airman mans a GPMG on board a Sea King helicopter.

Left: Sea King helicopters of 46 Squadron aboard the Royal Fleet Auxiliary Argos.

On Thursday morning, G+4, the division was ordered forward to cut the Basra road and enter Kuwait City. Hours later the Iraqis requested and were granted a cease-fire.

The British conducted themselves admirably throughout the 100 hours of battle, and indeed during the months preceding it. They lost only 17 men killed,

Above: Refuelling and rearming a Lynx helicopter.

Right: British troops found a wide variety of ammunition natures in captured Iraqi stock.

Far Right: A British major examining a stock of captured ammunition.

fewer than die in a major NATO exercise, and managed to finish the war with 95 percent of their fighting vehicles operational. Yet they were fighting a dispirited army, virtually defeated before the commencement of hostilities. Their intelligence was not always accurate and much of their newest equipment faulty. Their major asset, the controversial Challenger tank, performed superbly however, proving itself an able match for any main battle tank in the world.

INDEX

Longer entries for countries list name of fighting force followed by names of battles fought.

TACTICAL SYMBOLS

All armies use systems of symbols to mark maps to show the disposition of units. The most widely used is the NATO system, based on that developed by the U.S. Army. In this system a tactical unit is depicted by a rectangle ☐, with the size of the unit above it, e.g. ☐ (a company); the type of unit indicated by a symbol inside the rectangle: ☒ (an infantry company) and the unit designation to the right: ☒A (Company A). Where a unit is shown as a subordinate of another, the smaller unit appears on the left, the larger on the right: 1☒9 1st Battalion, 9th Infantry Regiment.

Size is indicated by:

•	Section	I	Company	x	Brigade	xxxx	Army
•••	Platoon	II	Battalion	xx	Division		
		III	Regiment	xxx	Corps		

A bridge across the size symbol indicates an all-arms team:

Team/Combat Team

Task Force/Battle Group

The type of unit is indicated by a symbol, illustrative of the role:

Infantry
Mechanized infantry
Armour
Cavalry/Scout
Helicopter/Aviation
Marine
Artillery
Parachute unit

A rectangular symbol on its own indicates a unit in the area it is placed. In the NATO system friendly units are indicated in blue/black and hostile units in red. An area occupied by a unit is indicated by a line demarking the area and one of the size symbols described above. Thus,

Area occupied by a company

Area occupied by a battalion, with companies as shown

Vehicles can also be shown:

Light tank
Light, tracked APC
Medium tank
Medium, tracked APC
Heavy tank
Heavy, tracked APC

Further symbols include: Direction of advance Minefield

PICTURE ACKNOWLEDGMENTS

Associated Press Ltd: 66 top; Aviation Photographs International: 170 top, 186 top, 186 bottom, 187 centre, 187 bottom, 188, 189 top, 189 centre, 189 bottom left, 189 bottom right, 190 bottom, 191 top, 191 bottom, 192 top, 192 bottom, 193 top, 193 bottom, 194 left, 194 right, 195 top, 195 bottom left, 195 bottom right; BTPH: 99, 100 top, 115 top, 117 bottom, 138 top, 138 bottom, 140 top, 140 bottom, 156, 158 top, 158 centre, 158 bottom, 141 left, 141 right, 142 top, 142 bottom left; BTPH/USNA: 50 top, 50 centre, 50 bottom, 51 top, 52 top, 52 bottom, 53 top, 53 bottom, 55 top, 55 bottom; BTPH/IWM: 56 bottom, 57 bottom, 58 top, 58 bottom left, 58 bottom right; Department of Defense, Washington D.C: 2-3, 4, 9, 67, 68, 69 top, 69 bottom, 118 top left, 118 top right, 118 bottom, 119 top left, 119 top right, 119 bottom left, 119 bottom right, 120 bottom, 121 top, 121 bottom, 122, 125 top, 125 bottom, 126, 162 top, 162 centre, 162 bottom; Robert Hunt Library: 17 top, 19 centre right, 28 top, 29 bottom, 32 top, 34, 37, 43 bottom, 44 top, 46 top, 47 bottom, 51 bottom, 65 top, 65 bottom, 66 bottom left, 93, 95 top, 95 bottom, 96 bottom, 97 top, 97 bottom, 98 top, 98 bottom, 131, 133 top, 133 centre, 134; Imperial War Museum: 10, 12 top, 12 centre, 12 bottom, 22 top, 22 bottom, 23 bottom, 24 top, 24 bottom, 25 top, 25 bottom, 27 top, 27 centre, 27 bottom, 28 bottom, 29 bottom, 31 top, 31 bottom, 32 bottom, 35 top, 35 bottom, 36 top left, 36 top right, 36 bottom, 38, 40 top, 40 bottom, 41, 42 top, 46 bottom, 47 top, 48 bottom, 49 top, 49 centre, 56 top, 57 top, 57 centre, 58 centre, 60 top, 60 bottom, 61 top, 61 bottom, 74, 75, 76 bottom, 78 top, 78 bottom, 79 top, 79 bottom, 80, 87, 89 top, 89 bottom, 90 top, 90 bottom, 91, 92 top, 92 centre, 92 bottom, 104, 135, 136 bottom, 137 top, 137 bottom, 155 bottom left; Israeli Army: 100 bottom, 101; Keystone: 49 bottom; Leslie McDonnell: 106 top, 106 bottom, 107 right, 108 top, 108 bottom, 109 top, 109 bottom, 110 top, 110 bottom, 114 left, 114 right, 133 bottom left, 136 centre, 151 top, 152 top, 152 centre, 152 bottom; Popperfoto: 83 top, 85, 86, 127, 128-129, 142 bottom right, 143 top, 143 bottom, 149 top, 160 top, 166 top, 166 bottom, 168 top, 168 bottom, 169 top, 170 bottom, 171 top, 171 bottom, 172 top, 172 centre, 172 bottom, 174 top, 174 centre, 174 bottom, 175 top, 175 centre, 175 bottom, 176 top, 176 bottom, 177 top, 177 bottom, 178/179, 180 top, 180 bottom, 181 top, 181 bottom, 182, 183 top, 183 bottom, 184 bottom, 185 top, 185 bottom, 190 top; Rex Features: 123, 124 top right, 124 bottom, 132; Yves Robins: 17 bottom, 19 centre left, 19 bottom; TRH Pictures: 81 top, 82 top, 145 top, 150; TRH Pictures/B.I.F./U.N: 77; TRH Pictures/DOD: 71 bottom, 83 bottom, 159 top, 159 bottom, 160 bottom left, 160 bottom right, 161 top, 161 bottom, 163 top, 164 top, 164 bottom, 165 top, 165 bottom; TRH Pictures/IWM: 21, 66 bottom right, 113; TRH/RM: 151 bottom left, 151 bottom right, 154 bottom, 155 top, 155 bottom right; TRH Pictures/SAS Regt. Assoc: 62 top, 63 top, 63 centre, 63 bottom; TRH Pictures/T.A. Davis: 144 top left, 144 top right, 144 bottom, 145 bottom, 146 top left, 146 top right, 146 bottom, 147 top, 147 bottom left, 147 bottom right, 148 bottom; TRH Pictures/US Army: 81 bottom, 82 bottom, 85 bottom; TRH Pictures/USMC: 73 top; TRH Pictures/US Navy: 7 top, 7 bottom, 42 bottom, 43 top, 44 bottom, 71 top, 73 centre bottom.

MAPS

Brian Sandford 8, 11, 15, 18, 23, 30, 39, 45, 54, 64, 70, 80, 102, 105, 111, 116, 139, 148, 153, 173
Guy Taylor F.R.G.S. 21, 26, 33, 48, 59, 72, 75, 84, 94, 107, 112, 124, 128, 132, 136, 154, 157, 163, 167, 187